Visionary San Francisco

Visionary San Francisco

Edited by
Paolo Polledri

With contributions by

Gray A. Brechin, William Gibson, Joe Gores,
Daniel P. Gregory, Mark Helprin, Paolo Polledri, Richard Rodriguez,
Kevin Starr, and Sally B. Woodbridge

San Francisco Museum of Modern Art

Prestel

This book was published on the occasion of an exhibition of the
same name organized by the San Francisco Museum of Modern Art and shown
at the museum June 14 - August 26, 1990.

Visionary San Francisco is supported by the Challenge Program of the California
Arts Council; the Design Arts Program of the National Endowment for the Arts, a
Federal agency; Santa Fe Pacific Realty Corporation; the LEF Foundation; and
Mr. and Mrs. M. Arthur Gensler. Educational programs are made possible by the
Metropolitan Life Foundation, the California Council for the Humanities, and
San Francisco Beautiful.

Front cover: *John Kriken, Skidmore Owings & Merrill,* Mission Bay, *1990.*
Ink and Prismacolor on paper. Courtesy John Kriken.

Frontispiece: *View of San Francisco's Financial District from*
Twin Peaks, 1990. (Photo: Ben Blackwell, fig. 4, pages 14 and 15)

Prestel-Verlag, Mandlstrasse 26, D-8000 Munich 40, Federal Republic of Germany
Tel. (89) 38 17 09 0 Telefax (89) 38 17 09 35

Distributed in continental Europe and Japan by Prestel-Verlag,
Verlegerdienst München GmbH & Co KG,
Gutenbergstrasse 1, D-8031 Gilching, Federal Republic of Germany
Tel. (81 05) 21 10 Telefax (81 05) 55 20

Distributed in the USA and Canada by te Neues Publishing Company,
15 East 76th Street, New York, NY 10021, USA
Tel. (2 12) 288 0265 Telefax (2 12) 570 2373

Distributed in the United Kingdom, Ireland and all other countries by Thames &
Hudson Limited,
30 - 34 Bloomsbury Street, London WC1B 3QP, England
Tel. (1) 636 5488 Telefax (1) 636 4799

Library of Congress Cataloging-in-Publication Data is available:
Library of Congress Card Number: 90-61342

CIP-Titelaufnahme der Deutschen Bibliothek

Visionary San Francisco : [June 14 - August 26, 1990] / San Francisco
Museum of Modern Art. Paolo Polledri. – München : Prestel, 1990

ISBN 3-7913-1060-7

NE: Polledri, Paolo [Mitverf.] ; San Francisco Museum of Modern Art

Edited by Janet R. Wilson

Designed by Dietmar Rautner

Separations and Lithography by GEWA-Repro GmbH, Gerlinger und Wagner, Munich
Typography by Fertigsatz GmbH, Munich
Printed by Wenschow-Franzis Druck GmbH, Munich
Bound by R. Oldenbourg GmbH, Kirchheim near Munich
Printed and bound in Germany
ISBN 0-918471-15-X (Softcover, not available to the trade)
ISBN 3-7913-1060-7 (Hardcover)

Table of Contents

Foreword

San Francisco inspires dreams. The remarkable natural splendor of the city's location, the bountiful opportunities proffered by the American West and the Pacific region, and the idealism and optimism that characterize the attitudes of many individuals who have left their mark on California have all shaped the ways in which an uncommonly beautiful urban place has been attained. The distinctive character of San Francisco is as much conceptual as it is material; its physical development into a collection of buildings, streets, and open spaces has been importantly affected by utopian urban design ideas, both realized and unrealized. It is these visions that are here the subject of the first major exhibition and publication project to be organized by the San Francisco Museum of Modern Art's newly established Department of Architecture and Design.

Paolo Polledri, founding Curator of Architecture and Design, proposed "Visionary San Francisco" in 1987 as an element of the plan in which he would define a unique role for the Museum's new curatorial department. He urged the development of a program dedicated in both its collecting and exhibiting activities to a very broad notion of "regionalism," encompassing nothing less than the huge geographic area of the Pacific and concentrating on architecture and design in California as well as in the cultures of Latin America and Asia, which have strongly influenced the built environment here. The exhibition and this accompanying publication are his idea. It was he who established the liberal parameters of the project, ranging from historical to contemporary components, and he who invited the many collaborators in the exhibition whose participation has distinguished and enlivened it. He also set as an important item on his agenda — utopian in its own right — that "Visionary San Francisco" should contribute to helping people join together to find a new expression of what they want for their city, a task made even more urgent in the aftermath of the earthquake of October 17, 1989.

In addition to recognizing Mr. Polledri, I offer special thanks to the lenders to the exhibition, to the schol-ars, authors, and designers who have contributed texts and projects to the undertaking, to Prestel-Verlag, the co-publisher of this book, to Michael Blackwood, Robert Colo, and Hilary Grimm, who independently produced an accompanying film and kindly made available portions of the footage for the Museum to use in the exhibition installation, and to Jeannette Redensek and Janet Bishop of the Museum's staff, whose dedication to "Visionary San Francisco" has gone far beyond the bounds of professional commitment. I thank, too, the many individuals and organizations credited by Mr. Polledri in his acknowledgments who were helpful in bringing "Visionary San Francisco" to fulfillment.

With great appreciation I acknowledge the generous support of the California Arts Council, the California Council for the Humanities, the National Endowment for the Arts, Santa Fe Pacific Realty Corporation, the LEF Foundation, Mr. and Mrs. M. Arthur Gensler, the Architecture and Design Forum of the San Francisco Museum of Modern Art, and — through the Beaux Arts Ball benefit events of 1988 and 1989 — the American Institute of Architects, San Francisco Chapter, and the Modern Art Council of the San Francisco Museum of Modern Art, without whom this very worthy and ambitious project would have remained unrealized.

John R. Lane
December 6, 1989   Director

Acknowledgments

I remember an evening, a few years ago, when my wife and I were driving across the Bay Bridge from Berkeley. This experience alone—to be on the upper deck of the bridge, under the pylons and their sweeping tendons—was exciting. At the exit of the Treasure Island Tunnel the city came into view, its illuminated skyscrapers cloaked in fog, appearing almost like a tridimensional computer image of a mythical city. This image conjured up an unexpected pride of ownership, the feeling that one could touch the city, guard its beauty, and change it at will. This is the image of San Francisco I carry with me even though I now live here. While the idea for this book and for an exhibition with the same title started about two and a half years ago, it is this image, or vision, that supports it. Other people, I reasoned, must also have seen it as a dream city.

Indeed San Francisco must exert a powerful appeal on many people, since many have collaborated in making this book. First, those who have contributed by means of writing, research, and ideas, and whose names appear throughout the text; they have invested more than time and effort in this project, they have revealed their passion for the city. Gray Brechin, Daniel Gregory, and Sally Woodbridge have carried out most of the historical research and have assisted in organizing parts of the exhibition; above all, their constant help and advice have made this book a reality.

In the course of their research they were helped by Waverly Lowell, of the National Archives and Records Administration; Gladys Hansen and Pat Akre of the San Francisco Archives in the Main Public Library; Jerry Wright of the California Historical Society Library; Caitlin King of the College of Environmental Design Documents Collection, University of California, Berkeley; Tom and Jean Moulin of Moulin Studios; Mary Hanel of the Caltrans Library in Sacramento; Robert David of the Golden Gate Bridge, Highway and Transportation District; Douglas Brookes of the Treasure Island Museum; Bonnie Hardwick and Lawrence Dineen of the Bancroft Library, University of California, Berkeley; Mary Woolever of the Burnham Library, The Art Institute of

Chicago; Joyce Connolly of the Frederick Olmsted National Historic Site; Lauren Bricker; Edward H. Bennett, Jr.; John and Milton Pflueger; Michael Goodman; Eleanor Morrow Mead; and Mrs. Chesley Bonestell.

Joe Gores shares with Mario Gandelsonas and Diana Agrest an interest in cities. Cities are composed of many layers of meaning, which intersect and offer the opportunity for extraordinary events to occur at the intersections. Richard Rodriguez, Sohela Farokhi, and Lars Lerup are interested in contrasts in contemporary society heightened by private and public languages that mold our perception of the world and our relationship with society. Mark Helprin and Barbara Stauffacher Solomon share poetic visions of the world—visions that are grounded in real sites, true gestures and histories, yet their cumulative effect conjures up fantastic cities. William Gibson, Ming Fung, and Craig Hodgetts share a vision of the future, ultimately optimistic, but strongly reminiscent of today's world.

They and especially I were helped by the considerable talents of Janet Bishop and Jeannette Redensek, who have advised, critiqued, and coordinated the text and images with Florence Lipsky while preparing the manuscript. Shannon Cameron has held all the pieces together. Janet Wilson, who has edited the text, has been able to achieve almost the impossible, a coherence among all the sections of the manuscript. Jack Lane and Graham Beal saw the merits of a primitive idea, nurturing and supporting it to its completion. Rozanne Stringer, Gail Indvik, Inge-Lise Eckmann, Kent Roberts, Tina Garfinkel, Barbara L. Phillips, Barbara Levine, Kara Kirk, Catherine Mills, Mindy Holdsworth, and Sandra Stumbaugh coped with my requests for time, resources, and commitment far beyond their professional duties.

Outside the San Francisco Museum of Modern Art, many people supported this project. Among these, Kevin Starr deserves special credit: it was his ideas that gave me the courage to develop mine. Many friends in San Francisco's architectural scene listened to these ideas and rendered valuable assistance: Vernon

DeMars, Mario Ciampi, Romaldo Giurgola, John Kriken, and Allan Temko have witnessed, at various stages, many of the events narrated in this book and all have been generous with ideas and practical advice. Stephen Tobriner and Spiro Kostof, both my teachers at the University of California, Berkeley, directed me to sources hitherto unknown. Prestel Verlag kept me on my toes while preparing the manuscript for publication; I am grateful for their high standards. Rosemary Klebahn and Thomas Swift were instrumental in developing the support that has made the Department of Architecture and Design a reality at the Museum; because many believed them, many helped me.

Sharon Lee Polledri, with maddeningly accurate criticism, has assisted me in more ways than I am able to acknowledge. Naturally, this book and the exhibition would not have been possible without the generosity of all who have loaned material; they had the vision to preserve what we can show.

The talent and passion of all those who, directly or indirectly, have participated in preparing this book will make it worth reading. The shortcomings are, of course, my responsibility.

Paolo Polledri

December 19, 1989

View of Financial District from the James Lick Freeway, 1990
(Photo: Ben Blackwell)

Kevin Starr
Preface

Cities envision themselves. Cities think and dream. How this occurs remains mysterious, for there is no commonly accepted definition of what a city is. In a model of civil polity, cities envision themselves through the dreams and speculations of their individual inhabitants. The city serves as the context and stimulus for individual thought. In a sociobiological model, cities are alive, and the collective thoughts and dreams of their citizenry constitute a process whose identity is greater than the sum total of its parts.

This process of self-envisioning, whether considered from the perspective of individual dreamers or taken as a whole, synergizes fact and symbol to achieve an art object: the imagined city functioning as an expression of identity and aspiration. Beginning with the limits and possibilities of site, topography, and climate, city envisioners proceed next to the historical and socioeconomic components of civic identity. Certain very basic questions are asked. Who came to this city, and when, and for what reasons? How did the city, once founded, serve its region? What industries grew up? What were its patterns of business and finance? In sorting out these elemental forces, city envisioners soon discover that the realities of geography and economics are less significant than a cache of founding metaphors (fig. 2). The Puritan metaphor, for example, learned and moralistic, rests at the center of the Boston experience. New York has always meant money and the definition of taste. Savannah is the South as eighteenth-century utopia, benign and rational. Atlanta and Omaha are railroad cities: depots, ports of entry and of exchange for their regions, whether by rail or jet aircraft. Chicago is the greatest crossroads city of them all, the heart and brawn of the American continent. The founding metaphors of Los Angeles revolve around evangelical piety and show business—a most unusual combination that has given to the City of the Angels its Oz-like quality.

This exhibition and its scholarly catalogue are concerned with the process of envisioning San Francisco, both historically and in the present. More than most great American cities, San Francisco seems a figment of its own imagination. The city should not have been here in the first place—on the isolated edge of a waterless, treeless peninsula. In the nineteenth century the East Bay would have been a more logical site for the emergence of a great city in Northern California; indeed, Oakland, not San Francisco, was the destination of the transcontinental railroad. Passengers then took ferryboats to San Francisco. For more than one hundred fifty years, San Franciscans have been forced to rearrange their environment to make it habitable. Not until 1934, for example, with the completion of the Hetch Hetchy project, did the city finally solve its water problem. It took more than thirty years for San Francisco to agree upon an adequate source of water, the Tuolumne River, and then to decide to create a dam and reservoir in the Hetch Hetchy Valley near Yosemite. It took another thirty years to complete the dam and the aqueduct. Similarly, the eccentric visionary Joshua Norton was talking about spanning the Bay with two bridges as early as 1869. Not until the late 1930s was the city linked to its surrounding regions by great bridges.

And yet, despite these limitations, great visions were already in place when San Francisco began its existence as an American territory in 1846. In 1847, two years before the Gold Rush, Jaspar O'Farrell, surveyor-general of Alta California, prepared a map of the San Francisco peninsula that constituted an heroic act of imaginative projection (fig. 3). Retained by the federal government, O'Farrell did not merely delineate the unpretentious adobe and wood frontier settlement of Yerba Buena, as San Francisco was known until January 1847. Far from it: he filled out his map

1   San Francisco from the air, 1988.
Courtesy Aero Photographers, Sausalito.
(Photo: Ed Brady)

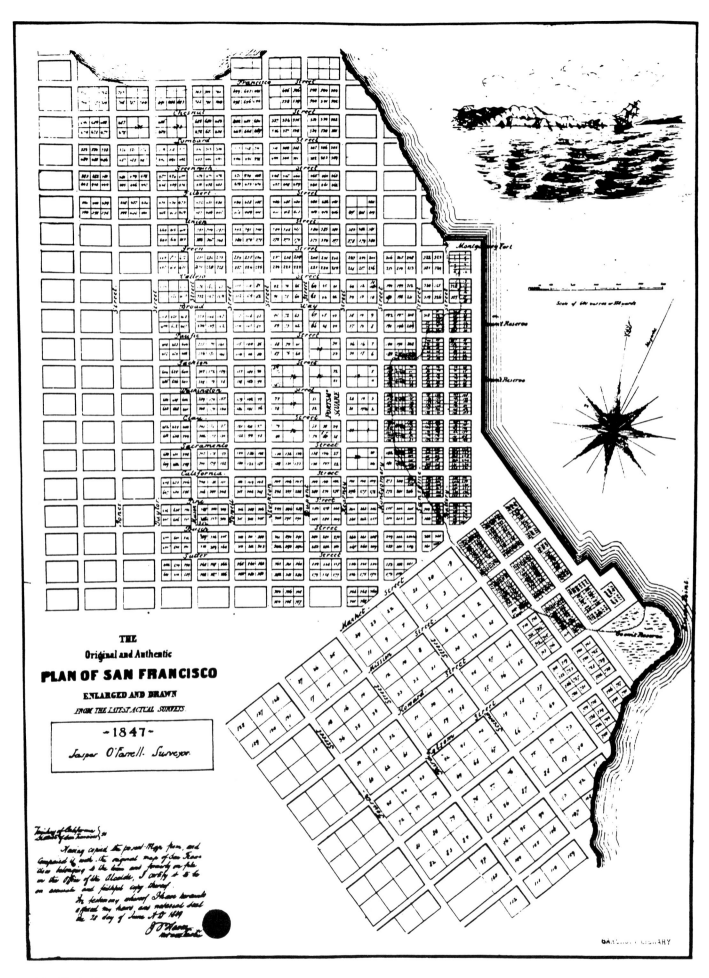

THE
Original and Authentic
PLAN OF SAN FRANCISCO
ENLARGED AND DRAWN
FROM THE LATEST ACTUAL SURVEYS

~1847~
Jasper O'Farrell. Surveyor.

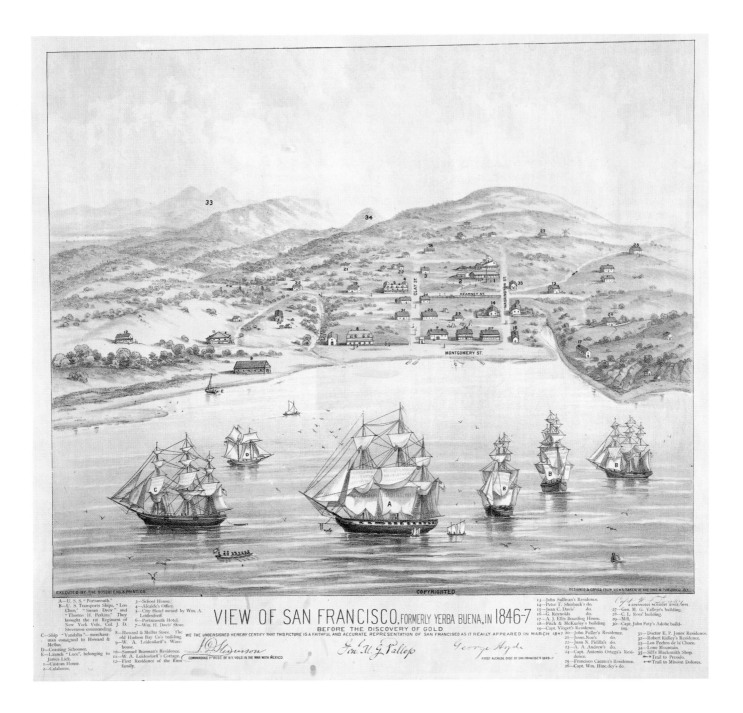

2 Capt. William F. Swasey. View of San Francisco, formerly Yerba Buena, in 1846-7, *1886.*
Collection of the Library of Congress, Washington, D. C.
In the 1840s San Francisco already displayed some of today's urban character. Even though the city had a small population, the street grid is clearly delineated.

3 Jaspar O'Farrell, Surveyor. The Original and Authentic Plan of San Francisco Enlarged and Drawn from the Latest Actual Surveys, *1847.*
Courtesy The Bancroft Library, University of California, Berkeley.
The plan delineated future areas of the city before any settlement actually occured in those sections.

with the streets and boulevards of a grand city—the very same grid that exists to this day. He ran Market Street down from Twin Peaks on a diagonal across the grid, and he envisioned the avenue now called Van Ness as another grand concourse moving at a right angle through the streets named by O'Farrell himself.

A city that was still a frontier town when it set aside Golden Gate Park, a city that constructed the Palace Hotel long before its hundreds of rooms could be filled, a city that surveyed water sources fifty years before construction could commence, a city that built churches, synagogues, and an opera house with seats for thousands was a city ever on the lookout for its

4　*View of San Francisco's Financial District from
Twin Peaks, 1990. (Photo: Ben Blackwell)*

future, ever envisioning itself. Since frontier times, San Francisco has been the achieved product of its own self-invention. San Francisco has been the best and final symbolic statement of itself.

To mention San Francisco is by definition to evoke metaphors of grandeur and civility. The founding metaphor of San Francisco, in other words, is not the Puritanism of Boston, the financial power of New York, or the subliminal glitter of Los Angeles, frequently known as the City of Dreams. The founding metaphor of San Francisco is the urban metaphor itself. Everyone who came to this peninsula during the Spanish, Mexican, and early American eras somehow envisioned a city rising from the tip of the peninsula like Atlantis being born from the sea. This urban dream emanated from the peninsula itself. It was obviously energized by San Francisco Bay, with its promise of a great world port, but in the long run Oakland would capture that function more comprehensively. Something about the very shape of the peninsula—its

seven great hills, its sand dunes and tidelands—challenged the city-building instinct.

Very rapidly, with the Gold Rush, the urban metaphor was actualized. For more than half a century, before the rise of Denver, Los Angeles, and Phoenix, San Francisco stood in splendid isolation, the most achieved urban polity west of Chicago, like a Greek city-state in the Mediterranean—America's only urban hold on the Pacific Rim. This splendid isolation gave rise to a tendency toward narcissism that has been frequently and justifiably criticized. But even as we chide San Francisco for its self-absorption, we must also remember that the city began as an heroic act of self-determination in defiance of topography and distance from other urban centers. Without this strong inner metaphor of achieved urbanism, San Francisco might have dilated outward into amorphous suburbanism, surrendering its physical and political identity to the surrounding metropolitan region when it began to emerge in the early twentieth century. This self-regard

led to the construction of a city along the most ambitious lines of urbanism.

As the essays in this catalogue demonstrate with such learned enthusiasm, this process of self-envisioning has continued through the decades, from the mid-nineteenth century to the present. Like a great Pythagorean entity, San Francisco has always been dreaming of itself and calling these dreams into being. Other selections in this catalogue suggest through autobiographical and/or fictive statement the shimmering play of metaphors and identities still resonating in the city. Reading these selections, studying the visual components of this exhibition, we circle slowly in a descending arc toward a central point of symbolic reference, which is San Francisco itself. The moment San Francisco is separated into its component parts, it recoalesces around this persistent symbolic identity. The fact that this identity is so elusive in its final meaning, that it refuses to be packaged and given one name, adds to the continuing vitality of San Francisco as a city of fact and a city of imagination and dream. It is sometimes frustrating to live in a city that so persistently hides its central metaphor. Neither history nor present-day circumstances have conferred upon San Francisco a clear-cut definition.

And yet the search continues. It is evident in the work of the architects and planners that is chronicled in this catalogue and exhibition. It emanates from the individual experiences chronicled in the fictional and autobiographical selections. Who knows? Someday the final metaphor of San Francisco may be found. But I doubt it. San Francisco began as the dream of a city on windswept, ocean-girded hills. The dream materialized across the decades in a thousand real and imagined shapes. Like a platonic archetype conferring existence in the material world, this imagined San Francisco haunts us still. Paradoxically, it is also a very real place. We enjoy it day by day, year by year. In so many ways, as this catalogue suggests, the imagined San Francisco is more real than reality itself (fig. 4).

Paolo Polledri

Visionary San Francisco: Dreamscape and Reality

"…what he sought was always something lying ahead, and even if it was a matter of the past it was a past that changed gradually as he advanced on his journey, because the traveler's past changes according to the route he has followed: not the immediate past, that is, to which each day that goes by adds a day, but the more remote past. Arriving at each new city, the traveler finds again a past that he did not know he had: the foreignness of what you no longer are or no longer possess lies in wait for you in foreign, unpossessed places."
— Italo Calvino, *Invisible Cities*

It is unusual when an art museum takes an active interest in cities, not merely parts of a city but the myriad of buildings, parts of buildings, daily experiences, talk, business, dreams, and grittiness that together form the urban environment. One can imagine the half-whispered question: is art not the domain of a museum,

and is it not better to leave all urban questions—well known to be complex, controversial, and often unanswerable—to planners and politicians?

To add to the puzzle, this title is ambiguous: why not simply "San Francisco" rather than "Visionary San Francisco"? Are these visions of the past or of the future? Does this visionary quality still exist? Does being visionary refer to evoking wishful thinking, insulated from reality, or is being visionary a virtue? Are these visions ineffable dreams, literary utopias, political and social agendas, or are they visions of the physical city? Finally, why visions at all when we need deeds?

To begin with, we need a vision to point us in the right direction. The year 1990 marks the beginning of a new decade, traditionally the opportunity for a fresh start. It is also the beginning of the last decade of the

1   *View of San Francisco's Financial District from Potrero Hill, 1990. (Photo: Ben Blackwell)*

present millennium, a word that by itself is sufficient to evoke images of anxiety and anticipation. This beginning requires not only a freshly minted cliché to distinguish it from the previous years—the "rebellious" 1960s, the "me-generation" of the 1970s, the "yuppies" of the 1980s—but also a carefully prepared balance sheet of past activities and future prospects.

Unease rather than the tempered optimism of the previous two decades has characterized the 1980s. These have been years of uncertainty and indecisiveness compared to the history of the earlier part of this century when, amid natural disasters, economic dislocations, wars, and soul-searching, San Francisco achieved the role of capital of the Pacific (fig. 2). Now that this role seems momentarily lost, there is some groping for a new vision to direct the future.

In an article published in 1988, Kevin Starr attributed this feeling of unease to the loss of public identity in San Francisco during the late 1970s and 1980s.[1] Large-scale public works such as the Civic Center, the Produce Market, and the Sutro Baths (fig. 3) were not only picturesque landmarks but also social and cultural points of reference. With their demolition, part of the collective soul of San Francisco is also gone. New public or semi-public development areas such as the Yerba Buena Center and the huge Mission Bay project

are plagued by factionalism; new ventures such as the home port for the battleship *U.S.S. Missouri* and the candidacy of San Francisco for the 1996 Olympic Games have been blocked by conflicting interests. The public focuses on parochial rather than public issues. Private enterprise, once the source of philanthropy in San Francisco, is viewed with distrust. A new vision to bind the public spirit seems to be lacking.

So rampant is the skepticism about improving our condition that when new opportunities present themselves, we immediately anticipate wasting them. With the closing of the U.S. Army base at the Presidio (fig. 4), the federal government will bequeath 1,400 acres of park and unspoiled coast to San Francisco. Architectural critic Allan Temko has expressed the fear that although the Presidio offers an unprecedented opportunity to adopt a new, visionary plan, its future could be undermined by the lack of vision and the parochial interests of petty bureaucrats, technocrats, and "populist nuts."[2]

To focus only on immediate surroundings or interests, to seek only the short-term gain, and to lose sight of a broader perspective seems to be endemic to contemporary American culture. The agendas of groups, individuals, or city government officials, even when legitimate, polarize viewpoints not shared by the whole

2 *Jules Guerin.* Civic Center, *1916.*
Watercolor on paper, 78 × 72 in. (198.1 × 182.9 cm).
Collection of the San Francisco Public Library.
(Photo: Ben Blackwell)
From the early years of this century, San Francisco
seemed destined to fulfill the role of capital of the Pacific.
At its administrative and political center, the most
important civic buildings are neatly framed by long
avenues, each terminating against another significant
building. The architectural style was inspired by that of
European capitals, but the sweeping urban vision is the
result of American planning principles.

3 *Sutro Baths. Courtesy Gabriel Moulin Studios, San*
Francisco.

Many of San Francisco's historic buildings, such as the
Sutro Baths, have disappeared. These buildings accom-
plished much more than their designated function; they
were social and cultural icons as well.

community. Along with a lack of consensus comes strong opposition. The decision-making process slows to a standstill. The history of the Yerba Buena Center—mentioned in Kevin Starr's article and discussed in Sally Woodbridge's essay in this book—provides a strong example. Yerba Buena Center was launched as a powerful vision shared only by some and opposed by many.[3] As a result, after more than thirty years the project is still largely unbuilt.

A shared vision for the city is necessary. This book and the exhibition it accompanies aim at reconstructing such a vision. They examine the history of visionary projects for San Francisco in this century and show that it is still possible to conceive a vision for the city.

There is a history of San Francisco as its inhabitants have wished it to be, which keeps pace with the history of the city as it has become. This is a *shadow* history, chronicling not the desire for a particular urban form but for an impulse toward constantly creating new forms.[4] Some of the visions that constitute this history have spawned other projects; some have been powerful

catalyzers of public efforts on behalf of their own realization.

Since its beginnings, San Francisco has often appealed to visionaries who have seen it as the bridgehead of civilization in the West and have sought a status befitting this role. Heralded as the "Paris of the West" in the early part of the century (fig. 5), it was subsequently viewed as the prominent city of an expanding metropolitan area and, more recently, as a gateway to the Pacific region and the Far East. These visionaries have proposed ambitious, but often unfulfilled, plans for the city's development. Even though these plans may not have been realized, they have nevertheless influenced architects' and planners' visions for San Francisco; what began as an unfulfilled dream has often molded what was built. These visions usually did not refer to an imaginary future but to the present. By showing alternatives to the city of their time, these visionaries focused on what it lacked and, by so doing, directed their efforts toward supplying their need (fig. 6).

As Gray Brechin indicates, to transform San Francisco into a twentieth-century capital, a "Paris of the

West," architects, urban designers, and planners shared their efforts with civic leaders, wealthy businessmen who held a commitment to the quality of life in their city, and philanthropists. At times this bond between patrons and architects resulted in a vision strong enough to create a political consensus unmatched in the history of this city.[5] Gradually, in the 1920s and 1930s, as the attention of planners and architects shifted from the city as a whole to practical problems related to individual areas, public attention also turned from visionary goals to finding the means to resolve everyday problems. As Daniel P. Gregory writes, politicians, architects, and planners enthusiastically prescribed visions that took into account an in-

creasingly complex urban reality by employing increasingly complex technologies. Attention to the particular rather than to the general, however, did not ignite the consensus that was necessary to achieve even modestly scaled results. Lack of consensus became particularly obvious after World War II during the period examined in Sally Woodbridge's essay. Yerba Buena Gardens was preceded by other projects, such as the Ferry Building and other redevelopment areas, which are still being questioned thirty, forty, or even fifty years after their conception. As politicians, planners, and architects attempt to address particular problems, they often lose sight of the whole, the vision that could inspire the rest of us, that could create public

4   View of the Presidio from the top of the Golden Gate Bridge.

5 *View of Market Street toward the Ferry Building,*
1989. (Photo: Paolo Polledri)
Market Street is the urban spine of San Francisco. In the
view of planners such as Daniel Burnham and architects
such as Willis Polk, it was to become a grand boulevard
like the Champs-Elysées.

consensus. When people make this vision their own,
leadership becomes a coordination of efforts toward
the same goals and ceases to be imposition.

The city's *shadow* history documents an essential part
of our history. This desire for a better life, a better
environment, has been an integral part of the history of
Western civilization since the poetic vision of the lost
Eden. Plato's *Republic* represents the first systematic
attempt to rationalize the complex realities of the
Greek *polis:* moral principles, political and social dynamics, and aesthetics form the blueprint for a perfect
urban mechanism. During the Renaissance the inspiration drawn from the literature of antiquity came to
fruition: rulers, subjects, and such men as Leonardo,
Leon Battista Alberti, and Antonio Filarete, who combined the roles of architect, engineer, planner, and
artist, found the medieval city inadequate to embody
the ambitions of a new type of ruler and a new society.
Their admiration for the architecture of antiquity was
not only an aesthetic choice but also reflected the belief that it was the most appropriate solution for social
and political problems. Alberti gave architecture first
place in the hierarchy of the arts on the grounds that
the architect alone could coordinate every urban activity. Architecture and engineering treatises were also

political treatises, as they attempted to describe an
environment in harmony with its inhabitants. New
theories found a practical application during the Italian Renaissance in such cities as Rome, Pienza, and
Venice.[6]

Architects were not the only people to prescribe a
different, usually better, environment. Political philosophers such as Thomas More, Tommaso Campa-
nella, and Francis Bacon also discussed their visions
but located them in vaguely defined lands, usually
with an ocean separating imagination and reality. The
choice of these locations manifested optimism for the
geographical discoveries of the fifteenth and sixteenth
centuries but also reflected the total incompatibility
between the ideal society described and the prevailing
political and physical environment of their time—its
rulers, class divisions, and limited justice. Therefore it
was necessary to imagine a completely new environment, hence their use of the name "utopia"—no place.

There is a difference between the architect's—even
the social architect's—vision and the political writer's
utopian blueprint. The ideal city of the Renaissance
consisted of individual buildings—private residences,
public buildings, and open spaces—that were rede-
signed according to a more decorous architectural language but remained substantially similar in function
and name to their medieval predecessors. The goal of
architects was not to create a perfect society but to
prescribe an environment more attuned to the society
of their time. For them, the physical form caught up
with the world of ideas. In contrast, political writers
such as Thomas More conceived a totally different,

Visionary San Francisco 21

6   *Arthur Mathews*. Modern City, *n. d.*
Watercolor and pencil on paper, 27⅞ × 21 in.
(70.8 × 53.3 cm). Collection of the Santa Barbara
Museum of Art, gift of Harold Wagner.

Mathews shows a city immersed in fog and vaguely re-
sembling the San Francisco of his day. Large on the
horizon loom palatial structures. Although unfinished,
this painting reflects the ambition for a city still largely
to be developed.

7   *Camille Pissarro*. Boulevard des Italiens, Morning,
Sunlight, *1897.*
Oil on canvas, 28⅞ × 36¼ in. (73.2 × 92.1 cm).
Collection of the National Gallery of Art, Washington;
Chester Dale Collection.

At the end of the nineteenth century, Paris became the city
that Baron Haussmann and Napoleon III had envisioned.
Large streets lined with trees became the model that
planners and architects sought to imitate in their cities.

alternative reality, immune to the defects of the one in which they lived. Usually the physical settings were described too vaguely to be recognizable. Whereas the architects' visions were practical and prescriptive, the philosophers' utopias were theoretical.[7]

Rarely, however, were visionaries and utopists completely incompatible. Sometimes their views overlapped, and even social utopias exerted influence on the physical environment. In the eighteenth century, in the climate of the European Enlightenment, philosophers, political writers, and even architects such as Claude Nicolas Ledoux questioned the social institutions of their time and proposed radically different ones based on a strict logic of social justice.

The distinction between vision and utopia became increasingly blurred. During the nineteenth century Baron Haussmann's plans for the urban renewal of Paris (1850-1870) also illustrated an aesthetic goal for other European as well as American cities (fig. 7). In

the twentieth century, architects and planners—such as Ebenezer Howard (*Garden Cities of Tomorrow*, 1902), Tony Garnier (La Cité Industrielle, project, 1904), Le Corbusier (La Ville Radieuse, project, 1928), and Frank Lloyd Wright (Broadacre City, project, 1935), among others—accommodated the requirements of new activities, transportation, building technology, and smaller living spaces. Recognizing that many cities had reached the saturation point in terms of population and size, they struggled to find new, more appropriate forms of urban environment. In the twentieth century, the ideas of urban designers and architects lagged behind a world of new forms.

Not unlike Renaissance architects, early twentieth-century architects and planners developed visions to resolve practical problems, to halt the deterioration of urban life, and to meet new social demands. Unlike Renaissance architects, however, they envisioned new building types made possible by new technologies.

New technology allowed a concentration of people in high-rise apartment towers; the advent of the automobile made commuting possible; and the need to overcome urban congestion suggested that the countryside could also offer the amenities of urban life. Before then, the city had maintained its traditional structure, with working and living quarters in close proximity. Architects and planners instead proposed a new type of urban environment, with rigidly zoned areas designed for living, working, and leisure. Because of the new means available to them, their vision was practical and utopian at the same time. Their utopia, however, differed substantially from More's; it was not the heavenly citadel isolated from the corrupting influence of the external world but the prototype of an environment for a new society.

More recently, the vision of a world regulated by technology has revealed fundamental flaws. Technology has been exposed as a byproduct of human culture and is only as sound and effective as the individuals who have forged it. The subtly seductive nightmare of the film *Blade Runner* explores the complex interaction between technology, city dwellers, and the urban environment. As William Gibson shows in his short story "Skinner's Room," this interaction produces unpredictable results; technology becomes as useful and as flexible as scrap metal in a junkyard.

The history of visions and utopias is as important as the history of actual urban changes. By ignoring it, we cannot accurately evaluate our current condition, and we fall prey to misleading ideologies. Unless we know our history and become aware of our present, we cannot make decisions for our future.

Architects, urban designers, and planners have been most successful in inspiring others, it seems, when they regard the city as a work of art—an environment that can reflect their purpose, talent, skill, thinking, even control, just as a painting does for the artist. It is therefore appropriate for a museum to focus on a city, since behind each project lurks a creator. But a city is also much more than a painting or a piece of sculpture.

All cities are recognizable as forms—forms in the landscape, forms against the sky, and forms reflecting the status, habits, and culture of their inhabitants. One can think of Rome as a city of churches, piazzas, and obelisks; Paris as a city of long and rectilinear boulevards, the Opéra, and—why not?—the Eiffel Tower; New York as the city of a thousand spires, where one looks for the familiar outlines of the Empire State and the Chrysler buildings. San Francisco is perhaps one of the best examples of a very complex form (fig. 8). Varied in topography, it is ordered by a strict grid of similarly shaped building blocks. Yet, although deceptively similar if seen on a map or from the air, these blocks appear strikingly different at street level. Differences between Russian Hill, the Castro district, or the Tenderloin blur from the air, but if one looks closely, these areas reveal a different texture that tells much about their inhabitants.[8]

The artistic quality of a city, however, does not reside only in its form. As Mark Helprin writes in this book, a city is not composed merely of a set of formal components. Rather, the artistic essence of a city is found in much more elusive attributes—the view from a hilltop, the silhouette of a bridge against the sky, the glimpse of people and traffic in the distant landscape, and the memories we have of all of this: of driving along a street, of walking through the park, of friends and buildings.

The memory of the city's past embraces not only an awareness of its history—the burden of its tradition, some might call it—but also our memories or fragments of memories of it. To paraphrase T. S. Eliot, our appreciation of today's city requires a sense of its history, not only its past but also the impact of the past on our present.[9] We look down the street and see the traffic, the pedestrians, the sequence of short and tall buildings receding in the distance. If we examine a photograph of San Francisco dating from the turn of the century, for example, we immediately become aware of the difference between those buildings, people, and vehicles and present-day ones. If we look at the same area today, we might not be aware of the relationship we establish with the past, but we know that the buildings, cars, and people belong to today's world. By looking we establish a connection, however tenuous, between all of these elements.

The memory of a particular urban environment remains with us, together with all of the other memories we have of the city throughout our lives. We will add it to the memory of what we read about the city. Indeed, we see cities through the eyes of writers—novelists, poets, essayists, and sportswriters. The city's history becomes our story, a personal as well as a common history. We may view it as a metaphor of the lives of its inhabitants, such as those plagued by AIDS, as Richard Rodriguez does in this book. The painted facades of Victorian houses become transparent and fragile, revealing their true nature: a screen barely concealing the anguish. Or we may look at the city as a puzzle made of a series of layers, stacked on top of one

8   *View of the San Francisco Bay Area from a satellite.*
Courtesy Space Shots, Los Angeles.

another, as does Joe Gores' private eye, Neil Fargo. The solution of the puzzle is not in peeling these layers but in finding where they intersect.

The form of the city eludes us also because we can never comprehend the whole, but we remember its parts. The city is made of different fragments—memories, perceptions, and emotions that intersect one another, as they do in a novel. We perceive a greater order from these apparently random parts. Even though our comprehension of the city is fragmented into a series of short narratives, we still "read" the city. Its appeal resides not in the whole but in each of its fragments. It is this essentially literary quality of the city and of its designs that makes it a work of art.

Quite unlike a painting or a sculpture, however, cities lack paternity or authorship. Even though we

9 *View of San Francisco from Treasure Island, 1989. (Photo: Paolo Polledri)*

think of a building, or a part of the city, as the work of an architect, we often discover that the architect did indeed have a major role, but that he or she also relied on the efforts of many other people—assistants, clients, engineers, city administrators, critics—so that the result is quite different from the initial idea.

Architects, urban designers, and planners, as they lay out their narratives, incorporate these memories and this collective will in a vision. These narratives begin as little more than abstractions—the designers' plans or projects. They impose a new order over an existing fabric. Their plans, however, conceal action, plot, drama, and emotion not conveyed by lines and numbers on a sheet of paper. The plan represents only the surface of things.[10]

What we call drama, emotion, and action are the sentiments, the beliefs that inspire the plan—in a word, the vision. The vision refers to the future, for, of course, a designer's blueprint illustrates something that does not yet exist. Yet the vision demarcates a narrow frontier between past and future because it is a reaction against the past that has given rise to the vi-

sion. Virtually every visionary project in the urban history of San Francisco reflects the past.

Urban forms are not fixed but rather dynamic forms in which the parts—buildings, open spaces, infrastructures—interact constantly with one another and with the whole. Each new building creates a new set of relationships with surrounding buildings, thereby altering the space around it. Other buildings are influenced by these alterations, as are the ways in which people use them, the activities performed in them, and the economy of the area. As a result, each new building starts a chain of events that strays well beyond its physical boundaries. Architecture, urban design, and planning are engaged in a mutual exchange. The difference between these disciplines is ultimately one of scale; buildings have an impact on the overall form of the city, and the city makes demands on individual buildings.

As with buildings, the city itself reflects a collective will. At different times buildings undergo changes in use and are transformed into different structures. Changes in the economy may cause entire areas to

become suddenly affluent or derelict. City dwellers spend most of their time in buildings, which are the physical manifestations of their labor and economic investment. Buildings promote or discourage the concentration of voters and shape the profile of electoral districts; finally, the built environment is directly responsible for the well-being of its inhabitants. In short, the urban environment is also a political environment.

This environment is as varied as the individuals who inhabit it. San Francisco is what each of us wants to make of it. To preserve without change is to ignore our tradition and to oppose the dynamism of the city. To encourage urban change without a vision is to neglect an essential component of our culture. Here lies our challenge and our greatest opportunity (fig. 9).

NOTES

1   Kevin Starr, "Commentary by historian Kevin Starr on San Francisco's loss of soul," *Image* magazine, *San Francisco Examiner*, May 1, 1988.

2   Allan Temko, "What to Do with the Presidio. Time is Now to Plan a Visionary Future," *San Francisco Chronicle*, May 15, 1989; "The Presidio Should Become a Center of Global Learning," *San Francisco Chronicle*, May 16, 1989.

3   Chester Hartman, *The Transformation of San Francisco* (Totowa, N.J.: Rowman and Allanheld, 1984).

4   The meaning of the term "desire" is that given by Italo Calvino in *The Uses of Literature* (San Diego, New York, London: Harcourt Brace Jovanovich, 1986), pp. 52-61.

5   William Issel and Robert W. Cherny, *San Francisco 1865-1932. Politics, Power, and Urban Development* (Berkeley and Los Angeles: University of California Press, 1986), p. 204.

6   For an original treatment of Renaissance thought see Eugenio Garin, *Scienza e Vita Civile nel Rinascimento Italiano* (Roma and Bari: Laterza, 1985. First ed. 1965), especially the chapter "La città ideale," pp. 33-56.

7   The difference between "vision" and "utopia" is discussed by Garin, op.cit., and by Karl Mannheim, *Ideology and Utopia* (New York: Harcourt, Brace and Co.; London: K. Paul, Trench, Trubner and Co., Ltd., 1936). Cf. in particular Chapter IV: "The Utopian Mentality." A review of urban utopian conceits is given by Ian Todd and Michael Wheeler, *Utopia* (New York: Harmony Books, 1978).

8   For a much more complete exposition of these ideas, see Aldo Rossi, *The Architecture of the City* (Cambridge, Mass., and London: MIT Press, 1984).

9   See T. S. Eliot, "Tradition and the Individual Talent." *Selected Essays* (New York: Harcourt, Brace and Co., 1950), pp. 3-11.

10   See Umberto Eco, *The Open Work* (Cambridge, Mass.: Harvard University Press, 1989), pp. 114-15.

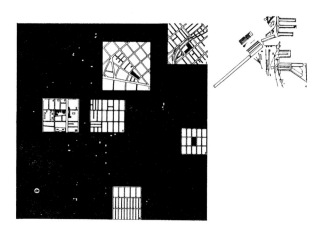

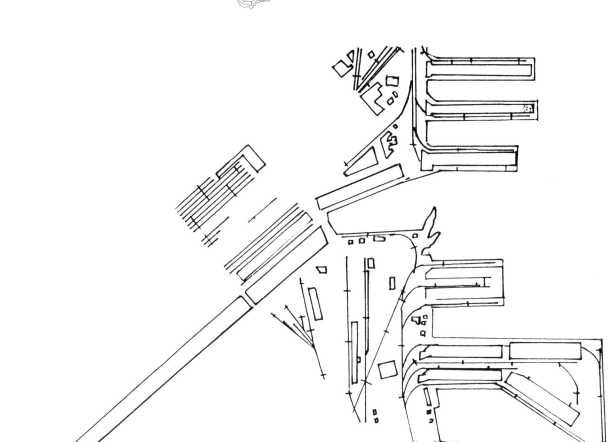

4

Joe Gores

Dance of the Dead

It was *La Noche de Muerte*. In San Francisco's Mission District, death jostled and capered on the sidewalks, spilled out over the curbs, crossed mid-street in front of honking cars. It hung on art gallery walls, as *exquisito pan de muerto* it was sold over the counters of the bakery shops. Beneath the ubiquitous wall murals, death shouted greetings in liquid Spanish, bought yellow marigolds—*flores de muerto*—lit candles, kept vigil, made *ofrendas* for *muertitos chicos* who by some cruel twist of fate had preceded their parents to the grave.

In the cantina the mariachi band's mournful brass crowded the dance floor with death sweating and stomping and flashing its eyes. Death-clad dancers crushed closer, tighter, until buttocks rotated sensually against unknown buttocks behind them. In that press of sweating bodies, you could lift your feet and be swirled around the room. Swirled against hired death and then away again as, grinning, it slid its stiletto blade delicately up between your third and fourth ribs, through your pleural cavity into your heart so you were dead, dead in your death's suit, dead as dust.

Dead. But El Muerto knows who. El Muerto knows why. El Muerto knows, and will tell. In good time. In the proper way.

---

1   *Diana Agrest and Mario Gandelsonas.* Drawing No. 1: Frame, *1989.*
Ink on Mylar, 24 × 24 in. (61 × 61 cm).
Courtesy San Francisco Museum of Modern Art.
(Photo: Ben Blackwell)

(a) A small piece of ground, generally used for a specific purpose. (b) A measured area of land, a lot. In plotting the scene of the crimes, a magnifying glass assists in exposing the urban fabric where violence is manifest.

2   *Diana Agrest and Mario Gandelsonas.* Drawing No. 1: Frame (detail), *1989.*
Courtesy San Francisco Museum of Modern Art.
(Photo: Ben Blackwell)

"El Muerto?" asked Neil Fargo in a neutral voice. "Sounds like Toneff wants me to go grave-robbing."

"Mr. Toneff," said Angelina Roydon automatically. "El Muerto is a group of *muralistas.*"

She had almost violet eyes that hinted at sins of a magnitude Yahweh might once have sacked a couple of cities over.

"They work in secret, then unveil their work anonymously. No one seems to know who they are, although our previous investigators learned that Esteban Gijon founded the group. Mr. Toneff feels only El Muerto can complete Gijon's mural at the China Basin Center without destroying the integrity of the work. Mr. Toneff feels that it is essential they be identified as soon as possible so work can recommence immediately."

"Gijon was political. He pissed off the power structure."

"If Mr. Toneff was 'pissed off,' as you say, he would hardly have offered Gijon a great deal of money to do the entranceway mural at the new center." She leaned back for a heavy file folder on the corner of the desk beside her. The movement emphasized the firm, rounded contour of her breasts. She held out the folder. "Mr. Toneff wants you to have these reports——"

"There'll be nothing in there for me."

Irritation appeared on her face again as Neil Fargo stood up. "Don't be such a smug bastard, Fargo. Other detectives are good at their jobs, too, you know."

He dropped the folder into the wastebasket.

"These weren't," he said.

"We got squat," Vince Wylie said with defensive savagery.

"Characterize squat for me," said Neil Fargo.

He was sitting on one corner of the cigarette-scarred desk in Wylie's third-floor homicide bureau cubbyhole in the gray boxy Hall of Justice on Bryant Street. Instead of responding, Wylie flopped open the folder on

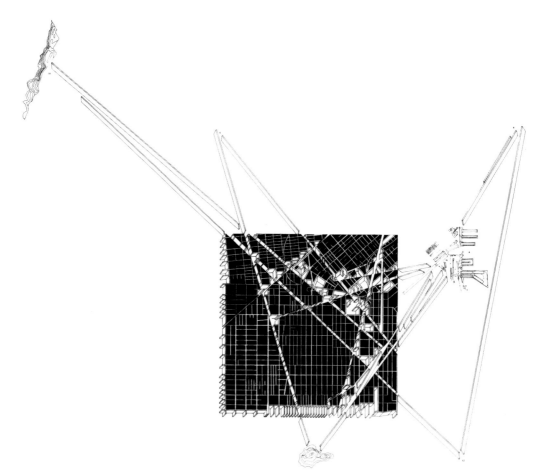

his desk to signal the discussion had ended. Neil Fargo leaned down toward him.

He said: "Milovan Toneff."

"Bullshit."

But uncertainty had entered Inspector Vince Wylie's eyes. Power was San Francisco's blood sport; Toneff was a top gun, Wylie but one of the hounds. Cautious now, he sighed and leaned back in his creaking swivel chair.

"Squat consists of one dead spic, Esteban Gijon, shivved between the ribs when he was on a dance floor with half the beaners in the Mission District—all of them dressed up like freaking skeletons."

"*La Noche de Muerte,*" said Neil Fargo.

"Squat consists of no perp, no weapon, no fingerprints, no witnesses, no motive."

It was a raw day, but the previous night's rain had stopped. Five big muscular dogs played on the wet grass of Precita Park. Over the Mural Art Center storefront was a mural featuring a Buddhist third eye and a landscape in primary water and greenery colors.

Paloma Escobar, a striking Hispanic woman in her early thirties wearing a paint-smeared smock, was working with furious concentration on a panel of wet plaster at a large easel in the chilly, barren room. She cast dark eyes over at Neil Fargo's entrance.

"You." Her voice accused an ex-lover. She tried to blow a strand of black hair from in front of her face.

Neil Fargo nodded at the panel. "Something new."

"I attended a workshop given by some people who worked with Diego Rivera in New York and got fascinated with the fresco technique." She gestured with the brush. "Just a test piece."

He nodded.

"I have to know about El Muerto."

"You're working for that pig Toneff?"

"Toneff's paying me. I work for myself."

3   Diana Agrest and Mario Gandelsonas. Drawing No. 2: Plot, *1989.*
Ink on Mylar, 24 × 24 in. (61 × 61 cm).
Courtesy San Francisco Museum of Modern Art.
(Photo: Ben Blackwell)
The series of events consists of an outline of the action of a narrative or a drama. The insertion of the plot onto the urban fabric subverts physical travel and generates boulevards of trespass. In this way the city is rewritten.

4   Diana Agrest and Mario Gandelsonas. Drawing No. 2: Plot *(detail), 1989.*
Courtesy San Francisco Museum of Modern Art.
(Photo: Ben Blackwell)

"He corrupted Esteban with his money. Now Esteban is dead."

He said softly, *"Morir por la libertad es vivir siempre."*

To Die for Freedom Is to Live Forever was the title of a mural she had done ten years before.

"Has Toneff corrupted you as well, Neil?" she asked softly.

"Do you really ask me that?"

She looked away first.

"The Feast of Our Lady of Guadalupe at Mission Dolores—you will dance again this year?"

"Five in the morning? In December?" She gave a harsh laugh of negation.

"You can't help yourself," he said.

Paloma wielded her brush for some time in silence. She finally spoke as if to the wet plaster, not to him.

"Eduardo Mesa knows who El Muerto is—if he will talk with you. Balmy Alley."

The face of almost every building in nondescript little Balmy Alley, which runs for a single block between 24th and 25th, was covered with living pictures in a remarkable variety of styles and colors. The defacement with spray-can graffiti had begun about five years before. Now Eduardo Mesa, a small round man with a bandido mustache and musical English full of Latinate vowels, worked to restore them.

"I need to know about El Muerto."

Mesa shrugged expressively. "A *muralistas* collective."

"That works in secret. The founder of which is dead."

"There is no connection."

"I'm a connection."

"Only with a man who wants us to finish Escobar's mural."

After dark, Neil Fargo tailed him to a restaurant called La Posta. Mesa split dinner and the bill with a tall, flame-haired woman. Knowing where to find Mesa, Neil Fargo followed the flaming hair to Hampshire Street, lost her when she got into a 1979 Datsun and drove away. Neil Fargo wrote his report, closing with a request for further instructions and Eduardo Mesa's residence address from the crisscross directory.

The DMV Searching Registration Service report showed the 1979 Datsun was registered to a Melody Manion in the 600 block of Rhode Island. She was waiting at the top of the inside stairs in a black workout suit. Neil Fargo pushed his hornrims down on his nose and

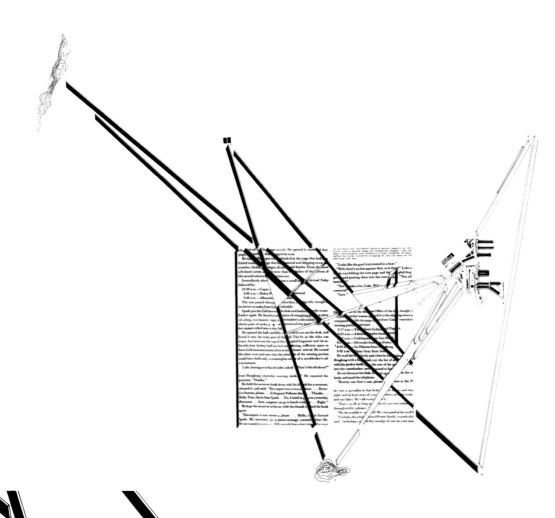

In mid-mass the feathered dancers weaved paganly up the
aisle like a sacred snake as flashbulbs popped; they had
been incorporated into Catholic ritual hundreds of years
before by rural converts clinging to the old ways as they
embraced the new.

"Looks like the gent's interested in a boat."

"Well, there's no law against that, or is there?" Luke Spade was folding the torn page and the crumpled fragment and putting them into his coat-pocket. "You all here now?"

"Yes. Thanks a lot, Luke. Will comes in?"

"Sure."

clas...ed-adv... ...s... page outside. He opened it, exam...d that page, ...nothi... ther... ...pped his eyes.

He tu...the... ...per over ...d looked at the page that had b...n folded inside... ...ge that he...nancial and shipping news, weather, births, ...riages, divorc... ...nd deaths. From th... ...wer left-hand corner, a... ...e more than t... inches of the ...ttom of the second column l... ...n torn out.

Immediately abov... ...was a small ca... a *Arrived Today* followed by:

   12:20 a.m.—Capac...

   5:05 a.m.—Helen P... ...enwood.

   5:06 a.m.—Albarado... ...don.

The tear passed throug... ...next line, ...ing only enough o... its letters to make *from Syd... ...* inferable.

Spade put the *Call* down o... ...he desk and looke... ...o the waste-basket again. He found a sm... piece of wrapping-p... ...a piece of string, two hosiery tags, a... ...berdasher's sale-ticket ... dozen pairs of socks ... ...ottom of the bas... ...p... ...of newspaper rolled into a tiny ball.

He opened the ball carefully, s... ...ed it out on the desk, and fitted it into the torn part of the ...ll. The fit at the sides was exact, but between the top of the c...mpled fragment and the inferable *from Sydney* half an inch wa... ...issing, sufficient space to have held announcement of six or se... boats' arrival. He turned the sheet over and saw that the other ...de of the missing portion could have held only a meaningless co... r of a stockbroker's advertisement.

Luke, leaning over his shoulder, asked: "...hat's this all about?"

...rom Hongkong yesterday morning, docke... ..." He repeated the ...uestion. "Thanks."

He held the receiver-hook down with his th...mb for a moment, ...eleased it, and said: "Davenport two o two o... ...ease. ... Detec...ive bureau, please. ... Is Sergeant Polhaus the... ... Thanks. ... Hello, Tom, this is Sam Spade. ... Yes, I tried to g... you yesterday ...fternoon. ... Sure, suppose you go to lunch with ...e. ... Right."

He kept the receiver to his ear while his thumb w...ked the hook ...gain.

"Davenport o one seven o, please. ... Hello, t... is Samuel Spade. My secretary g...t a phone-message yesterda... that Mr. Bryan wanted to see ...e. Will you ask him what tim... ...he most

SPA... ...ut to the Bu...ess Office of the C..., bought a ...pre...us day's issue, op...ed it to the ship...ng-news-p... compared ...with the page t...n from Cai... wastebas... missing portio...ad read:

   5:17 a.m.—Ta... from Sydney ...nd Pap...e.

   6:05 a.m.—Admira... ...oples from ...stori...

   ...7 a.m.—Caddopeak ...m San Pe...

   8:1... m.—Silverado from ...n Pedro.

   8:05 a... —La Paloma from H...gkong.

   9:03 a.m.—...aisy Gray from Sea...

He read the li... ...lowly and when he ha... ...ished *Hongkong* with a fin... nail, cut the list of ar... ...t... with his pocket-knife, ... the rest of the p... ...a... into the wastebasket, an... ...urned to his...

He sat down at his desk, lo... ...d up a... ...n the te... book, and used the telephone.

"Kearny one four o one, please. ...ere is the *P...

he's not a specialist in that field, ...e m...es and date... right, and at least none of your... ...orities or ...ir works... and-out fakes. He's all excite... ...r it."

"That's swell, as long as ... ...oesn't get too enthus... t through it if it's phoney.",

"Oh, he wouldn't—n... ...ed! He's too good at his stuff fo...

"U h-huh, the whol... ...nned Perine family's wonderful said, "including yo... ...d the smudge of soot on your nose handed her a card with the KQED educational TV logo on it and the name NESTOR FABIAN, with Producer written below.

"You're early," she accused. "I was dancing when—"

"Of course you were." His voice was that of a public television announcer trying to sound British without being overt.

In the living room, Neil Fargo sat down on the couch and crossed his legs. His socks were bright red. He wore a plaid cap and a tweed jacket with leather patches on the elbows, as if on his way to hunt elk with Teddy Roosevelt.

"El Muerto."

"You said you wanted to discuss the San Francisco mural scene for a possible feature piece. I don't know anything about El Muerto."

"You're one of them. You and Eduardo Mesa and—"

"Eduardo wouldn't have told you about—"

"Not Eduardo," agreed Neil Fargo quickly.

"And surely not—" In sudden realization of what she had almost done, she stopped. He said nothing at all, nor did he move. It proved irresistible to her. "Esteban's China Basin mural was to have a continual sound track." He was still silent. She demanded abruptly, "Why are you here?"

"I want to do a television feature story on... El Muerto's memorial mural by its surviving members."

"If you already knew about *Dance of the Dead*—"

"Being done in secrecy at a secret location... where? To be announced and shown publicly for the first time... when?"

But she voiced no further indiscretions.

5 Diana Agrest and Mario Gandelsonas. Drawing No. 3: Narrative, *1989*.
Ink and collage on Mylar, 24 × 24 in. (61 × 61 cm).
Courtesy San Francisco Museum of Modern Art.
(Photo: Ben Blackwell)
A secret plan is developed to accomplish a hostile or illegal purposer, or scheme. By allowing the urban plot to interrupt the narrative, the text is fragmented thus proposing new spatial organizations of utterance. The text interrupts itself, a pause in which to consider the implications of our reading of the city.

6 Diana Agrest and Mario Gandelsonas. Drawing No. 3: Narrative (detail), *1989*.
Courtesy San Francisco Museum of Modern Art.
(Photo: Ben Blackwell)

Eduardo Mesa lived in a rented room where Folsom pressed its nose against the rounded green breast of Bernal Heights. Since it was early December, it was still dark when he started down the hill from Mrs. Morales' house on his way to the day's work in Balmy Alley. An early jogger coming into Folsom on the dirt jogging path from the open land above struck Mesa a terrible blow on the side of the head with a length of iron bar, crushing the temporal bone and ripping off his left ear.

The jogger was a taut-bodied, open-faced man in his forties named Scread; his smile was dreadful in the same way that really bad breath is dreadful. He dragged the unconscious man into the bushes and kicked him to death.

When Neil Fargo heard the TV news account of the killing, he left an urgent message on Melody's machine, hit the street running. Mesa's death had to be more than a random mugging—and he had already phoned in his report on Melody. No answer at her door, no lights in her flat. *No entiendo* at the lower flat. He settled down in his car out front for a sleepless night.

By the light from the window of the bakery next door to the Strident Theater, Melody reread the *Examiner* story on the slaughter of Eduardo Mesa and shivered, not with the cold. She turned with quick relief when the theater door finally was opened from within by a Charlie Manson clone.

"Is Vikki in there?"

He nodded. "The Gay Blade is taking her over the hurdles."

She went past posters for *Charlie and Mrs. Olson* to black cloth baffles that herded incoming audiences around the bleachers and down a narrow aisle to the "intimate" floor-level stage. A waspish man in jeans and T-shirt and open pin-stripe vest was just leaping to his feet and throwing up his hands.

"This is destructive. *Destructive*," he exclaimed and stalked gracefully off.

Vikki, a brunette about Melody's age in jeans and sweater, started to giggle when she saw Melody.

"Poor Gay Blade, he thinks we're doing O'Neill."

She sobered when she saw that Melody's hands had begun unconsciously shredding the newspaper they held.

"Vikki, could... could I sleep over at your place for a few nights? No questions asked?"

It was dawn again. Scread went by the new Porsche parked beside an abandoned World War II gun emplacement on Presidio cliffs that fell away like a receding chin. Inside, the concrete bunker smelled strongly of urine and faintly of excrement. The Porsche owner stood with his forearms on the crumbling edge of the massive gun port, staring out over the Pacific.

Scread said to his back, "She didn't show."

The man whirled, startled, perhaps terrified, then said petulantly, "I thought Fargo was supposed to be good. He charges enough. If he got us a dead address——"

"The girl's still around—clothes, cosmetics still in her apartment. I waited there for her all night, then had to go out the bathroom window because Fargo had the place staked out."

"Why did I ever let myself be talked into this? First Mesa and now suddenly.... I don't want any more killing. Maybe we can just buy her off, like erasing a tape when——"

"Didn't you hear me? *Fargo was there.* We have to find her before he does. This isn't Memorex—there's only one way to erase a memory from a human mind."

The other man stared after him as if after a viper almost trod upon. He was sweating heavily in the dank air.

Milovan Toneff was sweating heavily as he parked his sports car across the sidewalk in front of his massive white three-story Queen Anne in the 2300 block of Broadway. It was slightly past seven a.m., the sunrise shadows long and dark across the rich Pacific Heights street. He looked his sixty-three years this morning; in the bungalow-sized living room he found Neil Fargo waiting.

"Who the hell are you supposed to be?"

"The Buddha, but I fucked up and can't get off the wheel until next time around."

"A nut case."

"Neil Fargo."

"You work for me," said Toneff almost accusingly.

"You pay me money. There's a difference."

"Not any more I don't. Not to that tone of voice."

"Yesterday Eduardo Mesa was found murdered. Day before yesterday I bird-dogged him for you. The second person from El Muerto I bird-dogged for you, a girl calling herself Melody Manion, is missing."

"You're a fool, Fargo. Or you think I am."

As he was angrily showing Neil Fargo out, the heavy oak door was jerked open from outside by a handsome black man of around forty. He wore a gray wool suit

and a paisley power tie and pointy-toed shoes with a spit-shine sheen.

Neil Fargo stuck out a hand, beaming. "Neil Fargo."

The black shook the hand automatically. "Larry Middleton."

Toneff made a face that almost might have had humor in it. Neil Fargo laughed aloud.

"Larry Middleton," he said. "Deputy Commissioner for Real Estate Development, City and County of San Francisco, eyes sparkling and breath Binaca'd, on the doorstep of Milovan Toneff, land developer anti-Christ, at"—he shot a cuff to check his watch—"seven twenty-four in the——"

"Now see here," began Middleton in a huffy voice, "there is absolutely no impropriety involved here. I am the city's action officer on Mr. Toneff's acquisition and development of the China Basin property."

"Lot of matching federal funds involved in the development of that particular piece of real estate," mused Neil Fargo.

He was gone before either of the men could react.

The China Basin Center was an ambitious commercial complex designed to revitalize the area between Third Street and the Bay, between the old Mission Railroad Yard and China Creek, where it passed under the Third Street Bridge. The reception building's arched walls and domed ceiling were up, but Esteban Gijon's mural, designed to cover the soaring prestressed concrete walls, had not progressed beyond the cartoon stage—to-scale outlines transferred to the walls from rolls of thin paper. Neil Fargo had two facts: Gijon had worked at night, alone, and for this mural he had planned something radical, a taped sound track.

For a half hour he lay waiting on his back on the scaffolding fifty feet above the floor where Gijon would have lain during his nocturnal work sessions. Finally two workmen passed below, voices echoing in the vast shell. After they were out of earshot, he played back their voices on the cassette recorder he had carried up with him. Excellent pickup.

Angelina Roydon glanced through the open connecting door to Toneff's still-empty office, picked up the phone, and said, "I've been expecting you for twenty minutes." She wrote NEIL FARGO on her scratch pad, underlined it twice. "To the *house*?" Her face became carved ivory. "Yes, I know how to reach her ahead of him. On an insurance app she listed for notification in case of accident an actress named Victoria Palmer."

Late morning sun slanting through the little kitchen made it bright and cheery, very far from nightmare. Vikki answered the phone.

"Yes, this is Victoria Palmer. You . . . *What*? Oh my God, of course! What? Where should I—" Vikki made frantic writing motions at Melody, began scribbling on the paper napkin provided. "In Oakland, yes. Two o'clock. I'll be there!"

She hung up and waltzed Melody around the kitchen.

"Tryout for a commercial!"

Melody helped her pick out clothes, find her folio and composite, and then lazed the day away. It was after six when she called her own phone for the message Vikki had promised to leave. A crisp female voice said Vikki would be tied up test-shooting until after ten p.m. Could Melody meet her at the Strident Theater at eleven? She had some great great great news.

It was raining again, the water drumming on the office roof like a thousand demented squirrels. The street door opened and closed; high heels started up the interior stairwell. Neil Fargo tilted the narrow green blinds to look down into Bush Street. Rain was splashing off the top of a long smoke-colored limo with tinted windows parked in the nearest traffic lane with its emergency flashers blinking. He turned back into the room.

"Toneff does the help well."

"On such a night, yes."

Angelina Roydon wore glittery red high heels and a full-length wild mink coat and matching cap jeweled with raindrops.

"Tonny wants you to keep looking." She slanted a look over at him from the corners of her eyes. "He hasn't told me why, but you can name your own price."

"Blood money."

"No, not that—whatever you might think."

"You didn't have to be driven all the way over here in the rain to tell me that."

She looked at him with what might have been sexual appraisal. "I had an idea, but on the way over decided it was a poor one."

Neil Fargo nodded as if in agreement. "I'll let you know."

He listened to her heels clattering down the stairs. When he looked down into Bush Street again, the limo was gone. He gave a single bark of laughter; then his face became closed and somber as if he had never laughed before in his life.

Melody sat on the edge of the low stage at the Strident Theater, swinging her legs. It was dim, somewhat menacing with no actors around. From behind her came the slightest of noises. She leaped to her feet. The stage was empty.

"Vikki? Where are you?"

Her response was a small scraping sound behind the folded-open curtain on stage left. She whirled toward it. The curtain began swaying almost imperceptibly. She ran toward the other wing, but as she went through the curtain off-stage right, toward the fire door, the smiling figure waiting there was on her with a grunt like a charging animal.

Neil Fargo heard it on the seven a.m. news report: an unidentified female, white, red hair, mid-twenties, had been found in the trunk of a stolen Cadillac on Cargo Way with her neck broken. Fifteen minutes later he was picking Melody Manion's door lock. The place had the dusty feel of a flat empty for several days. He listened to the phone tape, his own calls and that about the Strident Theater, replayed it, pocketed it. He found the 5 x 7 manila envelope taped inside the refrigerator motor's removable door.

Five Polaroids were spread out on Neil Fargo's desk, dates written on the backs that had to be when the dupes had been mailed off to Toneff. Nov. 10, Nov. 17, Nov. 24, Dec. 1, Dec. 8.

The November 10th photo was of a wall with the cartoon of a mural, an impressionistic rendering of the dance floor at El Rebozo on the Night of the Dead. Sketched into the center of the dance floor was a figure in a skeleton suit, half-slumped, being held up by the press of bodies around him. Penciled on the back of the photo under the date were the words DANCE OF THE DEAD.

November 17th: the background figures were painted in, the brass of the orchestra gleaming dully behind them. The slumping figure in the foreground was now painted in—without its face. TO DIE FOR FREEDOM IS TO LIVE FOREVER.

November 24th: a second foreground figure, also in a death suit, was painted in, just thrusting a stiletto into Gijon's heart. Like the slumping man, it had no face. TO KILL FOR WEALTH AND POWER IS TO BE DAMNED FOREVER.

December 1st: behind the killer was now a horned and tailed *diablo*, manipulating strings going to the killer's arms and legs. ALMOST DONE. PUBLIC SHOWING THIS MONTH.

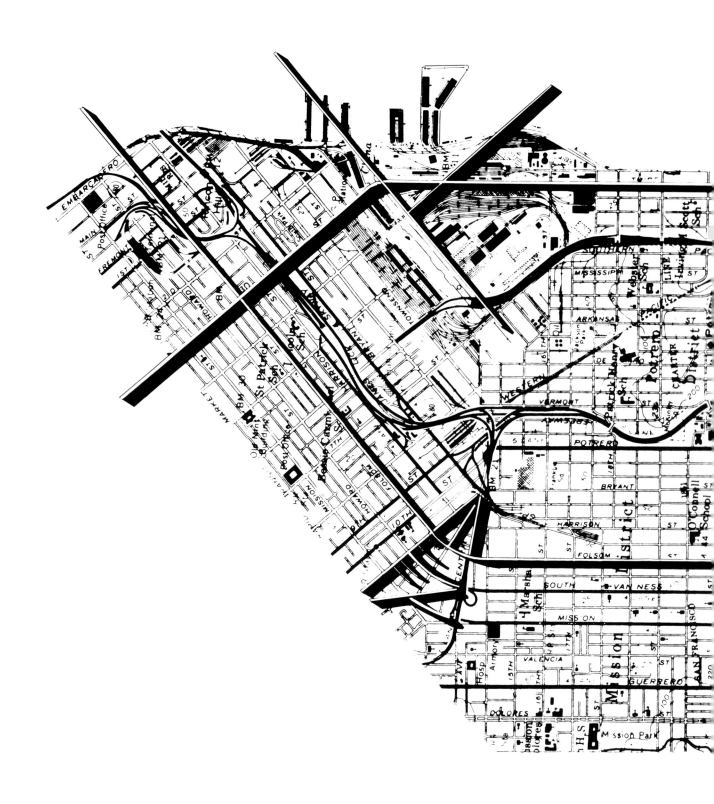

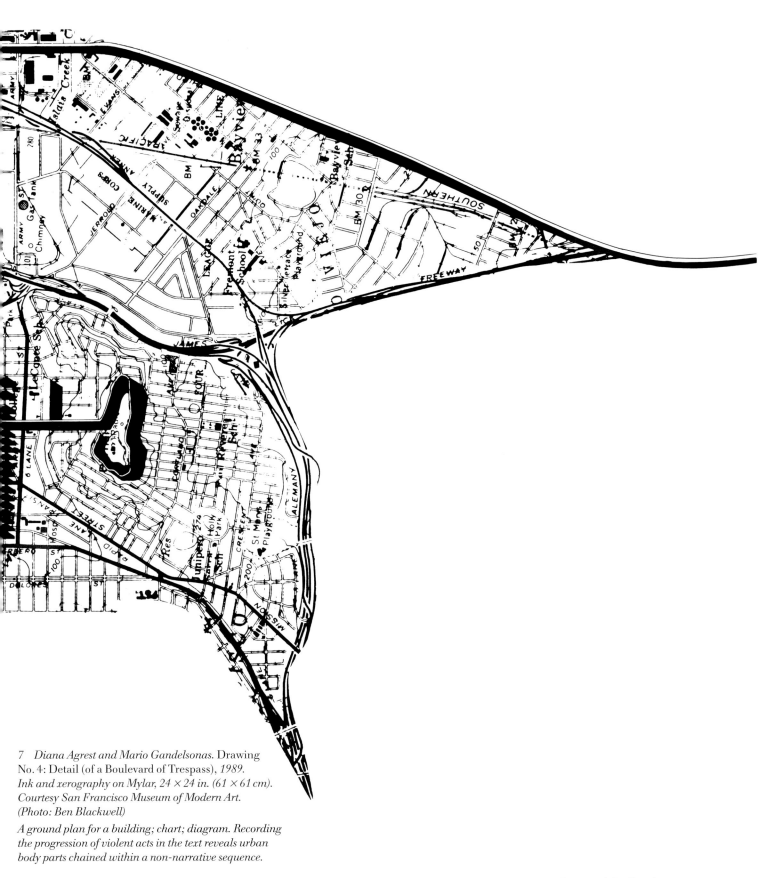

7   *Diana Agrest and Mario Gandelsonas.* Drawing
No. 4: Detail (of a Boulevard of Trespass), *1989.*
Ink and xerography on Mylar, 24 × 24 in. (61 × 61 cm).
Courtesy San Francisco Museum of Modern Art.
(Photo: Ben Blackwell)

A ground plan for a building; chart; diagram. Recording
the progression of violent acts in the text reveals urban
body parts chained within a non-narrative sequence.

December 8th: the slumping figure wore Esteban Gijon's face, realistic and unmistakable. Only the two murderers were faceless. TWO MURDERERS TO EXPOSE. WHO MIGHT THEY BE?

Neil Fargo would have been hired as soon as the December 1st Polaroid had reached Toneff's office.

He had located Eduardo Mesa. Mesa had died.

He had located Melody Manion. Manion had died.

The phone rang. "Fargo Investigations."

"Three-four-oh Eleventh Street." A woman's hoarse whisper strained through a handkerchief. "Old laundry. Go in through Norfolk Alley. Empty room in the back."

Neil Fargo listened intently to the voice. You disguised your voice only when you feared it would be recognized.

"Did Gijon make a recording?"

After a long pause, the voice finally whispered, "Yes."

"Have you heard it?"

No response.

"Do you know where it is?"

No response. A listening silence in which her exhalations and indrawn breaths could be heard over the wire.

Neil Fargo suddenly burst out, his voice tight with fury, *"Goddammit, don't play games with me!"* His hand was white around the phone, and the cords in his neck stood out. *"Three goddamn people are dead because—"*

"No and . . . no."

"Goddamn games," he said aloud after she had hung up.

The back of 340 Eleventh Street, facing Norfolk Alley in a light industrial area coming up fast, was fronted with old metal billboards fastened together and painted bright, alternating primary colors to form a high fence. There was a gate, but it was locked on the inside. Neil Fargo pulled himself up and rolled over to drop into the yard. Inside, flipping a light switch showed him a big boxy room with a two-story ceiling, concrete floor and walls, slit windows fifteen feet above the floor.

He stopped dead, dazzled.

The mural glowed with a dark inner light, somber yet shot through with radiance. The murderer's face was still blank, but the caped devil manipulating his strings wore unmistakable features for the world to see at the mural's public showing.

Milovan Toneff.

The face the woman caller believed had hired murder. Except without Gijon's recording, this was just a mural.

"Goddamn games," Neil Fargo said again aloud.

Gijon would not have expected to die, but he would have expected to have the tape looked for once its existence was known. He wouldn't have trusted—or endangered—anyone else with its possession. Back at the China Basin Center, Neil Fargo found the tape hidden at full stretch above the highest planks of the scaffolding, above the top of the mural where a pillar melded into the wall. He listened to it while driving around to find a working payphone. The voice he got on the phone after five rings was thick with sleep or passion.

"I hope this is important."

"I've identified the final member of El Muerto for you."

After the call was ended, he drove out to the 3300 block of Sixteenth Street and went to sleep in his car again.

As they had for each of the fifteen years since La sociedad Guadalupana de Mission Dolores had begun sponsoring a dawn Mass on December 12th, the feast of Our Lady of Guadalupe, the faithful began gathering in the cold, echoing, barnlike assembly hall behind the church at five a.m. Scread was enjoying himself; he had once been a Catholic. At five-thirty the music started and the dancers appeared on the stage. Three of them. They came down onto the open floor, began sinuous, stamping, intricate, almost shockingly physical dances. They wore huge, bright feathered Quetzalcoatl headdresses and not much else. The stamping feet were bare. The legs were bare, the men's chests were bare. Scread couldn't take his eyes off the woman. She was stern of face, stern as granite, but her body was lithe, beautifully shaped, her movements as old as humanity.

The music ended; the crowd lit one another's candles as they shuffled out for the slow procession around to the mission church. Candlelight illuminated devout faces; the sparkling river of light flowed up the broad steps and into the church itself, hundreds of candles glowing through clouds of incense from swinging silver censers.

Scread stayed just inside the huge open double church doors as the Mass started. In mid-Mass the feathered dancers weaved up the aisle like a sacred snake as flashbulbs popped: they had been incorporated into Catholic ritual hundreds of years before by rural converts clinging to the old ways as they embraced the new.

It was over. The *salida* began as the procession of the robed clergy was led down the aisle by the feathered dancers. She was coming to his embrace, the intimate moment when their bodies became one. The tip of his blade darted up into the very secret of her existence.

Neil Fargo's steel fingers handcuffed his wrist with the stiletto two inches short of her flesh. Scread twisted free. They circled. Scread's lips were skinned back, his breath whistled thinly through clenched teeth. The need to kill trilled his body as strong wind trills high-tension lines. Inside Neil Fargo's defenses, swift as a tiger. But his forearm was seized at full extension. Neil Fargo was behind him now, tremendously powerful arms up under the armpits for the full nelson. His head was being bowed toward his chest, his arms forced wide in a parody of crucifixion.

"Drop it."

Scread answered with curses. Before him was Paloma Escobar, feathered headdress moving with her anger. Her brown thighs no longer stirred him sexually; his vision was failing as the blood was cut off to his brain.

"You recognized my voice," Paloma said accusingly to Neil Fargo. "Told them who I was and where to find me so this . . . this animal would come after me."

"You played games with me, I played games with you."

She turned away, loathing on her face. Scread gave a final great heave, but the arms jerked taut like towing cables, separating nerves from spinal cord. For a moment Scread was a paraplegic; then his arms jerked again and he was a corpse.

Milovan Toneff raised his glass of champagne in a toast.

"To successful completions."

Angelina Roydon and Larry Middleton drank to that. Final approval of the federal matching funds for the China Basin Center had come through that morning; they were celebrating in one of Donatello's marbled dining rooms. Neil Fargo sat down in the empty chair at their table, still dressed for his night of foraging. The maître d' started his way with a horrified expression, but Toneff waved him off.

"I fired you day before yesterday," he said.

"And she rehired me night before last."

Angelina's face had gone bloodless. So had Middleton's. Neil Fargo put a cassette recorder on the table. Before pushing PLAY, he looked over at Toneff.

"Sometime this fall, you'll know when better than I, you're waiting to hear how you did on the competitive bids for the new stadium that's going to keystone the China Basin development. The reception building after hours—it's okay for them to be seen together, but they can't be overheard, so it's the perfect place. But up above, on his scaffolding, Esteban Gijon is checking out acoustics with a tape recorder for the sound track he wants to run with his mural. And he hears."

There was the rustling of papers; Larry Middleton's voice was unmistakable. "I have your competitors' proposals here for you to examine, Angelina."

Angelina's throaty chuckle. "You're a born thief, Larry."

"I'm not sure 'thief' is exactly the right word." His voice was slightly hurt.

"'Thief' is exactly the right word. I'm giving you a healthy percentage of my take to help me steal $2.5 million from Tonny and the City of San Francisco."

The tape recorder was still talking as Neil Fargo walked away. A dazed Toneff caught up with him at the elevator. He gestured over his shoulder, an astounded look on his face.

"There's cops there charging them with *murder*!"

"Gijon was going to expose them—to you, to the city. They had him killed. When El Muerto started after them, Angelina talked you into hiring me to identify El Muerto's members for their killer."

"But . . . all that I wanted was——"

"Someone to finish your mural. Right." He laughed bleakly. "All they had to do was sit tight. Paloma Escobar thought *you* had gotten Gijon killed, and if they hadn't tricked you into hiring me, no one ever would have found the cassette that proved otherwise. Of course they didn't know that. They'll be selling each other out before nightfall."

The elevator doors slid open. Toneff looked old, used up, not at all his usual *Wall Street Journal* dynamic-tycoon self.

"C'mon, old man," said Neil Fargo, "I'll buy you a beer and explain the facts of life on *my* side of the street."

Gray A. Brechin

San Francisco: The City Beautiful

San Francisco has seldom lacked for visions of what it might become. Its self-professed imperial destiny in the Pacific Basin—trumpeted by its leaders since the Gold Rush—demanded corresponding and permanent imagery. Yet that dream of durability, convenience, and beauty by deliberate design has largely eluded it. San Francisco became beautiful not because of but despite the men who built it.

Swiss surveyor Jean Vioget unwittingly locked the city's future growth into a relentless geometry when he laid down a grid of twelve blocks around Portsmouth Plaza in 1839. In subsequent decades that pattern would be extended east across the town's harbor and

seven miles west across rugged topography to the beach. When hills got in the way, they were blasted for bay fill (fig. 1).

The grid—containing and defining property lines—is ample proof of the dominance of paper over reality. Arbitrary and invisible as they are, property lines have repeatedly resisted both disaster and visions of a better city.

The Visionary Tradition

The half century following the Gold Rush produced no significant schemes for the public betterment of San Francisco other than the sporadic development of

Golden Gate Park. As the command post of Western exploitation, San Francisco thrived on mining and land speculation. Municipal government was notoriously weak and corrupt and the concept of public planning virtually synonymous with socialism for the city's builders.

The first act of monumental planning in the Bay Area was therefore undertaken by private initiative on an estate thirty miles south of the city. Leland and Jane Stanford's creation of a university complex in memory of their deceased son, utilizing the talents of landscape architect Frederick Law Olmsted and ar-

chitect H. H. Richardson (and his successor firm after his death), helped to trigger a series of events leading to the visionary re-creation of San Francisco in 1905.

Begun in 1888, the Stanford quadrangle (fig. 2) constitutes one of the most brilliant and original examples of nineteenth-century ensemble planning. Individual buildings organized on formal axes were linked by a continuous Romanesque arcade enclosing a sequence of plazas. One entered the quadrangle through a triumphal arch; a frieze depicted Leland and Jane Stanford leading the forward march of civilization against the recalcitrant force of nature.[1] (The arch is no longer there, having fallen down in 1906.)

Leland Stanford and his designers intended the original quadrangle to be extended indefinitely as the university grew, but his widow abandoned the plan at his death. The Stanford quadrangle forcefully demonstrated, however, what a few strong-willed individuals could achieve with sufficient capital on land free of subdivision lines.

As Stanford was being built, a group of young architects who were to exert a profound impact on the Bay Area arrived in San Francisco. Willis Polk, A.

1 *Eadweard J. Muybridge. Second and third plates of panoramic view of San Francisco, showing Russian Hill and the Bay from Mark Hopkins house, 1877. Albumen prints. Collection of Paul Sack. (Photo: Ben Blackwell)*

As San Francisco grew west, the grid of streets originally laid out around Portsmouth Plaza was extended relentlessly across hills, marshes, and dunes, indicative of the importance of land speculation in the western economy. Houses were built almost entirely of wood, giving the city a uniquely dense yet insubstantial appearance that alternately amazed and horrified visitors.

3   *Lewis Edward Hickmott.* World's Columbian
Exposition (Court of Honor), *1893.*
Oil on canvas, 51 × 80 in. (129.5 × 203.2 cm).
Collection of the Chicago Historical Society.

*The World's Columbian Exposition in Chicago marked
a sea change in American taste. It appeared as a revelation of classical harmony to Americans inured to dark
and dirty cities built by laissez-faire industry and commerce. For decades following it, classical architecture
was de rigueur for public and private buildings. Initiat-
ing the "City Beautiful" movement, the exposition made
urban planning possible for the first time in the United
States.*

4   *Orrin Peck.* Portrait of Mrs. Phoebe Apperson Hearst,
c. 1910-12.
Oil on canvas, 52 × 27 in. (132.1 × 68.6 cm).
*Collection of the University Art Museum, University
of California, Berkeley, gift of William Randolph Hearst, Jr.
(Photo: Ben Blackwell)*

*As widow and heiress of mining millionaire George Hearst,
Phoebe Apperson Hearst adopted the state university at Berkeley and sponsored an international competition to make it
the most beautiful in the world. A discriminating patron of
architecture and education, the former Missouri schoolteacher
was named the first woman regent of the University of California and, through countless benefactions, built it into a world-
renowned institution.*

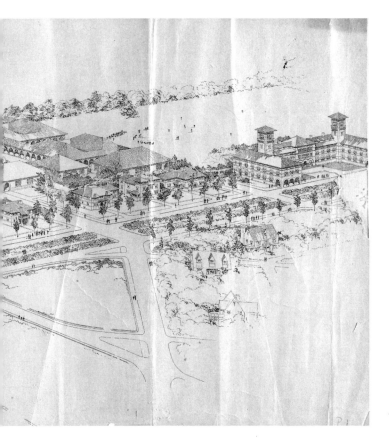

2   *Shepley, Rutan, & Coolidge and F. L. & J. C. Olm-
sted.* Perspective of Stanford quadrangles, *c. 1888.*
Sepia print with ink inscriptions, 10½ × 29½ in. (26.7 × 74.9 cm).
*Collection of University Archives, Stanford University.
(Photo: Ben Blackwell)*

*The proposed Stanford quadrangles were among the
most brilliant examples of nineteenth-century ensemble
planning, demonstrating what determined individuals
could accomplish on land free of subdivision lines.*

Page Brown, and Bernard Maybeck came to a city which they described as more fascinating than beautiful, a site of flagrantly missed opportunities.[2]

The arrival of well-trained architects coincided with the emergence of wealthy clients (many with second-generation fortunes) who desired a fitting image for their putative Queen City of the Pacific. Most of them witnessed the trend-setting World's Columbian Exposition in Chicago in 1893 (fig. 3) and wanted more of the same for their own hometown. The fair, as one observer recalled, was "a miniature of the ideal city . . . a unity on a single architectural scale"[3]—and an implied condemnation of the hideous growth and class warfare which laissez-faire economics had produced across America.

The Chicago exposition inspired *San Francisco Chronicle* publisher Michael deYoung to initiate a smaller world's fair in his own city for the following year. The Midwinter Fair of 1894 in Golden Gate Park, using leftover exhibitions from Chicago, was intended by deYoung to stimulate San Francisco's depressed economy and, architecturally, to express the exotic heritage of California in its farrago of Near Eastern and Mission Revival "palaces."

For San Francisco banker (later to be mayor) James Duval Phelan the fair was an impetus for urban greatness, but for other observers it was yet more proof of the city's provincialism. Boston's *Architectural Review* raked the fair as an example of mediocre architecture and incoherent planning. Willis Polk, who worked on the fair, described it as "a frightful nightmare."[4] The Midwinter Fair left no permanent mark besides the Music Concourse, a few sculptures, and the Japanese Tea Garden in Golden Gate Park.

Of more lasting significance was the convergence, in 1896, of Bernard Maybeck and Phoebe Apperson Hearst. Maybeck had recently settled in the Bay Area after a rigorous course of architectural study at the Ecole des Beaux-Arts in Paris. At his residential atelier in north Berkeley, Maybeck trained and inspired a group of young men and women who themselves would go to the Ecole and return to embellish the Bay Area. Phoebe Hearst had recently inherited the bulk of her husband's mining and real estate fortune and was embarking on a dynamic career of philanthropy and patronage.

Disgusted by the Victorian hodgepodge of buildings on the rural Berkeley campus, Maybeck proposed a

5   The Boulevard des Italiens, Paris, 1905.
Courtesy Préfecture de Paris and Norma Evenson.

By 1900 wealthy Americans and their favored architects
were well aware of what Napoleon III and Baron
Haussmann had accomplished in rebuilding the French
capital. With characteristic chauvinism, they took Paris
as a model for what Yankee know-how could do bigger
and better at home. San Franciscans called their city the
Paris of the Pacific and proposed to rectify earlier mis-
takes through coordinated planning.

6   Bird's-eye view of central Paris on the Right Bank.
Courtesy Institut Géographique National and Norma Evenson.

The grand boulevards cutting through the heart of Paris
in the mid-nineteenth century served as the model for
what Daniel Burnham and Edward Bennett proposed
as the ideal solution to San Francisco's traffic problems.
In addition, these streets would double as fire breaks in a
city dangerously full of wooden structures.

comprehensive plan modeled on that of the Chicago exposition. Hearing of Maybeck's idea, Mrs. Hearst (fig. 4) offered to finance an international competition for the state university, cost being no object.

How much Phoebe Hearst was motivated by rivalry with Jane Stanford is not clear, but it was *not* her intention to create a design specifically Californian, like Stanford University, but one fully in the mainstream of international taste. She would shake California from its provincialism.

Hearst sent Maybeck to Europe, where he met with architects and formulated a utopian program for the competition. Each entrant was invited to "record his conception of an ideal home for a University, assuming time and resources to be unlimited. He is to plan for centuries to come." The program concluded: "It is the intention to restore the artist and the art idea to their old pre-eminence. The architect will simply design, others must provide the cost."[5] Maybeck envisioned a Hearst-financed Renaissance on the Pacific coast.

In 1898 in Antwerp the jurors announced eleven finalists, all of whom were invited to inspect the site at Phoebe Hearst's expense. When they arrived, her own desire for imperial grandeur and order jumped the Bay. At a December 3 dinner for the architects at San Francisco's select Bohemian Club, Mayor James Phelan made a startling announcement. Mrs. Hearst, Phelan revealed, had told him of her intention to sponsor a second international competition "for plans by which

the city of San Francisco may be laid out, altered, and improved on artistic and scientific lines as Napoleon through Baron Haussmann laid out Paris" (figs. 5, 6). Engineers would be invited to submit plans for the grading of new boulevards, the creation of new parks, and the construction of a badly needed sewer system. Regent Jacob Reinstein announced that Mrs. Hearst was also considering the establishment of a department of architecture at Berkeley, "where young men should be trained especially for the carrying out of the plan for the beautification and fitness in every respect beneath and above the ground of this city of ours."[6]

Phelan's announcement was received with wild enthusiasm. The *San Francisco Call* headlined: "Would Build a City to Rival Rome of Old." The *San Francisco Examiner* predicted that the city would "rank with Florence, Constantinople, Edinburgh, and perhaps, thanks to her beautiful location, excel them all." Finalist Stephen Codman exclaimed that "the competition might be held up as a classic.... I feel that this is an epoch from which the growth of American architecture may date."[7]

Going even further, Mayor Phelan noted that the city had no municipal debt so there was no reason why the money to carry out the plans "could not be raised easily and willingly by self-imposed taxation."[8] More than a new San Francisco, Phelan anticipated a New Jerusalem.

It is unclear why Phoebe Hearst, then in Paris, did not follow through on her offer. Her biographer,

Judith Robinson, speculates that she may have been overextended in her charities. In 1905, complaining of the parasitism of San Franciscans and the unwillingness of other wealthy citizens to pull their own weight, she left the Bay Area to live for a period in Paris. Nonetheless, the enthusiasm generated by her announcement would lead Phelan to inaugurate the Burnham Plan for San Francisco in 1904.

The Hearst competition was officially concluded in San Francisco in August 1899 after what the London *Builder* called an "exceptional and perhaps unprecedented architectural competition."[9] The finalists' enormous Beaux-Arts drawings (fig. 7) were exhibited in a gallery of San Francisco's new Ferry Building, where their utopian example would not be lost on citizens.

Willis Polk scathingly denounced the competition as a megalomaniac waste of money, but he had his own plans for the Ferry Building. Because of the city's isolated position at the end of a peninsula, that terminus, completed in 1898, filled the role of the great train stations in other major cities; its monumental façade and clock tower bespoke its importance as one of the busiest passenger depots in the world. The building's handsome tower (possibly designed by Polk) had the added advantage of terminating Market Street, the

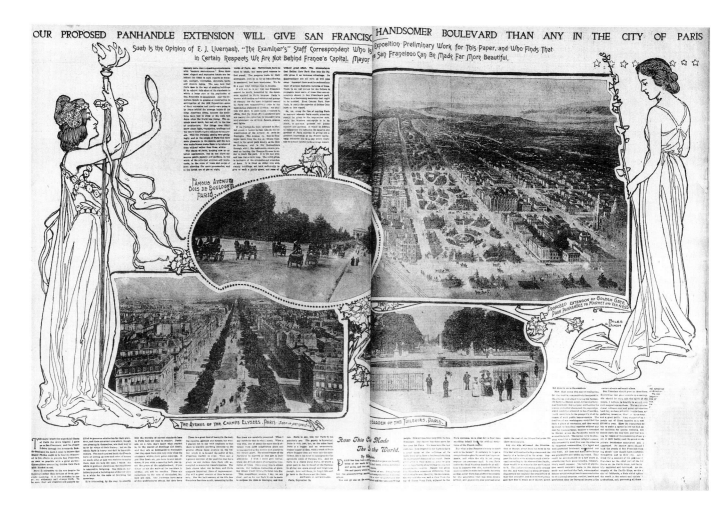

city's principal artery. Yet on leaving the depot, the transcontinental traveler's introduction to the self-styled Paris of the West was an encounter with severe traffic congestion amidst shabby waterfront dives, chandleries, and warehouses. Polk proposed to remedy the situation with a curved peristyle bowing out from the terminal, enclosing a forecourt modeled on that of Bernini's for St. Peter's in Rome (fig. 8). The peristyle would meet at a triumphal arch through which one would enter or leave Market Street.

First proposed in the weekly magazine *The Wave* in 1896,[10] Polk's peristyle and arch scheme repeatedly surfaced for at least the next fifteen years. In 1903 Bernard Maybeck recommended in the *Merchants' Association Review* that the complex be built of plaster over lath, as in contemporary exposition architecture, and gradually replaced with stone as money became available.[11]

At the other end of Market Street, both Polk and Mayor Phelan promoted an extension of the Golden Gate Park Panhandle. One city block wide, the Panhandle would, if extended thirteen blocks east, exactly meet the intersection of the two principal streets of San Francisco, Market and Van Ness.[12]

9 Panhandle Extension, San Francisco Examiner, September 24, 1899, pp. 26 - 27. Courtesy of the San Francisco Examiner. (Photo: Ben Blackwell)
Extending the Golden Gate Park Panhandle thirteen blocks east to the intersection of Market and Van Ness became a lasting obsession for James Duval Phelan and Willis Polk. It was actively promoted by the Hearst-owned Examiner.

In an article titled "How to Beautify San Francisco," Polk vilified the picturesque landscaping of Golden Gate Park and recommended the example of Versailles to the park commissioners for its redesign.[13] If the Panhandle extension were to be executed in the formal manner of Le Nôtre, he predicted, San Francisco would have its own Champs-Elysées (fig. 9), and the "hideous, crazy, bay windowed and begabled houses" facing the park would be replaced by more dignified and permanent buildings. In the same article, Polk endorsed another improvement close to the new intersection. The scheme was developed gratuitously by architect B. J. S. Cahill and published and promoted by William Randolph Hearst's *Examiner* in the fall of 1899.[14]

At that time the City Hall occupied a triangular lot largely on the site of the present main library, while the wooden Mechanics Pavilion stood on the neighboring block where the Exposition Auditorium now stands. Cahill proposed uniting these large structures and the dignified Hibernia Bank building north of Market Street with the ornate post office and federal courthouse then being built just south of the street.

Cahill's shotgun wedding of desirable structures required the demolition of all inharmonious buildings in the vicinity. A grand hotel and theater would be built on an island in the middle of Market Street, which would be split around it. Classical architecture, Parisian landscaping, ornamental lamp standards, and monuments would make that bleak neighborhood into a permanent world's fair and an architectural complement to the Ferry Building tower at the other end of the street.

Polk's peristyle, Cahill's civic center, and the Panhandle extension all were hot topics in 1899, stimulated, no doubt, by the climax of the Hearst competition, the prosperity promised by the Spanish-American War, and the mayoralty of James Duval Phelan.

The fastidious and scholarly son of a pioneer Irish banker, Phelan was a prototypical magnate of the American Renaissance. "Pericles could not have loved Athens more than this man loved San Francisco," eulogized one biographer.[15] As mayor (1897-1902), the bachelor prince launched a campaign for civic reform and artistic patronage with a sense of noblesse oblige matched only by Phoebe Hearst. Phelan patronized local artists, among them the director of the Mark Hopkins Art Institute, Arthur Mathews, who shared the mayor's hopes for San Francisco. When commissioned by the State Legislature in 1913 to decorate the rotunda of the State Capitol, Mathews envisioned the city of the future through the Greco-Roman lens he shared with his well-educated contemporaries. San Francisco's destiny was a fantasy not of sordid commerce and manufacture but of dancing maidens, busy artists, and a domed and colonnaded Byzantium by the Pacific. In one unfinished cartoon a penciled sculptor in the foreground suggests Mathews' own vision in its incipience.

As local Maecenas, Phelan paid for or promoted hortatory monuments in parks and on Market Street and donated a library building to the city. In his second inaugural message as Democratic reform mayor in 1899, he insisted that the Panhandle extension was an essential public improvement. Apparently inspired by Phoebe Hearst's offer, the Democratic platform of the same year recommended a master plan so that San Francisco would grow "on broad and liberal lines, that will ultimately conduce to the health, comfort, and prosperity of its inhabitants."[16]

Though Phelan stumped tirelessly for a renewed San Francisco, he accomplished little. In 1901 he was voted out of office for his role in breaking a violent waterfront strike and for his identification with leading local capitalists. The patrician mayor was replaced by Eugene Schmitz, the Union Labor Party's candidate, and by Schmitz's manager, "Boss" Abraham Ruef.

The Burnham/Bennett Plan for San Francisco

Out of office, Phelan had time to devote himself more fully to municipal reform and to its physical embodiment in a revamped San Francisco that would express its growing military and commercial role in the Pacific Basin. In the latter role, he worked closely with Willis Polk, the West Coast representative of Daniel Burnham of Chicago.

Phelan and Polk looked to Washington, D.C., for an object lesson in what imperial San Francisco could become. The Hearst competition drawings had toured the country for six months after being judged in San Francisco. In December 1900 they were exhibited at the Cosmos Club in Washington during the annual convention of the American Institute of Architects (AIA). Citing the competition and winning plan as "a clear idea of the effectiveness which may by produced by an intelligent grouping of buildings," the AIA directors recommended the formation of a commission to develop a plan for the nation's capital.[17] Burnham was appointed to head the Senate Park Commission for this purpose. Using Paris as the logical referent, the commission presented its grandiloquent plan to Congress in 1902.

On January 15, 1904, Phelan founded the Association for the Improvement and Adornment of San Francisco (AIASF), with many of the city's business and professional leaders as members. In May the association officially requested a plan from Burnham, who enthusiastically agreed. After surveying the city for a few weeks, he put his young assistant Edward Bennett in charge and hurried off to the Philippines to develop plans for occupied Manila and a new summer capital at Baguio.

While Burnham doubtlessly did some preliminary work on the plan that bears his name, he was, in fact, infrequently in San Francisco and would later give credit to his assistant. English-born Bennett had studied informally in Berkeley with Bernard Maybeck and had been sent to study at the Ecole des Beaux-Arts in 1895 by Phoebe Hearst.[18] From a Polk-designed "shack" high on Twin Peaks, Burnham and Bennett fabricated the imperial image that the city's businessmen wished to convey. Bennett's sketches for the plan survive at the Art Institute of Chicago.

Completed in 1905, the Burnham Plan is the most comprehensive vision ever formulated for the redevelopment and future growth of San Francisco (fig. 10).[19] Its changes in the city's existing land-use patterns are so numerous and audacious that they suggest the designers had applied the utopian program of the Hearst competition to an existing city.

Client Phelan's obsession predominated. "First in importance," began the plan, "is the extension of the Panhandle to the center of the city." From the semicircular civic center that would develop at its intersection with Market and Van Ness, radial boulevards would slash outward through the existing grid like a Parisian *rond-point*. The Panhandle would continue as a broad diagonal through the South of Market district to the Pacific Mail steamship docks. The grid pattern on the city's steepest hills would be redrawn on contour lines and their slopes built in tiers like Italian hill towns.

The park system was to be vastly expanded as well; a park would be developed for working-class residents on the site of their houses on Potrero Hill, and another park, three times the size of Golden Gate Park, would sweep from the summit of Twin Peaks down to the sea at Lake Merced. The crest of the Peaks would be leveled for a colossal statue of San Francisco gazing toward the Pacific in a plaza embraced by a colonnaded athenaeum: "a nucleus for the skirmish line of advance in civilization."[20] A meandering park chain would have followed the course of Islais Creek in the southeastern quadrant of the city and was likened to Washington, D.C.'s Rock Creek Park.

Imperial gestures were not lacking. Telegraph Hill would be cleared of its shanties and developed as a Palatine Hill with majestic stairs, luxury apartments, public buildings, and a monument to the pioneers in a formal garden at its summit (fig. 11). An immense stadium would occupy Cole Valley in the upper Haight, offering views of the Golden Gate recalling the vista from Delphi. A proposed bayside parade ground in the Presidio was a foretaste of Albert Speer's Zeppelin Field at Nuremberg.

The Burnham Plan was completed and presented to the Board of Supervisors on September 27, 1905. Though some estimated the cost at $50 million, Burnham assured the city's business leaders that the plan would more than pay for itself in increased land val-

ues, modernized transportation and port facilities, and, above all, by a flood of tourists eager to see and enjoy the world's most beautiful city.

So seductive was the overall concept and Bennett's drawings for it that even Michael deYoung's *Chronicle*, traditionally the voice of the bottom line, initially supported it. Others remained skeptical; the directors of the powerful Merchants' Association stated: "San Francisco is a commercial city, and while every effort should be made to beautify the streets, the city's growth and prosperity should not be sacrificed simply to give business districts an aesthetic appearance."[21]

Much as Burnham would have liked to play Baron Haussmann to Phelan's Napoleon III, neither of them had the power needed to realize their dream. Noble diagrams were largely futile against the sanctity with which the Constitution had endowed private property. Both were operating as well in one of the most contentious cities in the United States.

What English socialist Beatrice Webb observed in 1898 had been true of San Francisco since the Gold Rush. Noting that it was "isolated from and unconcerned with any other part of America," she went on to claim, "It has no standards, no common customs; no common ideals of excellence, of intellect or manners— only one universal anarchy."[22]

Social and political antagonisms fragmented San Francisco with particular intensity at the time of the Burnham Plan. The 1905 mayoral election had been unusually vicious, with Phelan, Fremont Older's *Bulletin*, and their associates charging widespread corruption in the Schmitz administration. Though Schmitz won in a landslide, Phelan, Older, and financier Rudolph Spreckels were secretly preparing an all-out graft prosecution in the spring of 1906 when the San Andreas fault delivered a surprise of its own.

The shock that rolled across northern California on the morning of April 18, 1906, ignited a firestorm that accomplished in three days what Burnham had estimated might take fifty years of deliberation and negotiation; it rid the peninsula of about half of built San Francisco. Burnham rushed to the Pacific coast from Europe to view the scorched tabula rasa on which he expected to realize his plan. After all, he reasoned, the radial boulevards were intended to double as firebreaks to prevent uncontrolled conflagrations. Burnham failed to reckon with the power of the grid, which remained imprinted on the land amidst the rubble.

In May and again in August Burnham and Bennett presented to the Committee for Reconstruction their plans for the realignment and widening of streets in

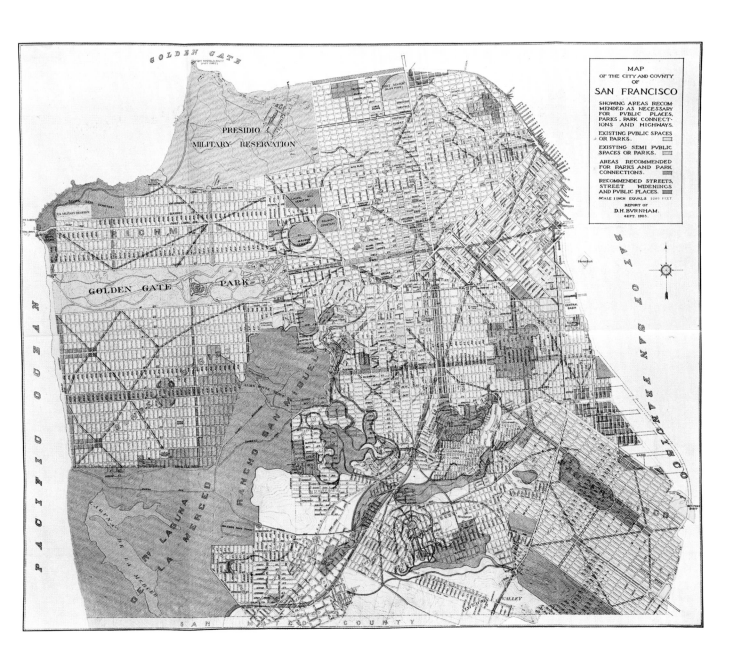

10   *Daniel H. Burnham.* Map of the City and County of San Francisco, *from* Report of D.H. Burnham on the Improvement and Adornment of San Francisco, *September 1905.*
Collection of Albert R. Schreck. (Photo: Ben Blackwell)

The 1905 Burnham Plan was the most comprehensive and audacious plan to redevelop San Francisco. Burnham, Edward Bennett, and James Duval Phelan envisioned it as the Paris of the Pacific in fact as well as in name. Red overlays on the existing street plan show new boulevards, while shaded areas stand for the expanded park system.

San Francisco: The City Beautiful   51

the burned section. The Panhandle would yet be extended across Market, as would Montgomery (now Columbus) Avenue. Curved streets would circumscribe the lower slopes of Nob and Russian hills. Many existing streets would be widened. Parks would be carved out of congested neighborhoods.[25]

Even as Burnham, back in Chicago a month after the fire, was exulting that the "San Francisco of the future will be the most beautiful city of the continent, with the possible exception of Washington,"[24] Michael deYoung was editorializing in his *Chronicle* that "the crying need of San Francisco today is not more parks and boulevards; it is business." Citing the example of London—rebuilt by the dictates of trade rather than on the baroque plan of Sir Christopher Wren after the Great Fire of 1666—deYoung stridently opposed the "unbusinesslike" schemes of Burnham and Phelan.[25]

The published Burnham/Bennett Plan of August 1906 demonstrates why it immediately self-destructed.[26] Street modifications were superimposed on a block book showing property ownership in the burned district. The property of hundreds of San Franciscans —among them the town's leading citizens, including deYoung—would have had to be condemned by the city. The cost was estimated at anywhere from $8 million to $40 million. In fact, there was almost no municipal government at the time to accomplish such a feat.

With an entire city to be rebuilt, Schmitz, Ruef, and their supervisors had sensed an unprecedented opportunity for graft in the granting of municipal franchises. Hardly missing a beat, Phelan, Older, and Spreckels zealously pursued the investigation and prosecution begun before the disaster. With extraordinary skill and extralegal means, the investigators cornered the grafters—then overreached themselves.[27]

Hounding the graft-givers as well as the graft-takers, Phelan and Spreckels invaded the highest realms of San Francisco society, where they were branded traitors to their class and ostracized. "Feeling on both sides is as embittered as were the feelings of the people of Florence in the days of the Guelphs and Ghibelines," reflected one chronicler of the prosecution.[28] Ultimately, only Abraham Ruef served time in San Quentin.

Within three years of the disaster, the city was virtually rebuilt with no significant changes; the Union Labor Party's Patrick McCarthy was swept into the mayor's office on the guarantee that *he* would make San Francisco "the Paris of America," by which it was generally understood that the vice squad would be curbed (fig. 12).

An eastern architect demurred: "Its citizens like to talk about it as the Paris of America. But French restaurants, electric lights, and a prevailing atmosphere of gaiety do not make a Paris. A metropolitan city must be tied together by a plan which provides for every essential economic and aesthetic need; and San Francisco still remains devoid of such a plan."[29]

12 *View of Powell Street from Market Street, c. 1930.*
Courtesy Gabriel Moulin Studios, San Francisco.
San Francisco was speedily rebuilt after the 1906 fire
with none of the changes suggested by the Burnham

Plan. What harmony exists in its downtown buildings
derived from a consensus of classical order and rational-
ity shared by architects and patrons rather than from
any central authority.

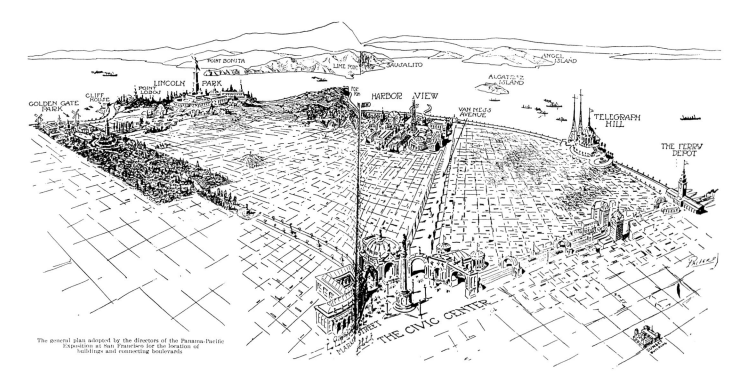

The general plan adopted by the directors of the Panama-Pacific Exposition at San Francisco for the location of buildings and connecting boulevards

The Panama-Pacific International Exposition

The social and political scars of the graft prosecution ran deeper than the physical wounds left by quake and fire. San Francisco was speedily rebuilt, but old friendships had been irrevocably damaged and the city's reputation and credit rating dragged through the mud. Thoughtful San Franciscans knew that they had missed a seismic opportunity to re-create their city in the way they wished it to be seen.

Department-store owner Reuben Hale had suggested a major world's fair a year before the Burnham Plan, but the quake, fire, and graft trials had sidetracked his proposal. With the city largely rebuilt by 1909, Hale's scheme was revived as the ideal way to bring the city's many factions together, repair its image, and, above all, stimulate business.[30]

It was also, at first, a belated attempt to realize some of the Burnham Plan. Initial proposals included turning the entire city into a world's fair with permanent improvements. Van Ness Avenue and Market Street would be transformed into Parisian boulevards converging with the Panhandle extension at a semicircular civic center (fig. 13). Burnham's Outer Boulevard would have entirely circumscribed the city's waterfront. Major exposition structures would be concentrated both at Harbor View (the Marina) and in the western half of Golden Gate Park.[31]

Though less grandiose than the Burnham Plan, the initial schemes still far exceeded available finances. For example, a marble replica of the Parthenon was to have been built on Telegraph Hill by Greek-Americans.[32] A 100-foot statue of "San Francisco Looking into the Future of the Pacific," intended for the bluff at Land's End,[33] was superseded by an 850-foot observation tower and lighthouse for the same site. The tower, with a beam visible 100 miles to sea, was to be financed

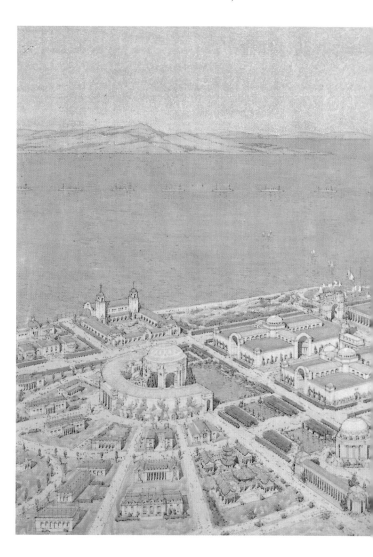

13 Bird's-eye Perspective of Entire City as World's Fair, Sunset Magazine, September 1911, pp. 338-339. Reprinted from Sunset Magazine, © Lane Publishing Co., 1990. (Photo: Ben Blackwell)

An initial proposal for the 1915 exposition sought to realize much of the Burnham Plan by turning the entire city into a world's fair. Costs proved too great, and the exposition was reduced to a square mile on the northern waterfront.

14 Jules Guerin. Bird's-eye View of the Panama-Pacific International Exposition, 1913. Ink and watercolor on paper, 49 × 97 in. (124.5 × 246.4 cm). Collection of the Exploratorium, San Francisco. (Photo: Ben Blackwell)

The block plan of the Panama-Pacific International Exposition, developed by Edward Bennett and Willis Polk, suggested Venice. Interior courtyards were connected to a waterfront esplanade. With its domes, towers, and continuous walls of travertine, the fair was deliberately exotic.

Edward Bennett prepared plans for the exposition. Willis Polk, Bennett's agent in San Francisco, was appointed supervising architect for the fair. Polk may have suggested the courtyard plan that was so remarkable a feature of the exposition, but sketches in Bennett's papers of the Piazzetta of San Marco indicate that Venice, rather than Paris, was his inspiration this time. For an academically trained architect, the waterfront site made the Venetian analog obvious.

Rather than the usual arrangement of detached structures around formal axes, Bennett's compact block plan incorporated three large courts contained within one superbuilding made up of eight exhibition "palaces" (fig. 14). The eighty-foot walls of the buildings broke the prevailing wind and fog pouring through the Golden Gate. Three elongated forecourts opened from the central courts onto the waterfront esplanade and the panorama of Mediterranean promontories and islands across the Bay (figs. 15, 16).

Other innovations set this, the last of the great Beaux-Arts American fairs, apart from those that had preceded it. Walls and columns were constructed of

privately at a cost of $1.5 million.[34] It, too, quickly vanished for lack of funding, and the exposition shrank to a square-mile strip along the northern waterfront in the Presidio and Harbor View.

16   *Jules Guerin.* Court of Honor, *c. 1912.*
Pencil and watercolor on paper, 26 x 65 in. (66 × 165.1 cm).
Collection of the San Francisco Public Library.
(Photo: Ben Blackwell)

The central ten-acre court of the Panama-Pacific Inter-
national Exposition was designed by the New York firm
of McKim, Mead & White. Here the two major axes of
the exposition met, leading the visitor to all sections of
the plaster "dream city."

15   *Jules Guerin.* Court leading to the Column
of Progress, *1912.*
Pencil and watercolor on paper, 50 × 37 in. (144.8 × 94.0 cm).
Collection of the San Francisco Public Library.
(Photo: Ben Blackwell)

Guerin's magnificent renderings of the exposition accu-
rately portrayed the fair as a collectively realized vision
of urban harmony, color, and imperial grandeur.

56   *Gray A. Brechin*

artificial travertine to give the fair the appearance of an ancient walled city of domes and minarets beside the Golden Gate. Jules Guerin, the artist who had worked closely with Burnham and Bennett on the Chicago Plan, color-coordinated everything from the architecture to landscaping and uniforms. The Panama-Pacific International Exposition was the first fair to be lit indirectly rather than with bare lightbulbs.[35]

Preservation efforts for some or all of the fair began almost the day it opened, February 20, 1915. That they largely failed is further testimony to the preeminent importance of land speculation. Only the Marina Green and Palace of Fine Arts were saved, the latter because it stood on Presidio land and the Army was in no rush to raze it. In the Palace of Fine Arts, however, San Francisco saved one of its archetypal creations.

The Palace instantly became the most beloved building of the exposition and launched Maybeck on a second career in his fifties. If the exposition was meant to give San Francisco a fantasy past, Maybeck went even further. The Palace was a brooding ruin, a polychrome Piranesi *capriccio* come to life. In the inseparable embrace of lagoon and building, in the plantings that sprang out of walls and were intended to erupt from entablatures, and in the "living walls" of ice plant that reached out from the rotunda, Maybeck blurred any distinction between art and nature (fig. 17). While housing art, the building spoke of the transience of civilization. While the rest of the fair celebrated the rebuilding of San Francisco, the Palace was a haunting memento mori of the city that had perished.

Mayor James Rolph and the Civic Center

After so many years of dissension and failure, the Panama-Pacific Exposition was a remarkable achievement of coordinated labor, design, and administration—a vision realized at last. That it was consummated without James Duval Phelan is not surprising; Phelan and his reformer associates were pointedly excluded from the exposition's board of directors, at least one of whom had been indicted in the recent graft trials.

The baton of municipal improvement had passed to James Rolph, Jr., upon his election as mayor in 1911. Rolph proved himself far more competent at realizing visions than James Phelan or Phoebe Hearst had been. Unlike Phelan, Rolph was a self-made millionaire who was raised and continued to live in the plebeian Mission District. Dapper, jovial, and nonpartisan, "Sunny Jim" was precisely what the divided city wanted and needed. Equally at ease with stevedores, bankers, and

Hollywood stars, he was adored by San Francisco, which gave him what he wanted.[36]

Rolph wanted not only an exposition but a permanent Civic Center to commemorate the event and to concentrate the city's administrative and cultural functions in one central location. San Francisco would be disgraced, Rolph told the voters, if it did not have a fitting city hall by the time of the fair to replace the one destroyed in 1906. He campaigned relentlessly, writing articles for the newspapers and even persuading Luisa Tetrazzini, the leading diva of the day, to plug the bond issue at her farewell performance on Market Street before the election. On March 28, 1912, the voters approved Rolph's bond measure by a margin of eleven to one.

While there was no organized opposition to the bond issue, the proposed site of the Civic Center continued to stir passions. No one seems to have taken seriously Arthur Mathews' schemes, published in his little magazine, *Philopolis*, to locate the Civic Center on Nob Hill near his studio.[37] A vocal minority led by Willis Polk continued to insist, however, that the Center should be built at Market and Van Ness, where Burnham had decreed it. The site seems to have been dictated by Phelan's deathless obsession with driving the Panhandle to that intersection.

The scheme developed by B. J. S. Cahill in 1904 and refined by him in 1909 would, instead, work within the existing grid pattern of the city (fig. 18). Cahill proposed that the City Hall be rebuilt on its old site facing a two-block plaza to its west. The space would be surrounded by other cultural and political buildings harmonious with, but subsidiary to, City Hall. The Panhandle would be jogged diagonally to Alamo Square. From there it would extend directly to the Civic Center on a widened and landscaped Fulton Street, which forms the central axis of the complex.

A committee of architects chaired by Professor John Galen Howard of the University of California at Berkeley adopted Cahill's plan but moved the proposed City Hall from its old site on Larkin Street two blocks west to its present site on Polk Street, thus creating a ceremonial entrance for parades from Market Street (today's United Nations Plaza). An embittered Cahill claimed his ideas had been stolen and stridently sought credit throughout the rest of his life.[38]

Mayor Rolph wanted his city hall in a hurry. Architects were invited to submit their credentials for a limited competition within a week of the bond issue. Less than three months later, a jury selected the plans of Maybeck's former students, John Bakewell and Arthur Brown, Jr., for a structure to cost $3.5 million.

The existing competition entries prove that the jury made the right choice. Over 100 firms entered the competition, but the majority of the entries were hackneyed and clumsy essays in French Renaissance monumentality. Bernard Maybeck was one of the few to submit a design without a central dome or tower; he placed a colossal sculpture in front of the main door and proposed an eccentric, inefficient spatial organization inside.

By contrast, the design by Bakewell and Brown invites favorable comparison with its French models. The scholarly and dignified elevation, detailing, internal organization, and, above all, the climactic rotunda with its ceremonial staircase, which appears to ooze over the marble floor, make San Francisco's City Hall the palatial symbol of a Pacific city-state. Moreover, in comparison with the jerry-built "cyclops" of a city hall that it replaced, the new building stood for the presumed rectitude of the Rolph administration, and for a city physically, socially, and morally regenerated. It was, San Franciscans proudly claimed, built without a dime of graft.

17   *Bernard Maybeck. Palace of Fine Arts, elevation, 1914.*
Charcoal on paper, 26 x 57½ in. (66 × 146.1 cm).
Collection of Hans Gerson. (Photo: Ben Blackwell)

While the Panama-Pacific International Exposition was
meant to create a fantasy past for San Francisco, Ber-
nard Maybeck's Palace of Fine Arts went even further.
His haunting vision of ruin blurred the distinction bet-
ween art and nature, between life and death. It was
saved from demolition and partially rebuilt in 1965 in
permanent materials.

18   *B. J. S. Cahill. Perspective of Memorial Court for*
Civic Center with Cannons, c. 1909.
Pencil on paper, 17 × 20½ in. (43.2 × 52.1 cm).
College of Environmental Design Documents Collection,
University of California, Berkeley.

Cahill developed and actively fought for a Civic Center
organized around a central plaza near the site of the old
City Hall, which was destroyed in 1906. His plan is fun-
damentally what exists today.

One preservation proposal would have rebuilt the Palace of Fine Arts across Van Ness Avenue from the new City Hall. The juxtaposition would have made a telling comment on the poles of San Francisco's culture: the academic correctness of City Hall versus the licentious imagination expressed in the Palace.[39] Yet both buildings used the same classical vocabulary, albeit to very different ends, and here they spoke for the fundamentally conservative nature of San Francisco's architectural taste as it matured. Not only was the Panama-Pacific International Exposition the last of the great Beaux-Arts American fairs but the Civic Center itself was one of the last monumental civic group plans to be initiated and executed in the United States.

The truly prophetic building constructed at almost the same time—Willis Polk's curtain-walled Hallidie Building of 1917, near Sutter and Montgomery streets —was largely ignored. Frank Lloyd Wright's 1912 project for a skyscraper on Market Street for the Spreckels family seems never to have been seriously considered. While wealthy Angelenos commissioned Wright, Irving Gill, Richard Neutra, and Rudolph Schindler to build their daringly modern homes, their counterparts in San Francisco continued to build stucco châteaux and villas in Pacific Heights and on the peninsula.

When the lights went out on the exposition on December 4, 1915, thousands openly wept. As the Great War began to rage, bringing with it the belated twentieth century, San Francisco seemed to hang back, reluctant to relinquish the lovely vision that it had collectively achieved at last.

The final panel painted by Arthur Mathews for the State Capitol at that time depicted a future beyond skyscrapers, beyond the machine. For painter and patron, the hope of the city's future lay in the past (fig. 19).

NOTES

1 Paul V. Turner, Marcia E. Vetrocq, and Karen Weitze, *The Founders and the Architects: The Design of Stanford University* (Stanford, Calif.: Department of Art, Stanford University, 1976).

2 Richard Longstreth, *On the Edge of the World: Four Architects in San Francisco at the Turn of the Century* (Cambridge, Mass.: MIT Press, 1983).

3 Charles Zueblin, *A Decade of Civic Improvement* (University of Chicago Press, 1905), pp. 60-61.

4 Longstreth, op.cit., p. 229.

5 Loren Partridge, *John Galen Howard and the Berkeley Campus* (Berkeley, Calif.: Berkeley Architectural Heritage Association, 1978), pp. 11-12. See also Longstreth, op.cit., and *California Architect and Building News* during the period of the competition.

6 "A New San Francisco to Rival All Cities," *San Francisco Examiner*, December 4, 1898. A Hearst paper, the *Examiner* carried the most complete coverage of the announcement. All other papers also carried the news on December 4.

7 Ibid.

8 "New Plan of Mrs. Hearst," *San Francisco Chronicle*, December 4, 1898.

9 Quoted in *California Architect and Building News* (March 1898), p. 34.

10 *The Wave*, July 18, 1896, p. 3.

11 Bernard Maybeck, "A Dream That Might Be Realized," *Merchants' Association Review* (November 1903), pp. 1-2.

12 See, e.g., *San Francisco Bulletin*, January 5, 1898; *The Wave*, Christmas 1899; *San Francisco Examiner*, September 24, 1899.

13 Willis Polk, "How to Beautify San Francisco," *The Wave*, March 10, 1900, p. 4.

14 *San Francisco Examiner*, October 7, 8, 12, 1899. Also see *California Architect and Building News* (October and November 1899).

15 Quoted in Carol Dunlap, *California People* (Salt Lake City: Peregrine Smith, 1982), p. 161.

16 Judd Kahn, *Imperial San Francisco: Politics and Planning in an American City, 1897-1906* (Lincoln: University of Nebraska Press, 1979), p. 66.

17 Mellior Scott, *American City Planning* (Berkeley: University of California Press, 1969), p. 49.

18 *Architect and Engineer* (November 1911), p. 53; Joan Draper, *Edward H. Bennett: Architect and City Planner* (Art Institute of Chicago, 1982).

19 Daniel Burnham and Edward Bennett, *Report on a Plan for San Francisco* (San Francisco, 1905); Mel Scott, *The San Francisco Bay Area: A Metropolis in Perspective* (Berkeley: University of California Press, 1959), pp. 95-108. See also Kahn, op.cit.

20 Edward Bennett. Typed draft of Burnham Plan in Bennett papers, Burnham Library, Art Institute of Chicago.

21 Kahn, op.cit., p. 118.

22 David Shannon, ed., *Beatrice Webb's American Diary: 1898* (Madison: University of Wisconsin Press, 1963), p. 141.

23 Mel Scott, *The San Francisco Bay Area*, op.cit., pp. 113-15.

24 *San Francisco Bulletin*, May 26, 1906, p. 4.

25 *San Francisco Chronicle*, May 23, 1906, pp. 6, 14.

26 Daniel Burnham and Edward Bennett, *Proposed Street Changes in the Burned District*, August 20, 1906. (Bound volume with color-coded overlays on contemporary block book.) San Francisco Public Library History Room.

27 Kahn, op.cit., and Walton Bean, *Boss Ruef's San Francisco: The Story of the Union Labor Party, Big Business, and the Graft Prosecution* (Berkeley: University of California Press, 1952).

28 Theodore Bonnet, *The Regenerators: A Study of the Graft Prosecution of San Francisco* (San Francisco: Pacific Printing Company, 1911), p. 6.

29 A. C. David, "The New San Francisco," *Architectural Record* (January 1912), p. 9.

30 Marjorie M. Dobkin, "A Twenty-Five-Million-Dollar Mirage," *The Anthropology of World's Fairs* (Berkeley and London: Lowie Museum of Anthropology and Scolar Press, 1983), pp. 66-93.

31 See, e.g., *Sunset* magazine (January 1912).

32 *San Francisco Chronicle*, June 2, 1910.

33 *The Architect and Engineer* (November 1911), pp. 53-55.

34 *Sunset* magazine (February 1912), p. 197; *The Architect and Engineer* (January 1912).

35 Gray Brechin, "Sailing to Byzantium," *The Anthropology of World's Fairs*, op.cit., pp. 94-113; Louis Christian Mullgardt, *The Architecture and Landscape Gardening of the Exposition* (San Francisco: Paul Elder & Co., 1915).

36 Joan Draper, *The San Francisco Civic Center: Architecture, Planning, and Politics*, Ph. D. thesis, University of California, Berkeley, 1979.

37 Arthur Mathews, "San Francisco and Its Civic Center," *Philopolis*, May 25, 1909.

38 See, e.g., B. J. S. Cahill, "Adventures in the Monumental," *The Architect and Engineer* (August 1918), pp. 38-97; Cahill, *The Architect and Engineer* (July 1933), pp. 47-48.

39 Willis Polk, "Willis Polk on the Preservation of the Fine Arts Palace," *The Architect and Engineer* (January 1916), pp. 100-3.

19   Arthur Mathews. The City (*sketch for mural in California State Capitol), c. 1913.*
Watercolor and pencil on paper, 27⅞ × 21⅞ in. (70.8 × 55.6 cm).
Collection of the Santa Barbara Museum of Art, gift of Harold Wagner.

Mathews' murals for the State Capitol in Sacramento depict the development of California from the prehistoric past to the future. In the final panel he envisioned a city of art and culture on the Pacific that would revive the classical tradition, a destiny beyond commerce and the machine. In doing so, he spoke for San Francisco's growing conservatism as it matured.

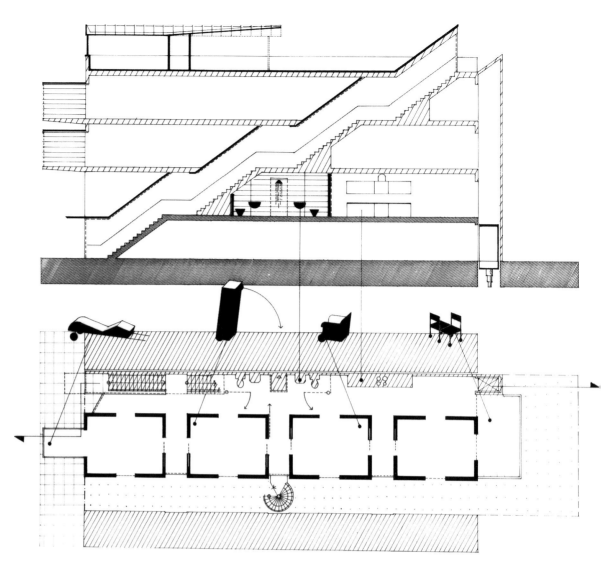

House of Flats
Sohela Farokhi and Lars Lerup

The drawings illustrate a proposal for a new House of Flats for San Francisco. Each flat with its movable furniture and rooms of obsession is a house for present and future San Franciscans, some of whom appear in Richard Rodriguez' essay. The reader/viewer may find parallels between the essay and house. Both may be read as text, in which the physical descriptions occur within the written word as well as in the drawn image.

The House of Flats was developed as a result of many conversations that we have had with Paolo Polledri and Richard Rodriguez. This project has its own "text," but since we find ourselves in the world of figures (artist/architect) rather than words (writer), we will only briefly outline the underpinnings.

The House stands firmly on the conceptual ground of the Victorian house of flats that remains the typical San Francisco house. Our house is an implicit critique of two facts: the inscription of the single family in the traditional plan of the Victorian house and the total rejection of the Victo-

rian house in the more recent development of houses and apartments. Consequently, our House of Flats attempts to erase the "family" from the plan while simultaneously utilizing the tremendous typological power of the Victorian house. The result is, in our mind, an excavation of the type, revealing an underlying stratum, a more fundamental plan if you will.

The flat consists of a wide hall (the old corridor) that contains stairs, bathroom and kitchen equipment, and an enfilade of rooms each separated from the next by a narrow anteroom—a time-out space that allows light to penetrate into the hall while simultaneously making each room an island unto itself. The venerated bay window has been elongated and stretched into a bay view, increasing visual access to both bay and street. This is the framework.

We have inserted our own obsessions into this framework, in a manner much as any occupant would his or her memories, dreams, and possessions: the room as a live-in painting and a world of postcards (the immigrant dream of always being

somewhere else). We have also rolled our ambiguous furniture onto the scene.

We hope that we have satisfied Richard Rodriguez' yearning for a structure; in the process of developing one for ourselves, we may forever have buried the open plan. It is with satisfaction that we find a nineteenth-century structure in our new plan. Erased is the Victorian plan with the compartmentalization of the industrial revolution, with its division of labor, sexism, and destruction of the family. In its place the doors swing open for the emergence of a new type of extended family, whose outlines Rodriguez sees in the wake of the AIDS crisis.

As utopian plans go, ours is not "a grand tale" because we do not believe there is one way of life, one kind of inhabitant, or one history that is relevant for all of us. Nevertheless, our tale is still utopian in light of contemporary San Francisco with its banks, planning departments, and zoning regulations.

Richard Rodriguez

Sodom: Reflections on a Stereotype

St. Augustine writes from his cope of dust that we are restless hearts and earth is not our true home. Human unhappiness is evidence of our immortality. Intuition should tell us we are meant for some other city.

Elizabeth Taylor, quoted in a magazine article of twenty years ago, spoke of cerulean Richard Burton days on her yacht, days that were nevertheless undermined by the elemental private reflection: this must end.

On a Sunday in summer, ten years ago, I was walking home from the Latin Mass at St. Patrick's, the old Irish parish downtown, when I saw thousands of people on Market Street. It was the Gay Freedom Day parade—not the first, but the first I ever saw. Private lives were becoming public. There were marching bands. There were floats. Banners blocked single lives thematically into a processional mass, not unlike the consortiums of the blessed in Renaissance paintings, each saint cherishing the apparatus of his martyrdom: GAY DENTISTS. BLACK AND WHITE LOVERS. GAYS FROM BAKERSFIELD. LATINA LESBIANS. From the foot of Market Street they marched, east to west, following the mythic American path toward optimism.

I followed the parade to Civic Center Plaza, where flags of routine nations yielded sovereignty to a multitude. Pastel billows flowed over all.

Five years later, another parade. Politicians waved from white convertibles. "Dykes on Bikes" revved up, thumbs upped. But now banners bore the acronyms of death. AIDS. ARC. Drums were muffled, as passing, plum-spotted young men slid by on motorized cable cars.

1   *Sohela Farokhi and Lars Lerup.* Section, Typical Plan, and Moveable Furniture, *1989.*
Ink on vellum, 14 × 17 in. (35.6 × 43.2 cm).
Courtesy San Francisco Museum of Modern Art.
(Photo: Ben Blackwell)

Though I am alive now, I do not believe an old man's pessimism is necessarily truer than a young man's optimism simply because it comes after. There are things a young man knows that are true and are not in the old man's power to recollect. Spring has its sappy wisdom. Lonely teenagers still arrive in San Francisco aboard Greyhound buses. The city can still seem, I imagine, by comparison to where they came from, paradise.

Four years ago on a Sunday in winter—a brilliant spring afternoon—I was jogging near Fort Point, while overhead a young woman was, with difficulty, climbing over the railing of the Golden Gate Bridge. Holding down her skirt with one hand, with the other she waved to a startled spectator (the newspaper next day quoted a workman who was painting the bridge) before she stepped onto the sky.

To land like a spilled purse at my feet.

Serendipity has an eschatological tang here. Always has. Few American cities have had the experience, as we have had, of watching the civic body burn even as we stood, out of body, on a hillside, in a theater. Jeanette MacDonald's loony scatting of "San Francisco" has become our go-to-hell anthem. San Francisco has taken some heightened pleasure from the circus of final things. To Atlantis, to Pompeii, to the Pillar of Salt, we add the Golden Gate Bridge, not golden at all, but rust red. San Francisco toys with the tragic conclusion.

For most of its brief life, San Francisco has entertained an idea of itself as heaven on earth, whether as gold town or City Beautiful or Treasure Island or the Haight Ashbury.

San Francisco can support both comic and tragic conclusions because the city is geographically in extremis, a metaphor for the farthest-flung possibility, a metaphor for the end of the line. Land's end.

To speak of San Francisco as land's end is to read the map from one direction only—as Europeans would

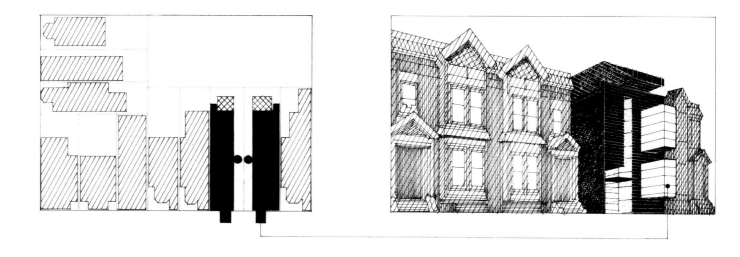

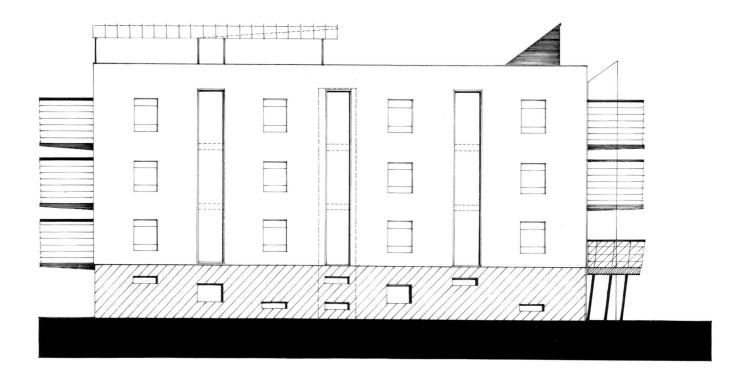

2   *Sohela Farokhi and Lars Lerup.* Site and View in
Context, *1989.*
Ink on vellum, 14 × 17 in. (35.6 × 43.2 cm).
Courtesy San Francisco Museum of Modern Art.
(Photo: Ben Blackwell)

3   *Sohela Farokhi and Lars Lerup.* Elevation in Re-
cess, *1989.*
Ink on vellum, 14 × 17 in. (35.6 × 43.2 cm).
Courtesy San Francisco Museum of Modern Art.
(Photo: Ben Blackwell)

read it or as the East Coast has always read. In my lifetime, San Francisco has become an Asian city. To speak, therefore, of San Francisco as land's end is to betray parochialism. My parents came here from Mexico, where they saw San Francisco as the North. The West was not west for them. They did not share the eastern traveler's sense of running before the past—the darkening time zone, the lowering curtain.

I cannot claim for myself the memory of a skyline such as the one César saw. César came to San Francisco in middle age; César came here as to some final place. He was born in South America; he had grown up in Paris; he had been everywhere, done everything; he assumed the world. Yet César was not skeptical of San Francisco, not at all. Here César saw revolution, and he embraced it.

Whereas I live here because I was born here. I grew up ninety miles away, in Sacramento. San Francisco was the nearest, the easiest, the inevitable city, since I needed a city. And yet I live here surrounded by people for whom San Francisco is a quest.

I have never looked for utopia on a map. Of course, I believe in human advancement. I believe in medicine, in astrophysics, in washing machines. But my compass takes its cardinal point from tragedy. If I respond to the metaphor of spring, I nevertheless learned, years ago, from my Mexican parents, from my Irish nuns, to count on winter. The point of Eden for me, for us, is not approach, but expulsion.

After I met César in 1984, our friendly debate concerning the halcyon properties of San Francisco ranged from restaurant to restaurant. I spoke of limits. César boasted of freedoms.

It was César's conceit to add to the gates of Jerusalem, to add to the soccer field of Tijuana, one other dreamscape hoped for the world over. It was the view from a hill, through a mesh of electrical tram wires, of an urban neighborhood in a valley. The vision took its name from the protruding wedge of a theater marquee. Here César raised his glass without discretion: To the Castro.

There were times, dear César, when you tried to switch sides if only to scorn American optimism, which, I remind you, had already become your own. At the high school where César taught, teachers and parents had organized a campaign to keep kids from driving themselves to the junior prom in an attempt to forestall liquor and death. Such a scheme momentarily reawakened César's Latin skepticism.

Didn't the Americans know? (His tone exaggerated incredulity.) Teenagers will crash into lampposts on their way home from proms, and there is nothing to be done about it. You cannot forbid tragedy.

By California standards I live in an old house. But not haunted. There are too many tall windows, too much salty light, especially in winter, though the windows rattle, rattle in summer when the fog flies overhead, and the house creaks and prowls at night. I feel myself immune to any confidence it seeks to tell.

To grow up homosexual is to live with secrets and within secrets. In no other place are those secrets more closely guarded than within the family home. The grammar of the gay city borrows metaphors from the nineteenth-century house. "Coming out of the closet" is predicated upon family laundry, dirty linen, skeletons.

I live in a tall Victorian house that has been converted to four apartments; four single men.

Neighborhood streets are named to honor nineteenth-century men of action, men of distant fame. Clay. Jackson. Scott. Pierce. Many Victorians in the neighborhood date from before the 1906 earthquake and fire.

Architectural historians credit the gay movement of the 1970s with the urban restoration of San Francisco. Twenty years ago this was a borderline neighborhood. This room, like all the rooms of the house, was painted headache green, apple green, boardinghouse green. In the 1970s homosexuals moved into black and working-class parts of the city, where homosexuals were perceived as pioneers or as block-busters, depending.

Two decades ago some of the least expensive sections of San Francisco were wooden Victorian sections. It was thus a coincidence of the market that gay men found themselves living within the architectural metaphor for family. No other architecture in the American imagination is more evocative of family than the Victorian house. In those same years—the 1970s—and within those same Victorian houses, homosexuals were betimes living rebellious lives to challenge the foundations of domesticity.

Was "queer-bashing" so much a manifestation of homophobia as a reaction against gentrification? One heard the complaint, often enough, that gay men were as promiscuous with their capital as otherwise, buying, fixing up, then selling and moving on. Two incomes, no children described an unfair advantage. No sooner would flower boxes begin to appear than an anony-

mous reply was smeared on the sidewalk out front: KILL FAGGOTS.

The three- or four-story Victorian house, like the Victorian novel, was built to contain several generations and several classes under one roof, behind a single oaken door. What strikes me at odd moments is the confidence of Victorian architecture. Stairs, connecting one story with another, describe the confidence that bound generations together through time—confidence that the family would inherit the earth. The other day I noticed for the first time the vestige of a hinge on the topmost newel of the staircase. This must have been the hinge of a gate that kept infants upstairs so many years ago.

If Victorian houses exude a sturdy optimism by day, they are also associated in our imagination with the Gothic—with shadows and cobwebby gimcrack, long corridors. The nineteenth century was remarkable for escalating optimism even as it excavated the backstairs, the descending architecture of nightmare—Freud's labor and Engels'.

I live on the second story, in rooms that have been rendered as empty as Yorick's skull—gutted, unrattled, in various ways unlocked—added skylights and new windows, new doors. The hallway remains the darkest part of the house.

This winter the hallway and lobby are being repainted to resemble an eighteenth-century French foyer. Of late we had walls and carpets of Sienese red; a baroque mirror hung in an alcove by the stairwell. Now we are to have enlightened austerity of an expensive sort—black and white marble floors and faux masonry. A man comes in the afternoons to texture the walls with a sponge and a rag and to paint white mortar lines that create an illusion of permanence, of stone.

The renovation of Victorian San Francisco into dollhouses for libertines may have seemed, in the 1970s, an evasion of what the city was actually becoming. San Francisco's rows of storied houses proclaimed a multigenerational orthodoxy, all the while masking the city's truly unconventional soul. Elsewhere, meanwhile, domestic America was coming undone.

4 *Sohela Farokhi and Lars Lerup.* House of Flats: Working Drawing #1, *1989.*
Mixed media on Bristol paper, 22⅝ × 30³⁄₁₆ in. (57.5 × 76.7 cm).
Courtesy San Francisco Museum of Modern Art.
(Photo: Ben Blackwell)

Suburban Los Angeles, the prototype for a new America, was characterized by a more apparently radical residential architecture. There was, for example, the work of Frank Gehry. In the 1970s Gehry exploded the nuclear-family house, turning it inside out intellectually and in fact. Though, in a way, Gehry merely completed the logic of the postwar suburban tract house—with its one story, its sliding glass doors, Formica kitchen, two-car garage. The tract house exchanged privacy for mobility. Heterosexuals opted for the one-lifetime house, the freeway, the birth-control pill, minimalist fiction.

The age-old description of homosexuality is of a sin against nature. Moralistic society has always judged emotion literally. The homosexual was sinful because he had no kosher place to stick it. In attempting to drape the architecture of sodomy with art, homosexuals have lived for thousands of years against the expectations of nature. Barren as Shakers and, interestingly, as concerned with the small effect, homosexuals have made a covenant against nature. Homosexual survival lay in artifice, in plumage, in lampshades, sonnets, musical comedy, couture, syntax, religious ceremony, opera, lacquer, irony.

I once asked Enrique, an interior decorator, if he had many homosexual clients. *"Mais non,"* said he, flexing his eyelids. "Queers don't need decorators. They were born knowing how. All this A.S.I.D. stuff—tests and regulations—as if you can confer a homosexual diploma on a suburban housewife by granting her a discount card."

A knack? The genius, we are beginning to fear in an age of AIDS, is irreplaceable—but does it exist? The question is whether the darling affinities are innate to homosexuality or whether they are compensatory. Why have so many homosexuals retired into the small effect, the ineffectual career, the stereotype, the card shop, the florist? Be gentle with me? Or do homosexuals know things others do not?

This way power lay: once upon a time the homosexual appropriated to himself a mystical province, that of taste. Taste, which is, after all, the insecurity of the middle class, became the homosexual's licentiate to challenge the rule of nature. (The fairy in his blood, he intimated.)

Deciding how best to stick it may be only an architectural problem or a question of physics or of engineering or of cabinetry. Nevertheless, society's condemnation forced the homosexual to find his redemption outside nature. *We'll put a little skirt here.*

The impulse is not to create but to re-create, to sham, to convert, to sauce, to rouge, to fragrance, to prettify. No effect is too small or too ephemeral to be snatched away from nature, to be ushered toward the perfection of artificiality. *We'll bring out the highlights there.* The homosexual has marshaled the architecture of the straight world to the very gates of Versailles—that great Vatican of fairyland—beyond which power is reduced to leisure.

In San Francisco in the 1980s the highest form of art becomes interior decoration. The glory hole is thus converted to an eighteenth-century French foyer.

I live away from the street, in a back apartment, in two rooms. I use my bedroom as a visitor's room—the sleigh bed tricked up with shams into a sofa—whereas I rarely invite anyone into my library, the public room, where I write, the public gesture.

I read in my bedroom in the afternoon because the light is good there, especially now, in winter, when the sun recedes from the earth.

There is a door in the south wall that leads to a balcony. The door was once a window. Inside the door, inside my bedroom, are twin green shutters. They are false shutters, of no function beyond wit. The shutters open into the room; they have the effect of turning my apartment inside out.

A few months ago I hired a man to paint the shutters green. I wanted the green shutters of Manet—you know the ones I mean—I wanted a weathered look, as of verdigris. For several days the painter labored, rubbing his water paints into the wood and then wiping them off again. In this way he rehearsed for me decades of the ravages of weather. Yellow enough? Black?

The painter left one afternoon, saying he would return the next day, leaving behind his tubes, his brushes, his sponges and rags. He never returned. Someone told me he has AIDS.

A black woman haunts California Street between the donut shop and the cheese store. She talks to herself—a debate, wandering, never advancing. Pedes-

trians who do not know her give her a wide berth. Somebody told me her story. I don't know whether it's true. Neighborhood merchants continue to tolerate her presence as the official vestige of dispirited humanity clinging to an otherwise dispiriting progress of "better" shops and restaurants.

Repainted façades extend now from Jackson Street south into what was once the heart of the black 'Mo—black Fillmore Street. Today there are watercress sandwiches at three o'clock where recently there had been loud-mouthed kids, hole-in-the-wall bars, pimps. Now there are tweeds and perambulators, matrons and nannies. Yuppies. And gays.

The gay male revolution had greater influence on San Francisco in the 1970s than did the feminist revolution. Feminists, with whom I include lesbians—such is the inclusiveness of the feminist movement—were preoccupied with career, with escape from the house in order to create a sexually democratic city. Homosexual men sought to reclaim the house, the house that traditionally had been the reward for heterosexuality, with all its selfless tasks and burdens.

Leisure defined the gay male revolution. The gay political movement began, by most accounts, in 1969 with the Stonewall riots in New York City, whereby gay men fought to defend the nonconformity of their leisure.

It was no coincidence that homosexuals migrated to San Francisco in the 1970s, for the city was famed as a playful place, more Catholic than Protestant in its eschatological intuition. In 1975 the State of California legalized consensual homosexuality, and about that same time Castro Street, southwest of downtown, began to eclipse Polk Street as the homosexual address in San Francisco. Polk Street was a string of bars. The Castro was an entire district. The Castro had Victorian houses and churches, bookstores and restaurants, gyms, dry cleaners, supermarkets, and an elected member of the Board of Supervisors. The Castro supported baths and bars, but there was nothing furtive about them. On Castro Street the light of day penetrated gay life through clear plate-glass windows. The light of day discovered a new confidence, a new politics. Also a new look—a noncosmopolitan, Burt Reynolds, butch-kid style: beer, ballgames, Levis, short hair, muscles.

Gay men who lived elsewhere in the city, in Pacific Heights or in the Richmond, often spoke with derision of "Castro Street clones," describing the look, or scorned what they called the ghettoization of homosexuality. To an older generation of homosexuals, the blatancy of sexuality on Castro Street threatened the

5   *Sohela Farokhi and Lars Lerup.* House of Flats: Working Drawing #2 (Lot Size and Type), *1989.*
Mixed media on Bristol paper, 22⅛ × 30³⁄₁₆ in. (57.5 × 76.7 cm).
Courtesy San Francisco Museum of Modern Art.
(Photo: Ben Blackwell)

discrete compromise gay men had negotiated with a tolerant city.

As the Castro district thrived, Folsom Street, south of Market, also began to thrive, as if in counter-distinction to the utopian Castro. The Folsom Street area was a warehouse district of puddled alleys and deserted streets. Folsom Street offered an assortment of leather bars—an evening's regression to the outlaw sexuality of the '50s, the '40s, the nineteenth century, and so on—an eroticism of the dark, of the Reeperbahn, or of the guardsman's barracks.

The Castro district implied that sexuality was more crucial, that homosexuality was the central fact of identity. The Castro district, with its ice cream parlors and hardware stores, was the revolutionary place.

Into which carloads of vacant-eyed teenagers from other districts or from middle-class suburbs would drive after dark, cruising the neighborhood for solitary victims.

The ultimate gay basher was a city supervisor named Dan White, ex-cop, ex-boxer, ex-fireman, ex-altar boy. Dan White grew up in the Castro district; he recognized the Castro revolution for what it was. Gays had achieved power over him. He murdered the mayor and he murdered the homosexual member of the Board of Supervisors.

Katherine, a sophisticate if ever there was one, nevertheless dismisses two men descending the aisle at the Opera House. "All so sleek and smooth—joweled and silver-haired—they don't seem real, poor darlings. It must be because they don't have children."

Lodged within Katherine's complaint is the perennial heterosexual annoyance with the homosexual's freedom from child-rearing, which places the homosexual not so much beyond the pale but relegates the homosexual outside "responsible" life.

It was the glamour of gay life, after all, as much as it was the feminist call to career, that encouraged heterosexuals in the 1970s to excuse themselves from nature, to swallow the birth-control pill. Who needs

children? The gay bar became the paradigm for the singles' bar. The gay couple became the paradigm for the selfish couple—all dressed up and everywhere to go. And there was the example of the gay house in illustrated life-style magazines. At the same time that suburban housewives were looking outside the home for fulfillment, gay men were reintroducing a new generation in the city—heterosexual men and women—to the satisfactions of the barren house.

Puritanical America dismissed gay camp followers as Yuppies—the term means to suggest infantility. Yuppies were obsessive and awkward in their materialism. Whereas gays arranged a decorative life against a barren state, Yuppies sought early returns, lives that were not to be all toil and spin. Yuppies, trained to careerism from the cradle, wavered in their pursuit of the northern European ethic—indeed, we might now call it the pan-Pacific ethic—in favor of the Mediterranean, the Latin, the Catholic, the Castro, the Gay.

The international architectural idioms of Skidmore, Owings & Merrill, which defined the skyline of the 1970s, betrayed no awareness of any street-level debate concerning the primacy of work or play in San Francisco, nor of the human dramas resulting from urban redevelopment. The repellent office tower was a fortress raised against the sky, against the street, against the idea of a city. Offices were hives where money was made, and damn all.

In the 1970s San Francisco was divided between the interests of downtown and the pleasures of the neighborhoods. Neighborhoods asserted idiosyncrasy, human scale, light. The gay movement rejected downtown as representing "straight" conformity.

San Francisco neighborhoods perceived downtown as working against their influence in determining what the city should be. Thus neighborhoods seceded from the idea of a city.

Was it possible that heterosexual Union Street was related to Castro Street? Was it possible that either was related to the Latino Mission district? Or to the Chinese Richmond? San Francisco, though complimented worldwide for holding its center, was in fact without a vision of its entire self.

In the 1980s, in deference to the neighborhoods, City Hall would attempt a counter-reformation of downtown, forbidding "Manhattanization." Shadows were legislated away from parks and playgrounds. Height restrictions were lowered beneath an existing skyline. Design, too, fell under the retro-jurisdiction of

6   Sohela Farokhi and Lars Lerup. House of Flats: Working Drawing #3 (Space Shaping), 1989. Mixed media on Bristol paper, 22⅝ × 30³/₁₆ in. (57.5 × 76.7 cm). Courtesy San Francisco Museum of Modern Art. (Photo: Ben Blackwell)

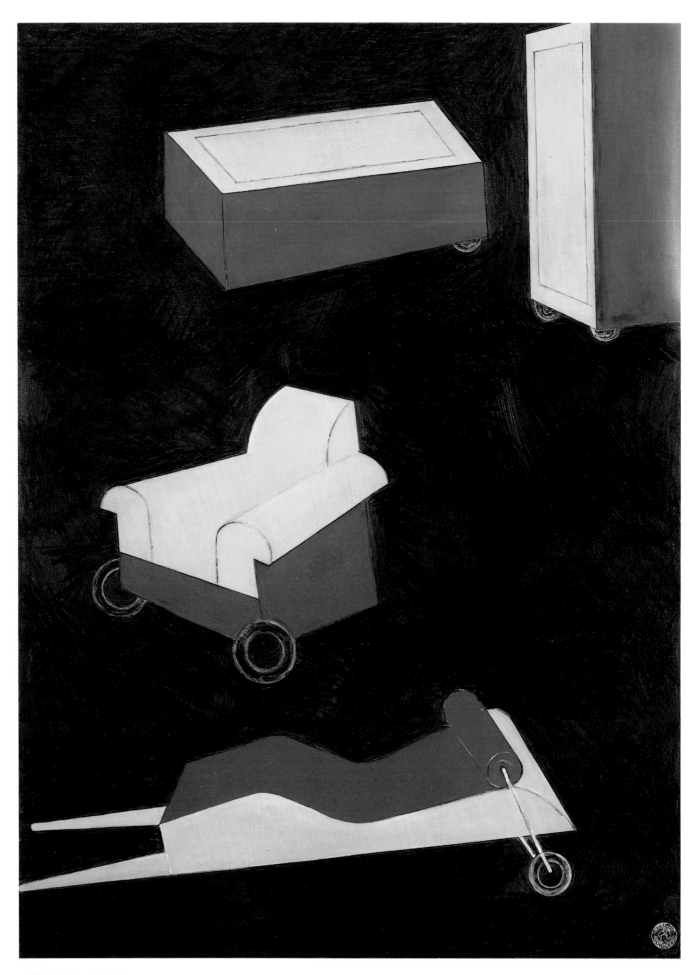

the city planner's office. The Victorian house was presented to architects as a model of what the city wanted to uphold and to become. In heterosexual neighborhoods, one saw newly built Victorians. Downtown, post-modernist prescriptions for playfulness advised skyscrapers to wear party hats, buttons, comic mustaches. Philip Johnson yielded to the dollhouse impulse to perch angels atop one of his skyscrapers.

I can see downtown from my bedroom window. But days pass and I do not leave the foreground for the city. Most days my public impression of San Francisco is taken from Fillmore Street, from the anchorage of the Lady of the Donut Shop.

I sentimentalize her into a picturesque. I look for her. Other days I may invest this raving black lady with powers of righteousness against the city, for she now often parades with her arms crossed over her breasts in an "X," the posture emblematic of prophecy. Such an impassive face.

And yet gather her madness where she sits on the curb, chain-smoking, hugging her knees, while I disappear down Fillmore Street to make Xerox copies, to mail letters, to rent a video, to shop for dinner. I am soon pleased by the faint breeze from the city, the slight agitation of the homing crowds of singles, so intent upon the path of least resistance. I admire the prosperity of the corridor, the shop windows that beckon inward toward the perfected life-style, the little way of the City of St. Francis.

Turning down Pine Street, I am recalled by the prickly silhouette of St. Dominic's Church against the scrim of the western sky. I turn, instead, into the Pacific Heights Health Club.

In the 1970s, like a lot of men and women in this city, I joined a gym. My club I've even caught myself calling it.

In the gay city of the 1970s, body-building became an architectural preoccupation of the upper middle class. Body-building is a parody of labor, a useless accumulation of the laborer's bulk and strength. No useful task is accomplished. And yet there is something businesslike about the habituees, and the gym is filled with the punch-clock logic of the work place. Machines clank and hum. Needles on gauges toll spent calories.

The gym is at once a closet of privacy and an exhibition gallery. All four walls are mirrored.

I study my body in the mirror. Physical revelation— nakedness—is no longer possible, cannot be desired, for the body is shrouded in meat and wears itself.

The intent is some merciless press of body against a standard, perfect mold. Bodies are "cut" or "pumped" or "buffed" as on an assembly line in Turin. A body becomes so many extrovert parts. Delts, pecs, lats....

I harness myself in a Nautilus cage.

Lats become wings. For the gym is nothing if not an attempt at transcendence. From homosexual to auto-sexual....

I lift weights over my head, baring my teeth like an animal with the strain.

...to nonsexual. The effect of the overdeveloped body is the miniaturization of the sexual organs—of no function beyond wit. Behold the ape become Blakean angel, revolving in an empyrean of mirrors.

The nineteenth-century mirror over the fireplace in my bedroom was purchased by a decorator from the estate of a man who died last year of AIDS. It is a top-heavy piece, confusing styles. Two ebony-painted columns support a frieze of painted glass above the mirror. The frieze depicts three bourgeois graces and a couple of free-range cherubs. The lake of the mirror has formed a cataract and at its edges it is beginning to corrode.

Thus the mirror that now draws upon my room owns some bright curse, maybe—some memory not mine.

As I regard this mirror, I imagine St. Augustine's meditation slowly hardening into syllogism, passing down through centuries to confound us: evil is the absence of good.

We have become accustomed to figures disappearing from our landscape. Does this not lead us to interrogate the landscape?

With reason do we invest mirrors with the superstition of memory, for they, though glass, though liquid captured in a bay, are so often less fragile than we are. They—bright ovals, rectangles, or rounds— bump down unscathed, unspilled through centuries, whereas we....

The man in the red baseball cap used to jog so religiously on Marina Green. By the time it occurs to me that I have not seen him for months, I realize he may be dead—not lapsed, not moved away. People come and go in the city, it's true. But in San Francisco in

7   Sohela Farokhi and Lars Lerup. Moveable Furniture: Closet/Chest, Club, Recorb, 1989.
Graphite and acrylic on Bristol paper, 22⅝ × 30³/₁₆ in.
(57.5 × 76.7 cm).
Courtesy San Francisco Museum of Modern Art.
(Photo: Ben Blackwell)

74   *Richard Rodriguez*

1989 death has become as routine an explanation for disappearance as Lyon Van Lines.

AIDS, it has been discovered, is a plague of absence. Absence opened in the blood. Absence condensed into the fluid of passing emotion. Absence shot through opalescent tugs of semen to deflower the city.

And then AIDS, it was discovered, is a nonmetaphorical disease, a disease like any other. Absence sprang from substance—a virus, a hairy bubble perched upon a needle, a platter of no intention served round: fevers, blisters, a death sentence.

At first I heard only a few names—names connected, perhaps, with the right faces, perhaps not. People vaguely remembered, as through the cataract of this mirror, from dinner parties or from intermissions. A few articles in the press. The rumored celebrities. But within months the slow beating of the blood had found its bay.

One of San Francisco's gay newspapers, the *Bay Area Reporter*, began to accept advertisements from funeral parlors and casket makers, inserting them between the randy ads for leather bars and tanning salons. The *Reporter* invited homemade obituaries—lovers writing of lovers, friends remembering friends and the blessings of unexceptional life.

Peter. Carlos. Gary. Asel. Perry. Nikos.

Healthy snapshots accompany each annal. At the Russian River. By the Christmas tree. Lifting a beer. In uniform. A dinner jacket. A satin gown.

He was born in Puerto La Libertad, El Salvador.

He attended Apple Valley High School, where he was their first male cheerleader.

From El Paso. From Medford. From Germany. From Long Island.

I moved back to San Francisco in 1979. Oh, I had had some salad days elsewhere, but by 1979 I was a wintry man. I came here in order not to be distracted by the ambitions or, for that matter, the pleasures of others, but in order to pursue my own ambition. Once here, though, I found the company of men who pursued an earthly paradise charming. Skepticism became my demeanor toward them—I was the dinner-party skeptic, a firm believer in Original Sin and in the limits of possibility.

Which charmed them.

He was a dancer.

He settled into the interior-design department of Gump's, where he worked until his illness.

He was a teacher.

César, for example.

César had an excellent mind. César could shave the rind from any assertion to expose its pulp and jelly. But César was otherwise ruled by pulp. César loved everything that ripened in time. Freshmen. Bordeaux. César could fashion liturgy from an artichoke. Yesterday it was not ready (cocking his head, rotating the artichoke in his hand over a pot of cold water). Tomorrow will be too late (Yorick's skull). Today it is perfect (as he lit the fire beneath the pot). We will eat it now.

If he's lucky, he's got a year, a doctor told me. If not, he's got two.

The phone rang. AIDS had tagged a friend. And then the phone rang again. And then the phone rang again. Michael had tested positive. Adrian, well, what he had assumed was shingles.... Paul was back in the hospital. And César, dammit, César, even César, especially César.

That winter before his death César traveled back to South America. On his return to San Francisco he described to me how he had walked with his mother in her garden—his mother chafing her hands as if she were cold. But it was not cold, he said. They moved slowly. Her summer garden was prolonging itself this year, she said. The cicadas will not stop singing.

When he lay on his deathbed, César said everyone else he knew might get AIDS and die. He said I would be the only one spared—"spared" was supposed to have been chased with irony, I knew, but his voice was too weak to do the job. "You are too circumspect," he said then, wagging his finger upon the coverlet.

So I was going to live to see that the garden of earthly delights was, after all, only wallpaper—was that it, César? Hadn't I always said so? It was then I saw that the greater sin against heaven was my unwillingness to embrace life.

It was not as in some Victorian novel—the curtains drawn, the pillows plumped, the streets strewn with sawdust. It was not to be a matter of custards in cov-

8   *Sohela Farokhi and Lars Lerup.* Moveable Furniture: Which Way Chair, *1989.*
Graphite and acrylic on Bristol paper, 22⅝ × 12¼ in. (57.5 × 31.1 cm).
Courtesy San Francisco Museum of Modern Art.
(Photo: Ben Blackwell)

9   *Sohela Farokhi and Lars Lerup.* Rooms of Obsession: Fragment of Room Painting, *1989.*
Gilded wood, graphite, and acrylic on Bristol paper, 30³⁄₁₆ × 22⅝ in. (76.7 × 57.5 cm).
Courtesy San Francisco Museum of Modern Art.
(Photo: Ben Blackwell)

10   *Sohela Farokhi and Lars Lerup.* 3 × 3 Postcards:
2 Kalmar Slott, Rutsalen; Ercolano, Casa del Tre-
mezzo di Legno; 3 Mantova, Castello, Sala degli Sposi;
2 Mantova, Palazzo Te, Sala dei Cavalli; Ercolano,
Casa del Mobilio Carbonizzato, *1989.*
Postcards, 12¼ × 17½ in. (31.1 × 44.4 cm).
Courtesy San Francisco Museum of Modern Art.
(Photo: Ben Blackwell)

ered dishes, steaming possets, *Try a little of this, my dear.* Or gathering up the issues of *Architectural Digest* strewn about the bed. Closing the biography of Diana Cooper and marking its place. Or the unfolding of discretionary screens, morphine, parrots, pavilions.

César experienced agony.

Four of his high school students sawed through a Vivaldi quartet in the corridor outside his hospital room, prolonging the hideous garden.

In the presence of his lover Gregory and friends, Scott passed from this life . . . .

He died peacefully at home in his lover Ron's arms.

Immediately after a friend led a prayer for him to be taken home and while his dear mother was reciting the 23rd Psalm, Bill peacefully took his last breath.

I stood aloof at César's memorial, the kind of party he would enjoy, everyone said. And so for a time César lay improperly buried, unconvincingly resurrected in the conditional: would enjoy. What else could they say? César had no religion beyond aesthetic bravery.

Sunlight remains. Traffic remains. Nocturnal chic attaches to some discovered restaurant. A new novel is reviewed in the *New York Times*. And the mirror rasps on its hook. The mirror is lifted down.

A priest-friend, a good friend, who out of naïveté plays the cynic, tells me—this is on a bright, billowy day; we are standing outside—"It's not as sad as you may think. There is at least spectacle in the death of the young. Come to the funeral of an old lady sometime if you want to feel an empty church."

I will grant my priest-friend this much: that it is easier, easier on me, to sit with gay men in hospitals than with the staring old. Young men talk as much as they are able.

But those who gather around the young man's bed do not see spectacle. This doll is Death. I have seen people caressing it, staring Death down. I have seen people wipe its tears, wipe its ass; I have seen people kiss Death on his lips, where once there were lips.

Chris was inspired after his own diagnosis in July 1987 with the truth and reality of how such a terrible disease would bring out the love, warmth, and support of so many friends and family.

Sometimes no family came. If there was family, it was usually mother. Mom. With her suitcase and with the torn flap of an envelope in her hand.

Brenda. Pat. Connie. Toni. Soledad.

Or parents came but leave without reconciliation, some preferring to say cancer.

But others came, one by one and in twos and threes. Sissies were not, after all, afraid of Death. They walked his dog. They washed his dishes. They bought his groceries. They massaged his poor back. They changed his bandages. They emptied his bedpan.

Men who sought the aesthetic ordering of existence were recalled to nature. Men who aspired to the mock-angelic settled for the shirt of hair. The gay community of San Francisco, having found freedom, consented to necessity—to all that the hypocritical world had for so long held up to them, withheld from them, as "real humanity."

And if gays took care of their own, they were not alone. AIDS was a disease of the entire city; its victims were as often black, Hispanic, straight. Neither were Charity and Mercy only white, only male, only gay. Others came. There were nurses and nuns and the couple from next door, co-workers, strangers, teenagers, corporations, pensioners. A community was forming over the city.

Cary and Rick's friends and family wish to thank the many people who provided both small and great kindnesses. He was attended to and lovingly cared for by the staff at Coming Home Hospice.

And the saints of this city have names listed in the phone book, names I heard called through a microphone one cold Sunday in Advent as I sat in Most Holy Redeemer Church. It might have been any of the churches or community centers in the Castro district, but it happened at Most Holy Redeemer at a time in the history of the world when the Catholic Church still pronounced the homosexual a sinner.

A woman at the microphone called upon volunteers from the AIDS Support Group to come forward. One by one, in twos and threes, throughout the church, people stood up, young men and women, and middle-aged and old, straight, gay, and all of them shy at being called. Yet they came forward and assembled in the sanctuary, facing the congregation, grinning self-consciously at one another, their hands hidden behind them.

I am preoccupied by the fussing of a man sitting in the pew directly in front of me—in his seventies, frail, his iodine-colored hair combed forward and pasted upon his forehead. Fingers of porcelain clutch the pearly beads of what must have been his mother's rosary. He is not the sort of man any gay man would have chosen to become in the 1970s. He is probably not what he himself expected to become. Something of the old dear about him, wizened butterfly, powdered old pouf. Certainly he is what I fear becoming. And then he rises, this old monkey, with the most beatific dignity, in answer to the microphone, and he strides into the sanctuary to take his place in the company of the blessed.

So this is it—this, what looks like a Christmas party in an insurance office, and not as in Renaissance paintings, and not as we had always thought, not some flower-strewn, some sequined curtain call of grease-painted heroes gesturing to the stalls. A lady with a plastic candy cane pinned to her lapel. A Castro clone with a red bandanna exploding from his hip pocket. A perfume-counter lady with a Hermes scarf mantled upon her left shoulder. A black man in a checkered sports coat. The pink-haired punkess with a jewel in her nose. Here, too, is the gay couple in middle age, wearing interchangeable plaid shirts and corduroy pants. Blood and shit and Mr. Happy Face. These know the weight of bodies.

Bill died.

. . . Passed on to heaven.

. . . Turning over in his bed one night and then gone.

These learned to love what is corruptible, while I, barren skeptic, reader of St. Augustine, curator of the earthly paradise, inheritor of the empty mirror, I shift my tailbone upon the cold, hard pew.

Daniel P. Gregory

A Vivacious Landscape: Urban Visions between the Wars

"Enthroned on hills, San Francisco captivates the stranger who sees it from the Bay by the vivacity of its landscape long before revealing any of its intimate lures."[1] So begins a travel booklet published by the San Francisco Chamber of Commerce in 1924. It is a telling statement.

In the 1920s and 1930s San Francisco's vivacious landscape—its hills and valleys and peninsular setting, its dramatic axial vistas across a gray-blue bay—helped stimulate new thoughts about the future city. The water-girded site served as both a physical constraint and a conceptual springboard. Newspaper editors, architects, engineers, and civic leaders believed that the San Francisco of the future would inevitably reach north and east across the Bay, forming the center of a great regional metropolis.

After World War I, San Francisco's outlook began to shift away from rebuilding and toward expansion. Faith in the future, in progress and growth, was strongly reinforced by the evidence of how far the city had already come. In the words of a newspaper editorial at the time of the city's Diamond Jubilee celebration of 1921, "From a handful of people ... we have grown in seventy-five years, to the metropolis of the Pacific Coast, the queen city of the West, to an aggregation of 600,000 people with palatial homes and magnificent public structures. The city that is is but a miniature of the city that is to be."[2]

Suavities of Outline: The Skyscraper Vision

As San Franciscans conceived momentous plans for the future of their city during the 1920s, a radical metamorphosis had already begun. The city's skyline grew dramatically during the boom years after the war. Downtown, the famous older landmarks, such as the ten-story Mills Building of 1891, the fifteen-story Ferry Building of 1898, and the eighteen-story Humboldt Bank Building of 1907, started to recede into the background as a new generation of larger and usually taller office buildings rose around them. (Immediately after the earthquake and fire in 1906 building heights had been limited to one and a half times the width of the street. This height restriction was removed in 1907.) Several unrealized skyscraper designs of the

1910s had pointed the way to a new urban scale, including Frank Lloyd Wright's unprecedented twenty-story slablike design of 1912 for the John Spreckels Building, Louis Christian Mullgardt's equally tall slab of 1916, and the more eclectic but also lofty design for another Spreckels Building by the Reid brothers.

By 1930 the downtown area sported an entirely new face. Along Market Street, the ten-story, block-long Southern Pacific Building (1917), the sixteen-story Matson Building (1924), and the adjacent seventeen-story Pacific Gas & Electric Building (1925) composed a colossal wall of resplendent, classically inspired corporate palazzi. Several blocks west and south of Market, the twenty-six story Pacific Telephone Building (1925) burst abruptly from a district of five- and ten-story buildings, its distinctive setback silhouette visible for miles.

In the financial district the change was equally evident. The twenty-two-story, mansard-roofed 111 Sutter Building (1927), the block-long, Gothic-ornamented thirty-one-story Russ Building (1927)—called "the largest building on the Pacific Coast"—and the twenty-two-story Shell Building (1929) formed an especially striking urban rampart. Closer to Union Square, the elegantly faceted twenty-six-story 450 Sut-

1 San Francisco, 1930.
Courtesy Gabriel Moulin Studios, San Francisco.
The clock-faced Ferry Building at the foot of Market Street, on an axis with Twin Peaks in the background, represents the city's older, smaller late nineteenth- and early twentieth-century scale. Taller, bulkier office buildings – like the flag-topped Shell Building – are beginning to overshadow it, creating a picturesque new cityscape all their own.

3 San Francisco, 1927.
Courtesy Gabriel Moulin Studios, San Francisco.

Seen from a ferry to the East Bay, the jagged, stock-
market graph of a skyline created its own hills and valleys, bringing to mind similar waterfront views of the
financial districts of New York and Chicago. At the far
left, the Pacific Telephone Building reigns over the
South of Market Street area as the city's first tall building designed to break away from classical precedents in
ornament and outline.

2 450 Sutter Building, 1989.
Courtesy Gabriel Moulin Studios, San Francisco.

One of Timothy Pflueger's most impressive structures,
this office building for dentists and doctors effectively
combined a variety of elements into a distinctive whole.
With its Manhattanesque verticality, its elegantly faceted outline, and its exotic and exuberant terracotta
cladding in what was at the time referred to as "the
Mayan-banana style," the building at once became a
modern San Francisco landmark.

80   Daniel P. Gregory

ter Building (1930) towered over all its neighbors (fig. 2).

The skyline was becoming more picturesque, enhanced by the newer, bigger towers with their distinctive belvederes, urn-studded cornices, and setback silhouettes meeting the sky. The statement in the Chamber of Commerce booklet of 1924 was just as applicable in later years: "Suavities of outline accent the horizons of San Francisco, where the skyscrapers take on fantasy as they pile up on hills and recede into vales."[3] Indeed, Gabriel Moulin's famous panoramic photographs of 1927 (fig. 3), looking west from the Bay —past the Ferry Building and up Market Street— show a wavelike effect: the towers along Market and north along Montgomery form two distinct hills of their own, adding to the rippling impression caused by the outlines of Telegraph, Nob, and Russian hills.

The perception of San Francisco as a romantic and modern city of towers came into sharper focus as architects grew less dependent upon Beaux-Arts ideals of beauty based on historical precedent and began to experiment with imagery more attuned, in their view, to the twentieth-century "Machine Age."

Several important events exerted a powerful influence on San Francisco architects during the 1920s, serving as catalysts for the discussion of an evolving modernism. The unprecedented New York zoning law of 1916 prescribed the maximum allowable building envelope for structures in particular zones and ultimately led to a new interest in setback silhouettes. The Tribune Tower competition in Chicago in 1922 provided an unusually clear-cut distinction between traditional and modern styles: the winning entry, by the New York firm of Howells and Hood, offered an exuberant adaptation of Gothic features to the tower form; runner-up Eliel Saarinen of Finland used a series of setbacks and expressed vertical lines to emphasize the building's height in a more abstract manner, which was perceived to be more modern. The Paris Exposition des Arts Décoratifs et Industriels of 1924-25 publicized the search for new ornamental forms as a way of expressing modernity.

Perhaps no other San Francisco architect was more dramatically influenced by these developments than Timothy Pflueger, partner in the firm of Miller and Pflueger. Pflueger gave San Francisco some of its most vivid images of skyscraper modernism during the 1920s and 1930s, both through his built work and through the presentation drawings he commissioned. Pflueger served as a sort of "cultural diffuser," bringing the latest skyscraper imagery to San Francisco from Chicago and New York and thereby offering his hometown a partial view of what the modern metropolis should look like (fig. 4).

6   Hugh Ferriss, delineator. Pacific Edgewater Club, *J. R. Miller and T. L. Pflueger, Architects, 1927. Charcoal on paper, 31¼ × 46¼ in. (80.6 × 119 cm). Courtesy Butterfield & Butterfield, San Francisco.*

Appearing to emerge from the fog and the craggy sea-swept site, Ferriss' marvelously melodramatic, almost Wagnerian depiction suggests that a quiet, convivial evening sipping cocktails at the club would lend new meaning to the phrase "bourbon on the rocks."

4   Hugh Ferriss, delineator. Winning Entry for the Pacific Stock Exchange Competition, *J. R. Miller and T. L. Pflueger, Architects, 1929. Pencil and charcoal on paper, 25¼ × 20⅜ in. (64.2 × 51.7 cm). Courtesy Butterfield & Butterfield, San Francisco.*

The sculptural piers show the influence of New York architect Bertram Goodhue, who designed the widely publicized Nebraska State Capitol of 1924.

5   Hugh Ferriss, delineator. Pacific Telephone & Telegraph Co. Building, *J. R. Miller and T. L. Pflueger, Architects, 1924. Charcoal and pencil on paper, 32½ × 20 in. (82.5 × 50.8 cm). Courtesy Butterfield & Butterfield, San Francisco.*

This powerful rendering of soaring solidity brought a romantic, "Manhattanesque" setback image to San Francisco for the first time.

With his associate, architect A. A. Cantin, Pflueger was beginning to work on the commission for the Pacific Telephone Building when, according to writer Harold Gilliam, he came across Eliel Saarinen's widely published second-place entry for the Tribune Tower competition in Chicago.[4] This scheme electrified the architectural profession with its expression of a soaring verticality simply and directly as a system of straightforward vertical piers, recessed spandrels, and setback outline. Pflueger adapted the design, wrapping it in gray speckled terra-cotta resembling Sierra granite. The chastely ornamented Pacific Telephone Building would bestow on San Francisco its first grand image of skyscraper modernism.

To give such a contemporary design the best possible chance of success with his clients, Pflueger hired the leading illustrator of the day, New York renderer and visionary architect Hugh Ferriss, to make a presentation drawing in 1924 (fig. 5). As architectural historian Carol Willis has documented, Ferriss' 1922 drawings illustrating the four stages of the zoning envelope (an analysis of the New York zoning law of 1916) had received wide exposure.[5]

Executed in his characteristic atmospheric style, the drawing presents the Telephone Building as a massive, glowing monolith rising out of the sidewalk and soaring into a darkening sky. Two low buildings with traditional detailing flank the new structure; in contrast to the sheer, brightly lit shaft between them, they are deeply shaded and give the drawing a heightened sense of drama by accentuating the contrast between old and new San Francisco. The city had no setback zoning ordinance comparable to New York's, so Pflueger was literally importing a setback style. Indeed, the Pacific Telephone Building had no need for setbacks to allow light and air to reach the ground because most of the adjacent buildings were no taller than ten stories.

A commission to design the Pacific Edgewater Clubhouse in 1927 (never executed) for a spectacular ocean-view site at Point Lobos, near the Cliff House, prompted Pflueger to hire Ferriss once again. The architect wanted a drawing that would help stimulate memberships and financial backing. Ferriss responded with an image that complemented his depiction of the Telephone Building (fig. 6). This time he concentrated on both the horizontality of the design and the ruggedness of the natural setting. The tiered, light-reflecting mass appears to have been chiseled out of the dark cliffs at its base. A crystalline geometry dominates the composition, broken only by two classi-

7 Timothy Pflueger, J. R. Miller and T. L. Pflueger, Architects. Perspective study sketches for a skyscraper, 1920s. Pencil and charcoal on paper; colored pencil and pastel on paper, 29½ × 12 in. (74.9 × 30.5 cm) each. Courtesy Butterfield & Butterfield, San Francisco. (Photo: Ben Blackwell)

Prism-like outlines hint at shapes of skyscrapers to come and echo the geometric tower forms being developed at this time by Hugh Ferriss for his utopian "Metropolis of Tomorrow."

cally inspired arcades. The drawing illustrates an architecture of geology: a building inseparable from its site, a Manhattan mountain at the edge of the world.

By the early 1930s Pflueger was ready to experiment more freely. He wrote, "We are beginning to recognize glass as an asset, and to develop a mass in which the glass takes form."[6] Three striking colored-pencil skyscraper studies from this period seem to illustrate these words (fig. 7). Each image presents the structure alone, without additional ornament of any kind, as if the architect had distilled his vision to the essential elements of steel, glass, and light. Just as the Depression curtailed most downtown building, Pflueger appeared to be reaching for a more radical, almost International Style approach.

8   *Downtown San Francisco, c. 1930.*
Courtesy Gabriel Moulin Studios, San Francisco.
This view down Montgomery Street, past the California Commercial Union Building by George Kelham and Kenneth MacDonald of 1923, with the Russ Building by George Kelham behind it, vividly captures the drama and disparities of scale along the urban canyon that San Franciscans proudly proclaimed to be their own Wall Street.

In 1940 the WPA guide to San Francisco described Montgomery Street as "the Wall Street of the West" (fig. 8). As "the narrow canyon between skyscrapers . . . neat and austere between sheer walls of stone, glass, and terra cotta, it is visible evidence of San Francisco's financial hegemony over the far West."[7] With the help of Pflueger and other skyscraper architects, San Francisco had acquired its own romantic, modern, Manhattanesque skyline.

When Pflueger designed a penthouse cocktail lounge for the Mark Hopkins Hotel in 1939—the Top of the Mark—all he had to do was make the walls disappear, using the skyline itself as the room's only ornamental mural: a view and a vision at the same time.

Visionary Pragmatism: Planning the Regional Metropolis

San Francisco experienced a sort of second Gold Rush during the 1920s, as a fever of "bridge-mindedness" swept the city. Support for civic beautification was combined with an aggressive boosterism to create an atmosphere of excitement and urgency about the future. Commercial rivalries with Los Angeles and other western cities heated up. Bridges, in particular, became synonymous with future growth and prosperity.

The automobile had come of age. Cadillacs and Packards gleamed in their palatial marble and glass showrooms along Van Ness Avenue. Suddenly motorists and automobile dealers wanted more and better roads, and, equally suddenly, San Francisco's splendid isolation came to be viewed less as a romantic feature than as an inconvenient anachronism. Ferryboats seemed especially old-fashioned, and they caused traffic jams by forcing motorists to wait in line on highways leading up to ferry slips. Architect Willis Polk summed up the feeling of many when he stated categorically: "San Francisco's ferry boats belong with the horse cars, the cobble stones, the cable cars, the turntable, and the old man with chin whiskers."[8] In other words, the modern city would be the automobile city: smooth, expansive roadways spreading outward in all directions regardless of terrain.

In the spring of 1921 the San Francisco Motorcar Dealers Association purchased a series of newspaper advertisements championing the need for bridges across the Bay to provide greater ease of movement and promote further growth. The *San Francisco Bulletin* was sympathetic and asked Polk for help in envisioning a future bridge-crossed Bay.

9 *Louis Christian Mullgardt. Bridge-skyscraper
proposal, 1924, from* The Architect and Engineer,
March 1927.
*Courtesy the San Francisco Public Library.
(Photo: Ben Blackwell)*

*The dizzyingly vast bridge piled high with apartment
houses would have joined San Francisco and the East
Bay in a single urban escarpment, forming an instant
megalopolis.*

Polk, who by the early 1920s had become perhaps
San Francisco's best-known architect, maintained that
the city had forsaken its most valuable asset: its splendid setting. The eagerness to grow had put that natural
beauty at risk. He therefore urged the city to make a
plan for the future that would incorporate a consistent
policy on beautification. And what could more em-
phatically call attention to the water-girded setting
than a series of beautiful bridges?

In a speech before the Commercial Club in January
1921, he referred to the Burnham Plan of 1905 and
asked why the city should not realize some of the civic
dreams outlined at that time. He stated: "We have by
nature the most picturesque site of any city in the
world but we are so used to it that we don't appreciate
it." His point, to the assembled businessmen, was sim-
ple: "City planning is good business."[9]

While Polk urged businessmen and civic leaders to
dust off the old "City Beautiful" concepts of Daniel
Burnham, he simultaneously proposed a variety of
schemes for crossing the Bay. Four such schemes appear in a single visionary image published on the
editorial page of the *San Francisco Bulletin* on May 24,
1921. The large bird's-eye sketch of the Bay Area
shows a Gothic-towered suspension bridge—reminiscent of the Brooklyn Bridge—spanning the Golden
Gate; a longer suspension span extending to Yerba
Buena Island, where it joins up with a drawbridge extending from the Oakland shore; a tunnel south of the
Goat Island span and parallel to it; and, south of that, a
low drawbridge extending east from near Candlestick
Point.

Inset at the right is a more detailed, though still
impressionistic, view of the Golden Gate Bridge concept, showing the massive towers treated as great
cathedral façades looming above the roadway. The
headline blares, "Break Through San Francisco's
Chinese Wall!" in a rather heavy-handed but graphic
comparison of the Bay to the Great Wall of China,
echoing the analogy used in a previous Motorcar Dealers Association advertisement. "It is not the drawing of
an engineer nor merely a dream," proclaimed the *Bul-*

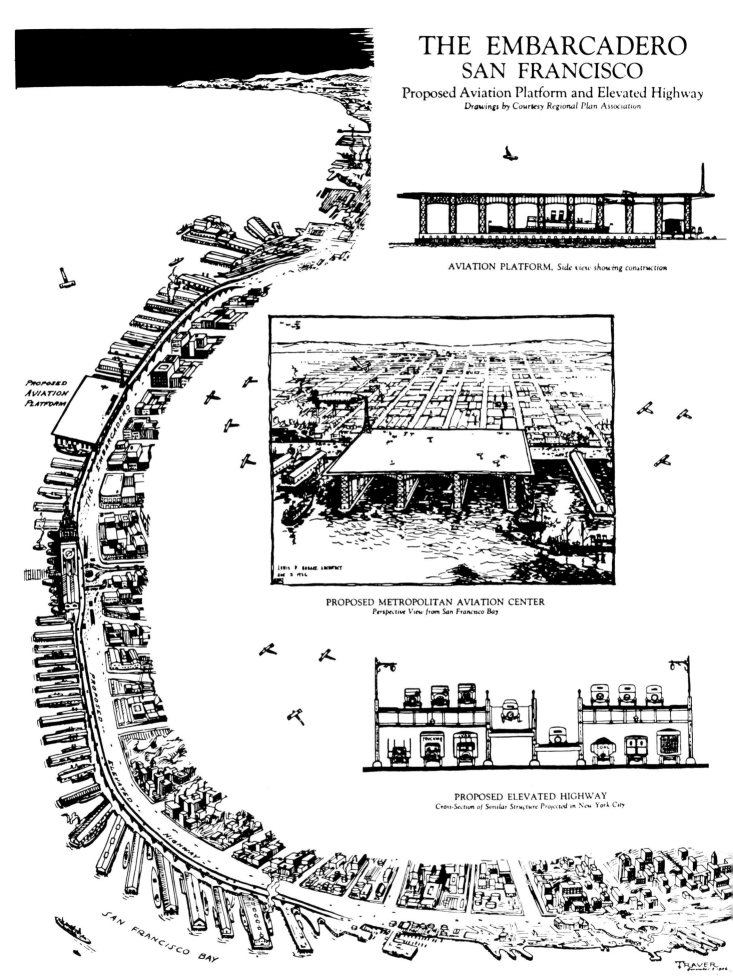

THE EMBARCADERO
SAN FRANCISCO
Proposed Aviation Platform and Elevated Highway

Drawings by Courtesy Regional Plan Association

AVIATION PLATFORM, *Side view showing construction*

PROPOSED METROPOLITAN AVIATION CENTER
Perspective View from San Francisco Bay

PROPOSED ELEVATED HIGHWAY
Cross-Section of Similar Structure Projected in New York City

PROPOSED AVIATION PLATFORM

THE EMBARCADERO

PROPOSED ELEVATED HIGHWAY

SAN FRANCISCO BAY

letin in the caption, "but is better than either; it shows what can and must be done to make San Francisco the city that some day is sure to be."[10] This grand trans-Bay vision united romance and pragmatism to present San Francisco as a sort of Manhattan of the West, the beginning and the end point for all transportation lines —a modern automobile city with a sense of history.

The mania for bridge proposals reached a peak in the middle of the decade when architect Louis Christian Mullgardt offered his extraordinary scheme for a Brobdingnagian Multiple Bridge with eleven spans, each 500 feet long, linking the area south of Market Street with Alameda (fig. 9). In several dramatically highlighted perspective sketches—recalling to some extent the imagery of Italian Futurism—Mullgardt proposed that multiple lanes and levels of traffic be supported on massive skyscraper piers. He envisioned these piers housing a wide range of functions, economically fitted into a steel and concrete structure: "The structures would have unrestricted light and air, from all directions. They would be directly connected with State highways above; also Pacific ocean steamers and smaller craft, which moor at their base. They may be palatial hotels, or great factories."[11]

Both the *San Francisco Chronicle* and the *San Francisco Examiner* reported on this remarkable proposal. Though most articles dwelt upon the "bridge-city" aspect, one emphasized Mullgardt's argument that such a structure would be an economical way to build new skyscrapers. Nothing came of the fantasy, however, and, according to architectural historian Robert Judson Clark, not long afterward Mullgardt "joined the ranks of the unemployed."[12]

Numerous more conventional proposals appeared during the mid-1920s, as consortiums sought the lucrative toll franchise. Such schemes built enthusiasm and support for bridging the Bay, priming the collective imagination for the colossal spans that would one day appear.

10   *Lewis P. Hobart, architect.* The Embarcadero, San Francisco, Proposed Aviation Platform and Elevated Highway, *1926.*
Courtesy San Francisco Archives. (Photo: Ben Blackwell)
This rather workmanlike series of images belies the imaginative, if implausible, concept of a downtown landing platform. The proposal embodies the enthusiasm and naïveté with which new technological developments were occasionally embraced.

Bay crossings were but one component of a much larger dream, that of a great regional metropolis with San Francisco at its center. This vision had only been hinted at by such men as Polk and Mullgardt. In 1924, at the urging of Senator (former Mayor) James Duval Phelan and San Francisco's Commonwealth Club, businessman and civic leader Frederick Dohrmann organized the Regional Plan Association, which articulated this vision more fully. Although the association remained fully active only through 1927, it lasted long enough to give San Francisco some of the most radical and far-reaching urban-design proposals of the decade.

Dohrmann served as a kind of benefactor-visionary, underwriting most of the association's expenditures and tirelessly lobbying on behalf of regional-planning principles among his wide circle of business and political contacts. Dohrmann and his association took on the monumental task of making "a comprehensive plan for the development of the San Francisco Bay Counties." According to the association's statement of purpose, such a plan should help unify port and harbor development, form a coordinated system of highways and scenic boulevards, bridge the Bay, connect all parts of the Bay Area with rapid transit, develop recreational areas, develop the water supply, remove the growing menace of Bay pollution, and institute regional zoning.[13] Like Polk, Mullgardt, and the Motorcar Dealers Association, the Regional Plan Association sought to assure continued growth and prosperity. No final plan was ever completed, but the Regional Plan Association did commission two nationally known planners to outline the new vision of San Francisco and the Bay Area as a single expansive metropolis of the future. Future greatness, according to Dohrmann and his planners, depended on carefully orchestrated growth and on San Francisco's leadership.[14] As planning historian Mel Scott points out, the clear San Francisco bias may have exacerbated traditional community rivalries, thereby eroding support for a truly regional point of view.[15]

In 1926 and 1927 "air-mindedness" reigned, prompting Dohrmann to develop his most visionary, if implausible, scheme: San Francisco should maintain its competitive edge over other Pacific ports by quickly becoming the center of commercial aviation in the Bay Area. He proposed that the city build a landing platform "from 150 to 200 feet above high water mark and about 1000 feet by 1000 feet in extent" on the Embarcadero south of the Ferry Building (fig. 10).[16] According to Dohrmann, it would be close to other forms of

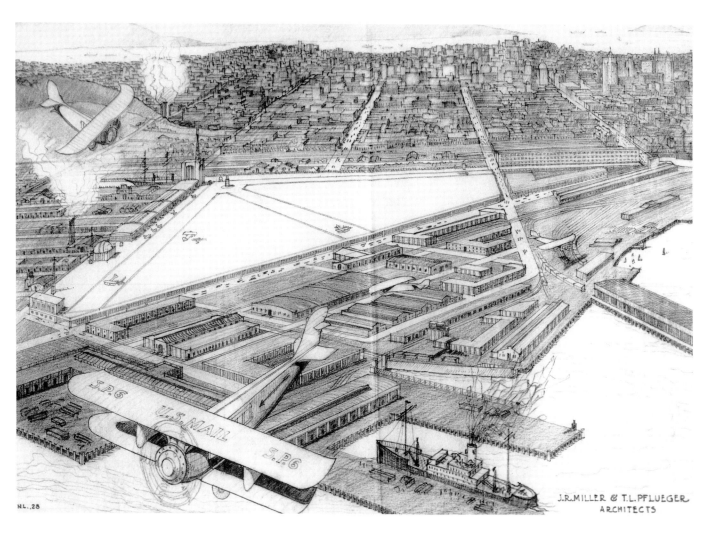

NL..28

J.R.MILLER & T.L.PFLUEGER
ARCHITECTS

11 J. R. Miller and T. L. Pflueger, Architects. Bird's-eye
View of the Proposed China Basin Airport, *c. 1928.*
Charcoal and pencil on paper, 14½ × 20¼ in. (36.8 × 51.3 cm).
Courtesy Butterfield & Butterfield, San Francisco.

Like the landing-platform idea – but not so compact –
this project would have combined airplanes and ocean
liners in a single transportation hub conveniently close
to downtown, on the waterfront south of Market.

transportation, a convenient transfer point for air mail,
and would serve "as the necessary terminal depot to a
large aviation field."[17] He described his plan to Secretary of the Navy Curtis D. Wilbur, admitting the lack
of precedent for such a structure, except perhaps an
aircraft carrier. Dohrmann even asked Wilbur if he
would let the association's engineers study firsthand
the design of an aircraft carrier.[18] The secretary heart-
ily endorsed Dohrmann's idea for a landing platform
while politely declining civilian inspection of his ships.

We may wonder today at the logic of building a
landing field near the center of a dense downtown area
(fig. 11). But it is important to understand the popular

excitement that aviation, and transportation technology in general, stimulated during the 1920s. Enthusiasm simply obscured practicality. In the romantic
age of airplanes and aviators, anything seemed possible, at least for the moment. The secretary of the
navy himself was so enthralled that, in his reply to
Dohrmann, he offered the opinion that a rotating platform, while obviously impractical, would be ideal.[19]

Architect Lewis Hobart drew up the association's
original stationary-platform scheme, including an elevated, double-deck street along the Embarcadero (to
handle the assumed increase in traffic once bridges
were built). The scheme became the centerpiece of a
publicity pamphlet on aviation and highway planning
for San Francisco published by the Regional Plan
Association. Charles Lindbergh endorsed the idea
shortly after his historic flight to Paris in 1927.[20]

The publicity was short-lived. San Francisco's Board
of Supervisors considered a variety of more realistic
landing sites and in 1927 settled upon Mills Field near
San Bruno (the present airport site), which was recommended by the airport committee because of its exten-
sive acreage, reliable weather, and convenient access

12 *Peter Stackpole*. Waiting for Rivets and Steel,
1935, from the portfolio When They Built the Bridge:
Photographs of the San Francisco-Oakland Bay
Bridge, 1934-1936, *1985, 12/35.*
Gelatin silver print, 7 × 9⅜ in. (17.8 × 23.8 cm).
Collection of the San Francisco Museum of Modern Art,
gift of Ursula Gropper. (Photo: Ben Blackwell)

Because of its proximity to downtown, the Bay Bridge
gave San Francisco a new urban dimension, especially
evident in early construction photographs. These images
of men at work, high above the city and oblivious to
their own danger, illustrated a brand of heroism that
became all the more powerful for its understatement.

to the new Bayshore Highway.[21] Machine-age technology had outrun the dream, though proposals for an airport close to downtown died hard. The architectural firm of Miller and Pflueger drew up a scheme in 1927 for an airport near China Basin, south of Market Street, and the organizers of the Golden Gate International Exposition of 1939 were convinced that after the fair Treasure Island would become an important airline gateway to the Pacific.

With a plan for the future, and the ability to take advantage of commercial opportunities such as aviation, Dohrmann believed that San Francisco and its neighbors would rule the West.

During the 1930s San Francisco achieved two of its most visionary goals by bridging the Bay to the north and to the east: the Bay Bridge was dedicated in 1936 and the Golden Gate Bridge a year later. As John van der Zee, Harold Gilliam, and other writers have documented, these bridges were true visionary projects in the sense that each had been an idea or dream long before achieving reality.[22] In two fell swoops the bridges themselves—which so radically altered the appearance of the city—seemed to transform San Francisco into the regional metropolis it had long sought to be. Reality outran the dream. As writer Felix Riesenberg put it in 1940, "The city of the day after tomorrow will, with these connecting spans, embrace all habitations on one hundred miles of harbor shores. This City of San Francisco Bay awaits the height of the Pacific Era."[23]

The building of the bridges put San Francisco and Bay Area residents in the curious position of watching a vision take shape before their very eyes. The reality of the construction process—from pouring monolithic island piers to spinning the vast webs of cable—seemed to make the concept of bridging the Bay not more mundane but more mythic. Reports of construction setbacks, tragic accidents, and engineering triumphs mesmerized a public who could check on building progress simply by looking out a living-room window or up from the deck of a commuter ferry. The Bay became an amphitheater focusing all eyes on a thrilling urban metamorphosis.

Photographers, architects, painters, and writers recorded each emerging detail and the day-to-day activities of the bridge builders as if attempting to dispel the feeling of disbelief. In a pamphlet published in 1936 by the United States Steel Company upon completion of the Bay Bridge, one observer of its construction is quoted as saying, "I cannot believe my eyes. I cannot believe you. It just cannot be so. It's too marvelous." But, the writer continued, "it was so. The unbelievable had been accomplished. The Greatest Bridge in the world had been completed."[24]

Peter Stackpole's famous Bay Bridge photographs record the duality with startling clarity (fig. 12). His images show workers matter-of-factly doing their jobs riveting, welding, or hoisting girders into place, and yet the new immensities of scale behind, above, or under them seem wholly divorced from the activity. The ordinary action appears unrelated to, and almost contradictory to, the extraordinary result.

The sheer magnitude of the task of construction—in terms of engineering complexity, organizational talent, financial commitment, and bridgeworkers' skill and daring—reinforced the visionary nature of each bridge. Simultaneous construction of two immense bridges during a time of economic cataclysm, the Depression, gave the bridges symbolic power as well. Even as they pointed to the future, they embodied a measure of victory over an adverse present.

Photographs could capture the magnificence, grandeur, and drama of the architecture and engineering, but only drawings and paintings could explain the mysteries of construction and describe the variety of forms to be assumed by the bridges. Such images could actually sharpen the vision and were often necessary to rally support from administrative bodies. A notable example is the extraordinary suite of paintings describing how the Golden Gate Bridge piers and

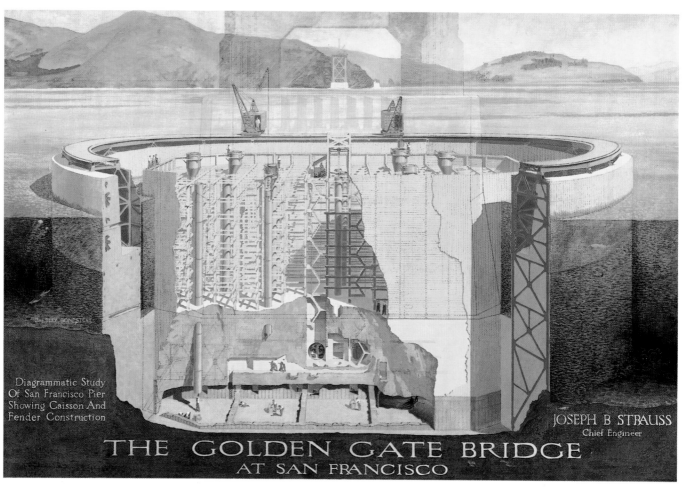

Diagrammatic Study Of San Francisco Pier Showing Caisson And Fender Construction

JOSEPH B STRAUSS
Chief Engineer

THE GOLDEN GATE BRIDGE
AT SAN FRANCISCO

A PROPOSED EASTERLY SAN FRANCISCO APPROACH TO GOLDEN GATE BRIDGE
PREPARED BY JOSEPH B. STRAUSS CHIEF ENGINEER

Chesley Bonestell

14   *Chesley Bonestell, renderer.* A Proposed Easterly
San Francisco Approach to Golden Gate Bridge, *c. 1932.*
Oil on canvas, 23⅛ × 31⅛ in. (58.7 × 79.1 cm).
Collection of the Golden Gate Bridge, Highway and
Transportation District, San Francisco.
(Photo: Ben Blackwell)

*Treating Maybeck's Palace of Fine Arts like a western
version of Paris' Arc de Triomphe (complete with its own
traffic circle) and the approach road as an extension of
the Champs-Elysées, Bonestell created a monumental
classical gateway to the modern bridge.*

13   *Chesley Bonestell, renderer.* Diagrammatic Study
of San Francisco Pier Showing Caisson and Fender
Construction, *Golden Gate Bridge, c. 1932.*
Oil on canvas, 39½ × 58½ (100.3 × 148.6 cm).
Collection of the Golden Gate Bridge, Highway and
Transportation District, San Francisco.
(Photo: Ben Blackwell)

*Immensities of scale are vigorously illustrated in this
cutaway view deep into the structural heart of the San
Francisco pier, which proclaims a measure of triumph
over nature. The tall vertical shafts of the inspection
wells are clearly visible. With its myriad steel and concrete braces and bulwarks laid bare, the pier resembles a
great urban monolith, a skyscraper under the Bay.*

towers were to be constructed. Undoubtedly commissioned to convince non-engineers—i.e., bridge directors—that the Golden Gate Bridge could in fact be
built, these paintings were done by the prolific renderer and architect Chesley Bonestell.

A San Francisco-born artist who had studied architecture at Columbia University, Bonestell worked
for Willis Polk during the planning and construction
of the Panama-Pacific International Exposition, then
as a renderer in New York during the 1920s. He returned to San Francisco in time to work for chief engineer Joseph Strauss on the Golden Gate Bridge.[25]

The cutaway views of the south-pier foundation are
especially remarkable (fig. 13). This pier presented the
greatest construction challenge because of its underwater depth and the swiftness of surrounding tidal currents. In one pier painting a vast drum-shaped coffer-
dam rises from the ocean floor. The sunlit cutaway
view reveals the many layers of defense against the
force of ocean currents: an immensely thick concrete
outer wall, multiple-story inspection shafts, and steel
cross-braced superstructures. The figures of men are
tiny but distinct, in control of and at ease with what
they have created. The engineer's vision is all clarity
and brilliance, an image of confidence and strength.

These paintings are almost transcendentalist visions of triumph and self-reliance, as if Bonestell and Strauss are saying, like latter-day Captain Ahabs, "Look down deep and do believe!" Strauss included one of the cutaway drawings in his final report of 1937.

Bonestell also drew schemes for treating the southern approach through the Presidio. Only three of these images are known to be extant. One shows the approach off Marina Boulevard much as it was actually built. The other two show a scheme to develop the Palace of Fine Arts as a sort of San Francisco version of the Arc de Triomphe in Paris, complete with traffic circle and a broad boulevard on an axis with it (replacing what is today Beach Street) (fig. 14).

Bonestell focused on demystifying and glorifying construction techniques, whereas architect Irving Morrow concentrated on dramatizing how the bridge would look when completed. His charcoal drawings of the towers, the roadway, and the entire span, done in 1930 and 1931, recall Hugh Ferriss in their use of shadow and light to emphasize scale and outline. Morrow, who had become deeply interested in aspects of modernism by the late 1920s and wrote on the subject for the local press, saw the bridge as a romantic ex-

15 The San Francisco end of the Bay Bridge, 1989. (Photo: Paolo Polledri)

16 Eudori, renderer. Cutaway view of central pier, San Francisco-Oakland Bay Bridge, The Architect and Engineer, October 1934. Courtesy Cal Trans Library, Sacramento.
This graphic illustration of the remarkable underground depth to which Bay Bridge piers were sunk contributed to the sense of wonder at the feat of construction.

pression of modern urbanism. Misty, ghostlike façades of a jagged modern skyscraper soar above a streamlined roadway suspended over a reflecting sea. In Morrow's deft hands, the Golden Gate Bridge could have fit into Ferriss' "Metropolis of Tomorrow."[26]

Images of the Bay Bridge conveyed similar themes of engineering and architectural heroics (fig. 15). Though occupying a less precipitous and rugged site, Bay Bridge piers had to be sunk much deeper into the Bay floor in order to reach bedrock. One of the westernmost piers had to be sunk 220 feet to bedrock, even though the water at this point was only seventy feet deep. The great center anchorage under the western crossing reached bedrock at a depth of 205 feet.

17 *Carl Nuese, delineator.* The San Francisco-Oakland
Bay Bridge Approach and Anchorage from Rincon Hill to
the Embarcadero, San Francisco, *1934.*
Pencil and charcoal on paper, 18 × 83 in. (45.7 × 210.8 cm).
Courtesy Butterfield & Butterfield, San Francisco.
The spare simplicity of the design expressed the bridge's
characteristics without an overlay of ornament to ob-
scure its essential modernity.

18 *Bernard Maybeck, architect.* West View Bay
Bridge, *c. 1939.*
Watercolor, ink, and colored pencil on illustration board,
30 × 20 in. (76.3 × 50.8 cm).
Collection of Timothy Tosta. (Photo: Ben Blackwell)
Maybeck was unconcerned by any apparent disparity
between modern engineering and classical architecture.
His was a more inclusive view aimed at enriching the
civic experience.

Such feats of underwater construction were unprecedented.[27] A widely published cutaway painting of the
central anchorage shows its cellular construction and
the great depths of water and mud in which it stands
(fig. 16). Unlike the Bonestell images, however, this
painting presents a more simplified view. The structure is complete, and though walls are carved out to
show what is behind them, no attempt is made to capture a moment in the process of construction.[28]

The Hoover-Young Commission, which in 1930 reported on the need for the Bay Bridge, made no
specific suggestions as to architectural character, noting simply that "the final design should be such that it
will conform with the scenic beauty of the San Francisco Bay."[29] Timothy Pflueger chaired the team of
three consulting architects who worked under Chief
Engineer Charles Purcell and, according to his brother
Milton Pflueger, argued for ornamental restraint. He
concentrated on refining and simplifying bridge approaches (fig. 17).[30]

The Bay Bridge acquired a more visionary quality
when artists took up the question of scale. Bernard
Maybeck proposed that monumental triumphal arches
be built where the bridge meets the city, extending the
scale of the structure into the urban fabric (figs. 18,
19). His romantic reprise of "City Beautiful" imagery

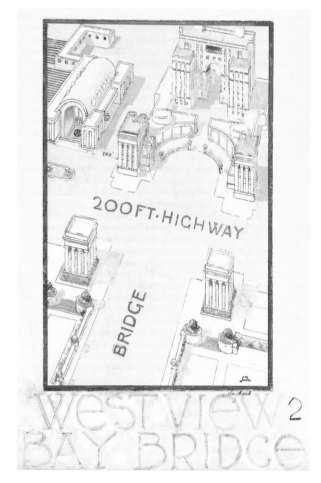

19   *Bernard Maybeck, architect.* San Francisco Ideal
City, *c. 1939.*
Watercolor ink, gold paint, and pencil on illustration board,
20 × 30 in. (50.8 × 76.3 cm).
Collection of Timothy Tosta. (Photo: Ben Blackwell)

Maybeck's eclectic, classically inspired concept would have
given the Bay Bridge a colossal triumphal gateway at its
San Francisco entrance, making arrival and departure as
visually exciting as the journey across the Bay.

gave the Bay Bridge approach what was already built into the approach to the Golden Gate Bridge: a classically inspired monument (his Palace of Fine Arts) marking a major gateway to the city.

A more futuristic image of the Bay Bridge appears in a poster by Paul Forster to announce the opening ceremonies on November 12, 1936. The view is up from the Embarcadero, past a stylishly dressed crowd of spectators who are themselves looking up, past the old and friendly but diminished Ferry Building to the huge new roadway leaping over it. A rainbow arches behind. This clever juxtaposition of old and new San Francisco—in reality the bridge crosses the Embarcadero far south of the Ferry Building—provides an emphatic welcome to the new and more monumental urban scale represented by the bridge. The proximity to downtown made the Bay Bridge towers visual extensions of the city's modern skyline, capturing the spirit of Mullgardt's fanciful skyscraper-bridge from the previous decade.

20 *E. A. Burbank, renderer. Site of the Golden Gate-International Exposition, "A Pageant of the Pacific," c. 1938. Collection of the San Francisco Archives. (Photo: Ben Blackwell)*

The siting of the exposition in the middle of the Bay on newly created Treasure Island turned the bridges and the Bay-fronting cities into the fair's biggest exhibits.

The Golden Gate Exposition and the Visionary Present

If the Bay and Golden Gate bridges added substance to the vision of San Francisco as a city of romance and modernity—a city at the heart of a newly joined regional metropolis—then the Golden Gate International Exposition of 1939-40 confirmed it by selecting the Bay itself for its site. Organized to celebrate the completion of both bridges, and as a public works project during the Depression, the exposition in fact celebrated the Bay Area (fig. 20).

The Treasure Island site—created by dredging up Bay mud and packing it over the Yerba Buena Shoals north of Yerba Buena Island—separated the fair from any single community and attached it to the region as a whole. Visible and accessible to all, the site would incorporate one bridge and allow views of the other. "A site should be chosen which involves no risk of sectional antagonism," wrote R. F. Allen, chairman of the exposition site advisory committee.

Such a site, on new land at the center of the Bay, would drive home the point that this was a fair celebrating the "whole complex of our institutions, life and progress in the San Francisco Bay Area." Allen even

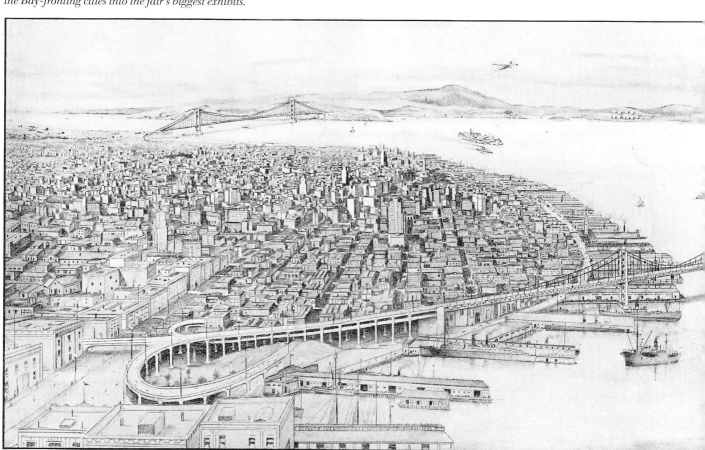

proposed that the exposition be given a quasi-visionary title: "The Golden Gate International New Age Celebration."[31]

The official report defending the Yerba Buena Shoals site restated and expanded Allen's themes, urging San Francisco to unite with her sister cities around the Bay "to achieve her destined greatness, now threatened by tremendous growth and enterprise of the cities of Southern California."[32] Frederick Dohrmann's dream of building a civic structure that would capture the imagination of the entire region had been realized to some extent in the construction of the bridges. An exposition on a prominent but neutral site might permanently seal the bonds of regional cooperation.

Outside observers agreed with the choice of the island site, viewing it as a fitting monument to the coming of age of a regional consciousness. *The Architect and Engineer* called the fair "a joyful celebration of the final unity of the cities around San Francisco Bay which are—at long last linked together by two of the most stupendous bridges in the world." The article called the new regional entity "the Greater San Francisco of the Future" and concluded that "it will be the metropolis of the Pacific and the second city on this continent."[33]

Although the process of planning for the exposition contained a strong visionary element, its architects carefully avoided futuristic imagery in favor of an exoticism loosely derived from the Far East. Monumental ziggurats crowned with elephant shapes, soaring simplified triumphal arches, and axial vistas through vast fountain-bedecked courtyards created a movie set for pageantry and processions. At night brilliant nebulas of color bathed every wall surface in a phosphorescent glow, adding to the cinematic effect (fig. 21).

The fair also functioned as a kind of theater for viewing the surrounding Bay. As painter and art critic Eugen Neuhaus wrote: "The many vistas from the island itself are stimulating parts of the whole Exposition scheme.... In the west, San Francisco's broken and somewhat jagged outline rises ghostlike, sending its verticals at unexpected places into a mellow sky."[34] The vistas turned the Bay Area into one vast exhibit in which the bridges played starring roles. Two photographs of the Bay Bridge appeared in the official guidebook to the fair, and U.S. Steel described the Bay Bridge as its most impressive display.[35]

Unlike most of the other exhibitors at the fair, U.S. Steel took the future as its theme, producing by far the most radical vision of San Francisco during the 1930s

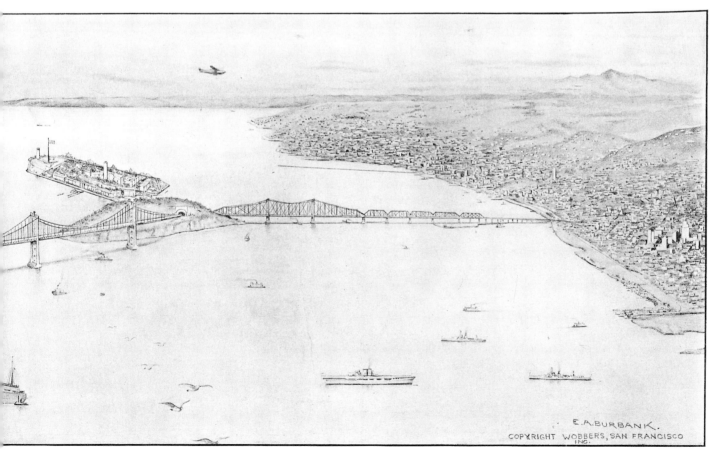

E.A.BURBANK.
COPYRIGHT WOBBERS, SAN FRANCISCO INC.

22 *Walter Dorwin Teague. U. S. Steel's exhibit, "San Francisco in 1999," Golden Gate International Exposition, 1939. Courtesy San Francisco Public Library.*

Teague's idea was to reinvent San Francisco as a Corbusian radial city, with cruciform towers standing in parks and a newly rationalized and centralized port combining all piers in a single monumental jetty, complete with airport.

(fig. 22). Behind tall, freestanding mock-ups of Bay Bridge towers—reinforcing the idea that the bridge was part of the display—stood a diorama, twenty-six feet long, entitled "San Francisco in 1999." It was designed by Walter Dorwin Teague, who also created the company's much larger exhibit at the New York World's Fair of the same year.

In Teague's San Francisco of the future, the only recognizable element from 1939—aside from the topography and the street grid—is a carefully detailed scale model of the Bay Bridge. The rest of the city is totally rebuilt along Corbusian lines, with cruciform towers in parks replacing the old downtown, and "all land, air, and water termini concentrated in one great pier system, leaving the waterfront free for parkway development."[36] By implication, only the bridges, and especially the Bay Bridge with its two levels of traffic and frankly structural design, expressed the rationalism and modernism needed for a futuristic vision of

the city. For Teague, and certainly for the steel manufacturer, the Bay Bridge embodied the beginning of an era of urban clarity, order, and new construction. The bridge would literally carry Bay Area residents to the future.

According to the press releases accompanying the exhibit, Teague's vision showed San Francisco "as it might appear if all building during the next 60 years followed a carefully conceived plan." An elevated highway resembling a modern aqueduct links the city's hills, which are crowned with rings of residential skyscrapers. Dramatic spiral ramps lead from the expressway down to surface streets.

One of the publicity drawings shows the corner of Howard and 7th streets, south of Market, as a dense intersection of streamlined sixty-story office buildings. Traffic was supposed to hurtle through the lower floors of the buildings (fig. 23). The diorama presented a vision of geometry, speed, and infinite technological progress—a small-scale version of the many dioramas and model cities illustrating the "World of Tomorrow" at the New York World Fair.

The exhibit left little, if any, impression on visitors. It must have seemed too farfetched to a community that felt it had already experienced the future by traveling across the Bay Bridge to get to the exposition. Anyway, the future had already arrived; why should it come

21 Chesley Bonestell.
Tower of the Sun,
*Golden Gate International
Exposition,
Treasure Island, 1938.
Oil on canvas 48¼ × 28¼ in.
(122.5 × 71.7 cm).
Collection of The Oakland
Museum.
With a stage-set exoticism
recalling the Panama-
Pacific Exposition's sig-
nature "Tower of Jewels,"
this tower functioned as
a sort of polychrome light-
house at night.*

again? In 1939 San Francisco looked complete. A new traffic network visibly united the communities of the Bay Area into a single region, and a picturesque but modern skyline embraced the landscape. "I like the looks of the city I call home," wrote San Francisco newspaper columnist Herb Caen in *Baghdad by the Bay*. "The imposing bristle of skyscrapers in the financial district, built on land that was once water—to me, they're arranged just so in just the right place to look like a city should look."[37] For a short while in San Francisco the futuristic and the familiar seemed to achieve a kind of equilibrium—the landscape vivaciously reshaped but ever the dominant feature, and more than ever boasting a suavity of outline. A metropolitan marvel had materialized (fig. 24).

23 Walter Dorwin Teague. U. S. Steel's exhibit, "San Francisco in 1999," Golden Gate International Exposition, 1939. Courtesy San Francisco Public Library.

This close-up view shows the intersection of 7th and Howard streets, with elevated roadways passing under each tower.

24 Aerial view of San Francisco, c. 1940. Courtesy Gabriel Moulin Studios, San Francisco.

The view from the crest of Twin Peaks down Market Street toward Treasure Island and the Bay Bridge reinforced the impression that San Francisco had become a great regional metropolis, spanning the Bay with the latest engineering triumphs. And if the so-called "Magic City" built for the Golden Gate International Exposition on Treasure Island seemed cloaked in the towers and temples of an exotic Far Eastern past, then the city's bridges and skyscrapers looked even more like a romantic Machine Age present and future.

NOTES

1 Fred Brandt and Andrew Y. Wood, *Fascinating San Francisco* (San Francisco Chamber of Commerce, 1924), p. 5.
2 Editorial, *San Francisco Bulletin*, June 27, 1921.
3 *Fascinating San Francisco*, p. 7.
4 Milton Pflueger, *Time and Tim Remembered* (San Francisco: Pflueger Associates, 1985), introd. by Harold Gilliam, p. 10.
5 Carol Willis, "Drawing Toward Metropolis," in *Metropolis of Tomorrow* by Hugh Ferriss, facsimile ed. (Princeton, 1986), p. 158.
6 Timothy Pflueger, "The Modern Office Building," *Architectural Forum* (June 1930), p. 785.
7 Works Progress Administration, *San Francisco: The Bay and Its Cities*, American Guide Series (New York: Hastings House, 1940), pp. 114, 178.
8 Editorial, *San Francisco Bulletin*, May 24, 1921.
9 "City Planning Is Good Business," *San Francisco Business*, June 28, 1921, in Willis Polk scrapbook at the California Historical Society Library, San Francisco.
10 Editorial, *San Francisco Bulletin*, May 24, 1921.
11 Louis Christian Mullgardt, "A Multiple Bridge for San Francisco Bay Between San Francisco and Oakland," *The Architect and Engineer* (March 1927), p. 69.
12 Robert Judson Clark, *Louis Christian Mullgardt, 1866-1942*, exhibition catalogue, The Art Gallery, University of California, Santa Barbara, 1966, p. 13.
13 Regional Plan Association, statement of purpose, February 10, 1925, in files of Regional Plan Association, The Bancroft Library, University of California, Berkeley.
14 Harlan Bartholomew, "Preliminary Report on Regional Plan Problems for San Francisco Bay Counties," Regional Plan Association, Inc., San Francisco, September 4, 1925, p. 9.
15 Mel Scott, *The San Francisco Bay Area: A Metropolis in Perspective*, 2nd ed. (Berkeley: University of California Press, 1985), p. 9.
16 Regional Plan Association, brochure.
17 Ibid.
18 Regional Plan Association, letter, June 9, 1926.
19 Regional Plan Association, letter, July 7, 1926.
20 Regional Plan Association, press release.
21 "San Francisco Airport: A Report" (San Francisco: Board of Supervisors, 1931), p. 12.
22 See John van der Zee's excellent and exhaustive biography of the Golden Gate Bridge, *The Gate* (New York: Random House, 1986); and also the chapter describing the construction of both bridges in Harold Gilliam's classic *The San Francisco Bay* (Garden City, N.Y.: Doubleday, 1957). Bay crossings had been debated at least since 1869 when the eccentric "Emperor Norton" issued a proclamation calling for construction of a span "to Sausalitoe [sic]." (Joshua Abraham Norton had made an unsuccessful attempt to corner the rice market in San Francisco in 1853, was bankrupted, and went mad, thereafter believing he was Norton I, Emperor of the United States.)
23 Felix Riesenberg, Jr., *Golden Gate* (New York: Alfred A. Knopf, 1940), p. 341.
24 "The San Francisco-Oakland Bay Bridge," United States Steel Company pamphlet, 1936, p. 8.
25 In New York, Chesley Bonestell worked for such architects as Cass Gilbert and William Van Alen. Interview, Mrs. Chesley Bonestell, April 7, 1989; and chronology in Frederick C. Durant and Ron Miller, *Worlds Beyond: The Art of Chesley Bonestell* (Norfolk/Virginia Beach, Va.: Donning, 1983).
26 Many of Irving Morrow's articles on contemporary architecture appeared in *The Architect and Engineer* during the 1920s.
27 E. Cromwell Mensch, *San Francisco-Oakland Bay Bridge: A Description in Ordinary Language* (San Francisco, 1936), p. 9.
28 This painting appeared in *The Architect and Engineer* in October 1934, p. 55, and in the United States Steel Company pamphlet on the bridge cited above.
29 "Report of the Hoover-Young San Francisco Bay Bridge Commission to the President of the United States and the Governor of the State of California," August 1930, p. 3.
30 Milton Pflueger, *Time and Tim Remembered*, p. 27.
31 Golden Gate International Exposition, Reports and Announcements, 1939; see Francis Allen's letter to J. W. Maillard, February 13, 1934, pp. 2, 5.
32 Yerba Buena Exposition Association, "A Site for the 1938 Exposition," undated, p. 6.
33 *The Architect and Engineer* (April 1939), p. 44.
34 Eugen Neuhaus, *The Art of Treasure Island* (Berkeley: University of California Press, 1939), p. 8.
35 Official Guidebook, Golden Gate International Exposition (San Francisco, 1939), pp. 3, 100; *Architectural Forum* (June 1939), p. 490.
36 Walter Dorwin Teague, *Design This Day* (New York: Harcourt, Brace & Co., 1949), fig. 120.
37 Herb Caen, *Baghdad by the Bay* (Garden City, N.Y.: Doubleday, 1949), p. 187.

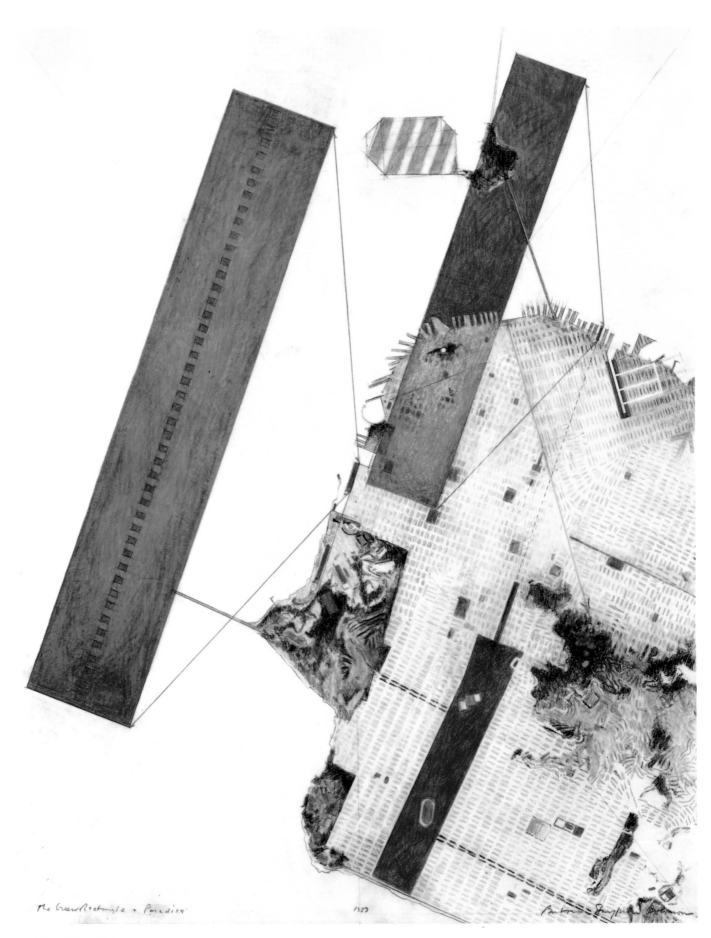

The Green Rectangle & Paradise   1959   Robert ....

Mark Helprin

The True Builders of Cities

Most great cities evoke from writers the kind of praise that takes the form of rhapsodic lists, perhaps because great cities are never without repetitions and variations of form that run through them like a melodic line, or because they are rich in qualities that, being intolerant of embellishment, need only be presented. But rather than a recitation and ode to San Francisco, let me set a scene.

I am standing at the entrance of an automatic car wash in North Beach, dressed in sneakers, Levis, a work shirt, and swimming goggles. It is twenty years before I will write this in a study overlooking a branch of the Pacific, silent but for the sounds of a fire, a grandfather clock, and an occasional ship's whistle. It is fifteen years before my father dies and my children are born, ten years before I meet my wife, five years before I am a graduate student at Magdalen College, Oxford, and not a very long time at all before I will be sleeping in mud, machine gun and grenades at the ready. The attendant is high on some sort of drug and thinks I must be surrounded by a car that he has blotted out. In the bay, deep in the fog, a carrier or two are tied up at Treasure Island, and gray ships from the Military Ocean Terminal in Oakland pass in the night, laden with supplies for the United States Army, Vietnam. I will shortly land myself in a great deal of trouble at Stanford when I tell my adviser that I want to be a frogman (I am not even in the biology department). In the Department of English and Comparative Liter-

ature, my future will be problematical. I have been working in the garlic fields near Gilroy, and walking, hitchhiking, and jumping on freight trains to get around the bay, even though I own a brand-new French car. It sits in a garage, cosseted like a Japanese beef cow or a queen bee. Each time I use it I wax it, polish the engine, and pick gravel out of the tires with a knitting needle. I will eventually sell it to a woman whose boyfriend appears to be a Black Panther and, though he is my age, insists that I call him "Mister Sir!"

"Turtle Wax?" the attendant asks.

"Thank you, no."

"Rust coating," he says urgently, as if the moving chains on the ground will imminently grip my tires.

"Just a wax," I answer, in italics.

After being banished from the apartment of a cocktail waitress because I was climbing on the fire escape and a hysterical pregnant woman almost blew me away with a 30.06, I have been living in a wooden shipping crate on the Embarcadero. I need a bath, and, being from the East, I am intrigued by automatic car washes, never having seen one before I arrived in San Francisco.

"Don't panic when the dervish wheel drops on you," the attendant says, emerging from his stupor. "It's soft."

I thank him and go forward to be attacked by wheels and spray, which is, like a lot of things in San Francisco at the time, tremendously exciting. Never having been through an automatic car wash in a car (which I would not subject to such insensitive handling), I cannot be sure that I am not going to be cut in two by the dervish wheel.

That evening I will have my standard dinner of carrots, jerked beef, and chocolate, the three basic food groups, and I will tour the record stores, trying to find a song I heard on the radio. It goes like this, I will say, and begin to sing my recollection of it:

1   *Barbara Stauffacher Solomon.* The Green Rectangle = Paradise, *1989.*
Graphite and colored pencil on vellum, 24 × 18⅞ in.
(61 × 47.9 cm). Courtesy San Francisco Museum of Modern Art. (Photo: Ben Blackwell)
"In San Francisco we are obsessed with nature and with paradise. We have decided that special rectangles in the ordinary grid of the city should be green. Hallowed. On these green rectangles we attempt to improve our bodies, perhaps our minds, and hopefully our chances for immortality." – B. S. S.

Guabi guabi buseray   Guabi guabi buseray
Lay obtini   Lay obtini
Meez abtingeray   Meez abtingeray
Tantoweeney   Tanto wee.

This, believe it or not, is an American folk song, by one Ramblin' Jack Elliott, a white man.[1] I will not find it until many years later when I don't care to listen to it. I have a deep conviction that I am Vietnam-bound. In fact I will go someplace else. A friend whom I will meet there will have spent two years in Leavenworth for refusing to put a wooden cutout of Rudolph the Red-Nosed Reindeer on the roof of the PX in the Presidio. The record clerks will look at me with wonder because I am soaking wet and my hair stands up like the quills of what my baby daughter now calls a "porky," or the fur of an electrocuted cat—because, after I was waxed, I had to walk through the wind tunnel.

That, although not a hundredth or even a thousandth of it, is youth. I came to know San Francisco in my youth, when both it and I were all passion and all love, and before we both, against all hope, became semi-respectable. I came to love it for a number of elements that, then, I could possess, and now I am able only to remember and explain. I, like many others, was convinced that it was the heart of the nation, and it may have been.

I went to San Francisco because it is a city of great beauty and because it arouses a feeling of intense well-being and equanimity that most American cities have taught their inhabitants to do without. I believe that beauty and equanimity need not be explained any more than anything else that is self-evident, but, then again, one need not walk through a car wash. I will try to see if I can explain to myself, as I go along, something of the origins of San Francisco's peerless equanimity, and begin to trace the elements of its beauty.

To do this, I first must leap back into the period just before the Renaissance, for this, I think, was the purest moment of the second great age of aesthetics in West-

ern art. The classical era was the first. Aesthetic criteria then were as eclectic and variable as the many competing cults of reason and religion. The world was superficially unified by Rome but so aesthetically and spiritually diverse that it could not retain its unity in the face of even purposeless assaults. One of the reasons Rome fell was the opposite of why the Church and Islam later were to rise: it was innocent of compelling beliefs. That the art of the ancient world was sometimes without parallel, sometimes charming, sometimes leaden, sometimes primitive, and sometimes inexplicable is not only appropriate to the structure of the ancient world but most telling, in that the themes and schools into which artistic endeavor always fragments were sovereign unto themselves rather than variations of a central conception.

The second great era began as gradually as the Roman world faded out and the world of the Church faded in, bringing with it the central conception that would be no less important for the art of the West than the sun is to the fields of Arles. It was a rich and immutable center that provided inspiration, technique, and a shared philosophy that became the common language of aesthetics. As simply as I can put it, the artist did not expect to create, but rather to uncover, as creation had already been accomplished perfectly, inimitably, and to the full. The task of the artist was to show, to reveal, and to praise the perfect works of God and nature.

Dante expressed this most perfectly in the second canto of *Paradiso*: *"Beatrice in suso, e io in lei guardava"* ["Beatrice looked upward, and I looked at her"]. The path is clearly illuminated. The object of Dante's love, desire, and (not least) description shines for him because she is reflecting the light of God, and she tells him, *"Drizza la mente in Dio grata..."* ["Direct thy grateful mind to God"].

We are now in the third era, when once again a central conception is lacking. Our art is eclectic, chaotic, and without sufficient confidence and tranquillity to balance its power. As his own ultimate authority, each artist is free to make up a new set of laws for each endeavor, to design universes between lunch and dinner, though even God, as far as we can tell, was humble enough to design only one. We arrived at our station as the impulse that led man to assert his powers in praise of what lay without him cultivated those powers to the point where the instrument displaced the object. It began in the Renaissance, was given wings in the Enlightenment, and took to the air in the industrial age, although, granted, the thread of it—in the rebel-

1 *Guabi Guabi*, arranged and adapted by Jack Elliott, 1964. Vanguard Records.

2 *Barbara Stauffacher Solomon. The Green Rectangle = Play-ground, 1989.*
Graphite and colored pencil on vellum, 24 × 18⅞ in. (61 × 47.9 cm). Courtesy San Francisco Museum of Modern Art. (Photo: Ben Blackwell)
"In San Francisco we are obsessed with ritual and with play. Both demand special ground and specific rules of the game. On green playgrounds temporary rules order the performance of assorted ritual games." – B. S. S.

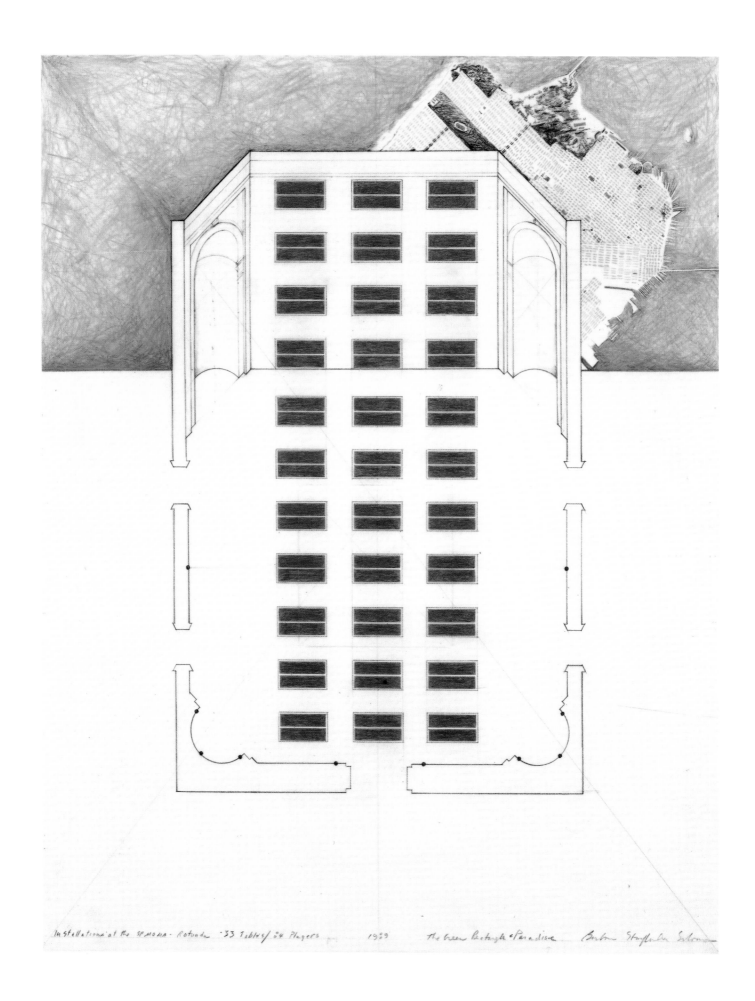

Installations at the SF MOMA – Rotunda · 33 Tables/ 24 Players   *1929*   *The Green Rectangle of Paradise*   *Barbara Stauffacher Solomon*

lions of the angels, in Icarus, in Hermetism—runs continually, even if at times weakly, through all history.

The quiet though strangely powerful time before the Renaissance is for me the emblem of the second age, when its underlying assumptions were young and undiluted. The artist was not self-conscious, and why should he have been? He was not a demigod as he is today, seeking credit for his "creations," but just an artisan in thrall to a master with whom he had no desire to compete. The art of the period was immensely powerful and tranquil.

I associate these two qualities—power and tranquillity—perhaps because, despite fraudulent assertions to the contrary, in great art you cannot have one without the other, just as a turbine cannot spin at high speed unless it is imperturbable. When any form of art is ascendant and strong, it has the attribute of not falling back on itself, of casting aside the tendency for self-examination. Instead, it surges ahead with what Kenneth Clark called "rhythmic assurance," as in the third Brandenburg, the curves of the Romanesque, the strong cadences of Dante, and the vigor and perfection of Raphael. This self-confidence, ironically, is the reward of humility; this excursion into uncharted space the gift of faith; this victory the child of surrender, for real power in art is neither arbitrary nor self-willed, but something afforded to those who seek and find the wild rivers of light unleashed by God in storm.

Why have I presented to you this abruptly encapsulated aesthetic? Certainly not because I hope to convince you. I haven't the space for argument, and, besides, I have long been acquainted with the futility of conversion. I have done so merely to clarify my assertions that today a great many architects—particularly those who dominate, and their imitators—unnecessarily forego the powers and spirits of architecture that informed their predecessors the Bramantes, Palladios, and Wrens; that a city is more a matter of God and nature than it is a matter of will; and that the same principles with which one can most powerfully envision a city are those that are also the eternal rules of architecture, which is not surprising, because the age

3 *Barbara Stauffacher Solomon.* Installation at the SFMOMA – Rotunda, 33 Tables/84 Players, The Green Rectangle = Paradise, *1989.*
Graphite and colored pencil on vellum, 24 × 18⅞ in.
(61 × 47.9 cm). Courtesy San Francisco Museum of
Modern Art. (Photo: Ben Blackwell)
"A drawing of an installation for the Rotunda of the San
Francisco Museum of Modern Art with a grid of 21 ta-
bles set up for playing table tennis on the ground and 12
paintings of table tennis tops on the back wall." – B. S. S.

in which they originated has as its hallmark the qualities of unity and consistency.

A famous architect once took me through a controversial structure he had designed for an arrogant institution. The building looked to me like one of the corpulent beach women in a sketch by George Grosz. It had tiny slit eyes near its flat top, massive unrelieved walls of fat, and an entryway that was a cross between a jukebox and a boa constrictor. The interior was nothing less than the union of *Flying Down to Rio* and the pyramid of Cheops. The hallways were illuminated by what looked like squadrons of UFOs ready for takeoff; the Zuni Indians had been allowed to design the furniture, and except for the obligatory battleship grays and international-architectural-cabal blacks, the colors had been chosen by Mae West.

As we toured this squat barbarous cube destined either for the blessed wrecking ball or to blight the earth for centuries, the architect could not stop talking for a second. I reminded him that this was my job, not his, and that although theory might be of some use before a building went up, after it was standing, theory had the same utility and the same ring as the Nuremberg testimony of the National Socialist elite.

As a philistine unfamiliar with the mysteries of what was au courant among architects, how could I possibly know what I was seeing unless he told me? I was probably one of those people who wanted a building to make me feel good when I looked at it rather than to offer itself as an armature for the display of my own erudition and glibness.

But I have been attentive all my life to that which is unfortunately called aesthetics. How is it that I am unaware of the beauty or genius in this building?

I could be Aristotle, Croce, or Leonardo, but I would not, could not, know *his* system, *his* theory, *his* ideas, and, to appreciate *his* building, I would have to listen to *him*, which was why he offered the preemptive defense. And there you have it; we have no common language. Each artist is sovereign in his own universe. Hence the torrents of explanation where once mere existence would have sufficed, since every building is its own solar system and the corpus of the architect's work its own universe. Quite apart from the limitations implicit in a system created by a man—a minute speck of dust, a desiccant mortal, a tiny raving ant—as opposed to the spacious, perfect, consistent, and full universe, this approach of polyglot aesthetic sovereignties requires above all interpreters and explainers, which is why architecture is commonly approached as an endeavor of ideas.

Table Tennis Installation at the Marina Green   1959   Barbra Stauffacher Solomon

But architecture is least of all about ideas. It is rather about sensations, associations, events, apprehensions, recollections, intuitions, emotions, a whole range of things other than ideas. Like every art, it is most successful in the context of a common language and a central conception, of which one need not be convinced but in which one must be versed. In medieval times when someone walked into a cathedral or spied the towers of a city, a deep spectrum of emotions, fears, and hopes was triggered in him, and enriched immeasurably what he saw. I am always amazed at the way architects view churches independently of (and at times even without reference to) the beliefs of the builders of churches and those for whom the churches were built. When these people saw the lights of stained glass, they felt the presence of God. The aesthetics of the structure and everything within were a road to that, not, as they are now, an end in themselves. Now, when we look at a city, we see the city itself, as an idea, when we should be seeing other things. We should be seeing history and the flow of time. We should be able to feel the presence of those we love, to bask in the light as it glances off the things we have built, to hear the music of form—something that, remarkably, exists in silence. (If that seems too metaphysical, consider the lunatic music critics who tell you that the sound means far less than the patterns of the notes on paper. Though in this case theory is an executioner's hatchet, music arising from the silent vista of a city is something else entirely, for the sound arises from the silence rather than being banished to it.)

Even in this fragmented age and in the absence of common beliefs, however, a common language exists nonetheless, underlying every fact and facet of art or aesthetics. That language requires neither translation nor recognition, for it is based neither on conception nor upon conceit, but on universal physical constants and effects (in light, proportion, color, etc.), and on the less precise but no less compelling permutations, accidents, and themes of the natural environment and of human history.

I believe that to envision a city—past, present, or future—one must draw as fully as possible upon those techniques of vision that relate to what is and will re-

main constant, and reject the fashions and follies that arise not from the great scope of things and the workings of natural law but from imaginations in need of flattery and offices in need of work. To envision a city —past, present, or future—one must seek the common language that runs in a golden thread through the history of cities to define them and to define what it is that makes them beautiful and great.

One of the dominant features of San Francisco is a joyous flow—the wind following the contours of the hills, the fog that crosses the terrain like a rapidly advancing army, currents seething through the Golden Gate, the winding, undulating, or serpentine streets. I have a photograph of my wife, in San Francisco in 1978, in profile, staring into the wind, an expression of love and elation on her perilously beautiful face, the wind pushing back her long lustrous hair as if she were diving through the waves. I doubt that she could have looked quite this way anywhere else.

For unlike Rome, Paris, London, or New York, San Francisco is dominated by the natural environment. Not only does nature in its inherent qualities and daily operations put a high gloss on the city, bathing it in semi-fantastic light and otherworldly fogs that put the greatest scene designers to shame, it has done things that in other cities are typically the province of other forces. For example, neighborhoods and districts in New York are almost entirely accidental, determined by the collision of patterns of European immigration and pure geographical availability, whereas, with some notable exceptions, the districts in San Francisco were determined by geography and the weather.

Even the way the city is perceived from a distance is determined in San Francisco more by natural forces than is the case in most other great cities, which tend to rise up from a plain and to be visually consistent from all angles. Apprehended from a distance, San Francisco has a hundred different signatures and all the complexity of a three-dimensional grid.

Once I went climbing in Wyoming and hitchhiked back to San Francisco, sleeping on the ground, trying not to inhale in Reno, eating raw eggs because I had only two dollars, baking and frying and loving every minute of it from Sacramento to Berkeley. My last ride put me down on California Street at the end of a workday. The color revealed by the light, the depth and quality of the air, and, doubtless, a long list of mundane characteristics that, disassociated, have all the charm and allure of the chemical analyses on bottles of Italian mineral water combined to offer the illusion of walking within a jewel, of floating somehow in clarity

4   Barbara Stauffacher Solomon. Table Tennis Installation at the Marina Green, 1989.
Graphite and colored pencil on vellum, 24 × 18⅞ in. (61 × 47.9 cm). Courtesy San Francisco Museum of Modern Art. (Photo: Ben Blackwell)
"A pre-earthquake drawing of the Marina Green with 30 Ping-Pong tables. Since October 17, 1989, no one wants to play." – B. S. S.

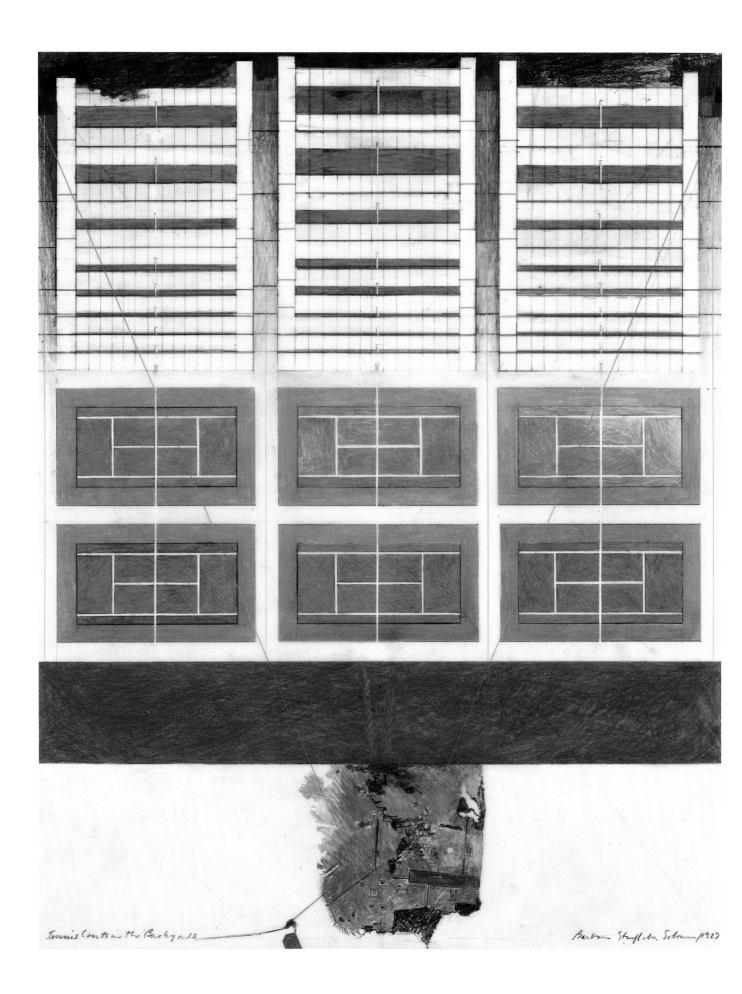

Tennis Courts in the Backyards

Barbara Stauffacher Solomon 1987

so intense that it had become substantive. The resistance, mass, and power of environmental elements that in other cities pass thinly by do many things for San Francisco that are rather extraordinary.

Not the least is the unusual balance they create in the duality of nature and artifice that makes a city. In New York, for example, the environment is beaten by and subsumed in artifice—there is no contest. But the rare light of San Francisco reveals a balance—a good example of which is the bridge. A bridge is a work that simultaneously elevates and subdues the space it crosses. The catenary, like the troughs and peaks of waves, masters both assertion and submission. A bridge is as fanciful as a jungle gym and yet primarily utilitarian.

The bridges are part of a long chain of the works of man that goes back at least to the Tower of Babel, but, unlike the Tower of Babel, they have risen vastly higher, they are beautiful, and they still stand. My temptation in this essay is to advocate surrender to the environment —indeed, that is the fashion and the only sensible conclusion if one were to rank man and nature—but when I think that only half a century ago these bridges arose from the hand of man, I want to rebel against what I most adore. To attempt to balance nature and artifice is to destroy the tension that is one of their chief benefits. You must choose one or the other. You cannot have a foot in both worlds, but a city is not mortal, and it can, if only because time is a force that acts upon a city differently from the way it acts upon people, and, over time, continual alternation can look a lot like compromise. But only over time. Time is the element that most ruthlessly takes the planning of a city out of human hands and returns the process to the other forces of nature that are its fraternal allies. The form of a city is always the result of battles between contending forces, and, as such, is less a matter of will than of the "accidents" that come clear after the smoke rises.

Because neither artifice nor environment is "right," except in the long term that lies beyond our will, the architect must choose at every juncture whether to surrender or to assert. In the absence of a central conception and a common aesthetic language, each architect makes his own independent determination. The methodology of surrender is what we commonly call utility, whereas that of assertion is commonly called fancy, and the tension between them probably cannot be reconciled in this age, when even the most steadfast advocates of utility, for example, push it to such an extreme that it becomes purely fanciful. I do not believe that, in the absence of a harmonious central conception, artifice or environment, utility or fancy, nature or the mechanical, and the dualities they foster and represent, can transcend their deadlocked balances, which amount to a kind of perpetual, motionless draw. Consider the sterility of the environmental and high-tech movements in modern architecture. They are theses and antitheses without the chance of syntheses. In recent times, San Francisco has become a battleground in this war and has suffered a kind of apoplectic eclecticism (if I may) that makes it superficially interesting, like a department store. If this goes on, the city will turn into Disneyland—here the Mediterranean village, here an ersatz Nantucket, here Le Corbusier's tomb, here an Alice-in-Wonderland Chippendale the size of Half Dome, standing on the street like a giant piece of furniture abandoned by extraterrestrial moving men.

And yet environment itself, apart from the will to design, built the city almost as surely as if it had been barking out instructions. The hills called for cable cars and houses oriented to the view and of a certain maximum height so as not to rise above the view of others. The peninsular geography demanded a waterfront and the bridges. The habits of the fog laid out the districts, and the quality of the light gave the city its color scheme.

The only thing that can save a city from uncontrolled eclecticism is the city itself, as a whole, transcending the limitations of its builders, organizing itself, slowly coming alive. A number of ways exist in which this remarkable process can be apprehended.

The battle between religion and science is bitter because it is a civil war. Science and theology, in their pure forms, have no boundary: they are like the ocean and the sea. In classical times, when human endeavor had not been mercilessly divided by the need to comprehend its overwhelming riches, this was understood.

After Pythagoras discovered the amazing principle that in a right triangle the square of the hypotenuse equals the sum of the squares of the two legs, he did not feel constrained to stop. He threw caution down and made a great many extrapolations. He noticed that

5 *Barbara Stauffacher Solomon.* Tennis Courts in the Backyards, *1989.*
Graphite and colored pencil on vellum, 24 × 18⅞ in.
(61 × 47.9 cm).
Courtesy San Francisco Museum of Modern Art.
(Photo: Ben Blackwell)
"A pre-earthquake drawing of the Marina Green and the grid of the Marina District furrowing up to Pacific Heights. The perimeter blocks enclose green rectangles of backyard tennis courts." – B. S. S.

the notes produced by a stringed instrument correlate exactly with the lengths of the strings, and he noticed much else, none of which would have justified his marvelous conclusion that the root of all things is not matter but proportion, and indeed it is, for if you dig deep enough or go high enough, as long as you look hard enough, you will see that there is nothing there but structures ultimately expressible in numerical ratios. Until someone materializes light, electricity, magnetism, and gravity, this truth will remain.

In Plato's *Timaeus* (which he derived from Pythagoras), everything is laid at the door of proportion. Kepler was similarly astonished. Indeed, the "second age" of which I speak accepted without much doubt the existence of a central underlying truth, that the various and darling constants discovered now and then in nature were but exfoliations of the ultimate reduction, that all songs were variations upon a single irreducible theme.

Perhaps I exaggerate, and you may know by now that I love exaggeration for the way it throws light on things, but the entire intellectual history of the world consists of discovering or utilizing the laws of proportion. Take music as an example. Music is the most beautiful city. All its elements are variations of proportion—the tempo, the frequency, and the strength of the notes, counterpoint, resonance, melodic structure, and whatever other patterns can be read or imposed. Music can convey the ineffable, and other burdens, and like a city, it makes sense and order from seemingly anarchic elements brought together in thematic repetition subject to the rules of proportion.

Poetry is no less dependent upon the breaks and spaces in melodic sound, weighted with a thousand categories of association. And painting depends not only on what is commonly understood as proportion but also on the proportional division of light into what we call color.

Needless to say, proportion and symmetry are to architecture what water is to rain. Their effects are not an idea or a theory, but purely empirical. Certain proportions have certain effects. Some are pleasing and some are not. When the architect has it right, you feel

6   *Barbara Stauffacher Solomon. After October 17th, 1989.*
Graphite and colored pencil on vellum,
24 × 18⅞ in. (61 × 47.9 cm).
Courtesy of the artist. (Photo: Ben Blackwell)
"A post-earthquake drawing of the Marina Green and Marina District. The filled land (formerly a lagoon and site of the 1915 Panama-Pacific Exposition) failed. In San Francisco we are now obsessed with 'the liquification of paradise.'" – B.S.S.

aesthetic pleasure in exactly the same way that you do when you listen to music or stare at a Raphael. The right proportions trigger something in your soul, something in your accumulated experience, something in both the part of you that you know and control and in that which you do not know and do not control, and a feeling takes hold (whether it is a chemical that blocks receptors or not is unimportant) that lifts you beyond life in this world.

The effective proportions are astoundingly versatile. They can inform and illumine any style of building, whether it has architraves or escalators. That which is so beautifully expressed in classicism is fully translatable into other styles. If it seldom is, it isn't the fault of variation but of architects who accomplish the variation improperly. Although the proportions that work are there for the taking, most architects simply do not try to find them, perhaps because the fashion is to disdain the kind of instinctive beauty that need not be explained, in favor of ephemeral theories crafted for the sake of individual buildings to which they do not even adhere beyond the time that the architect is there with his mouth open.

In Piero della Francesca's *Ideal Town* (which is entirely modest compared to the idealizations of Thomas Cole and Erastus S. Field that pump up classical architecture the way balloons are inflated for Macy's Thanksgiving Day Parade), public spaces are balanced with the private, the round with the square, the ornamental with the plain, height with breadth, light with shadow, etc. Standing in his piazza, you don't need to change focus or guess the sizes of buildings or wonder about how far something is (or how tall, or if it is going to keel over on you), for all the forms are anchored in a central harmony expressed in proportion and accessible via intuition.

From many viewpoints, San Francisco has become confusing. Everyone knows that quite a few colossal buildings are out of place. They trivialize the smaller buildings and "flatten" neighborhoods so as to rob them of their depth and prevent them from being places where one can become beneficially lost just by looking. San Francisco is remarkably full of chunks and blobs that ruin lines, block views, and terrorize the eye. As if by design, individual structures are often faulted in precisely the same ways in which they then fault the larger picture. I hate to kick a pyramid when it's down, but, really, it contradicts itself, it has all the grace of a dentist's drill, and looking at it is about as comfortable as having a staring contest with Rasputin. It is the rocket that isn't going anywhere, a hyperthyroid paperweight, the Cadillac of dunce caps, the triumph of one small idea over legions of graceful proportions. And who put that yellow thing on the Fairmont? Is it the same guy who tried to put the trailer hitch on Michelangelo's *David*? For intelligence about similar travesties you need only look out the window. The city is primarily a work of imperfection, as are all cities to greater or lesser degrees. And for a wide variety of reasons proportions have been honored mainly in the breach in American cities especially.

But the great thing, the sometimes astonishing thing —comparable to the disparate and seemingly anarchic elements of music combining to convey effortlessly what is otherwise ineffable, or the proteins that by some mystery organize and replicate themselves as if they (mere agglomerations of molecules) were possessed of purpose and will—is that even when proportion is neglected in individual buildings or in the haphazard growth of the city itself, it exists in the most unexpected moments in "random" views of the city.

New York is the best example of this that I know, for in New York sublime majesty arises from masses of incredible ugliness and confusion. With proper distance, at unexpected angles, the city transcends itself in a miracle of light, color, and form. How much other cities do the same depends on forces far outside anyone's control, for city planning can accomplish such miracles no more than it can overcome the forces of economy, necessity, and inertia that customarily paralyze it. The city evolves by itself, as it were, as if it were going someplace, as if it were more than thematic repetition upon thematic repetition, but something alive, something of will.

One has an infinite number of opportunities for discovering the totally unexpected visual fusions that make a city great far beyond the intent of its creators, which is the result of the city's tendency to elicit discoveries, whether from an airplane at 5,000 feet or upon close examination of the Presidio Wall. As far as I'm concerned, no place in the world surpasses New York in the raw power and spirituality that arise from seemingly inappropriate scenes, but San Francisco is hardly bereft of the same sharp angles and breathtaking surprises, even if they are in the colors of a dream.

After a prolonged absence, I returned to San Francisco via 101. I saw the city for the first time from just north of the Golden Gate. It was entirely different from what I had known. It was, first of all, suddenly immense. The huge face of a white cliff that simply had not been there before loomed beyond the Presidio and swept eastward. This was a new city that had grown up while I was away, and now, palpably great and vaguely sinister, it looked like something about to rear up on its hind legs and break away from the prison of all that had been intended for it. We do not get the opportunity to see mountains rise or seas collide as continents part (though in San Francisco, someday, we may). But cities evolve in front of our eyes, asserting themselves as if they were animals moving slowly as they awake. And as they arise they can, and often do, confirm those great laws of which we ourselves sometimes lose sight.

Despite and apart from human judgment, natural perfection asserts itself with omnipotent and astonishing power. It needs neither consent nor approval from philosophers and does quite well even in the face of discontinuity in human affairs, righting the ship time and again even after what are thought to be final storms. It is the original and sustaining calibration, or, if you will, the central conception, and it wells up in secret channels even after mocking repudiation.

Such is the power of light. In the early Middle Ages the fallen civilization of Europe had ahead of it what may have seemed like an interminable period of breathing slowly in the darkness, like a wounded animal, before becoming the equal and the better of Rome. In the many works of the twentieth century that deal with what the world is like after destruction —from H. G. Wells and Thornton Wilder to William Golding and Mad Max—the survivors are strikingly similar to the survivors of the fall of Rome. After the fall, these people were riveted on anything that preserved the light. They were obsessed with jewels, precious metals, amber, and, later, illuminated manuscripts. Italian miniaturists such as Franco Bolognese and Oderisi da Gubbio were the last of the tradition before the light it carried forward was amplified almost beyond imagination by the like of Dante and Raphael. The light of the Mediterranean was honored and preserved in jewels and gold, things that approach perfection, to rekindle civilization, which itself can be partially defined as the way man lives with light. I suppose that you might think of cities as enormous jewels in which light is captured and preserved.

Even before mirrored skyscrapers in cities of uncountable windows reflecting the light of the sun and sky like a reef filtering oxygenated surf, cities were creatures of the light, if only because they presented it with so many planes of colored and textured stone, so many angles, and so much in the way of diffusion, absorption, reflection, refraction, and shadow. Though it is not fully mature, San Francisco is very rich in this essential condition of civilization, for it is in many ways like a prism, a jewel, a "bright-work," something wrought to catch, echo, and play with the light.

Only in Greece and in the Sinai have I seen light quite as three-dimensional, dense, limpid, delicate, dreamlike, and clear. To say that much of San Francisco faces north over water only partially explains the effect. I have lived in Haifa, another city that faces north over water. From its hills one can see extraordinary light, but it is not like the light of San Francisco. It isn't as rich. The light of Rome is richer, but it isn't as clear. In Paris, the light does magical things but only in the sky and among the clouds, seldom descending. San Francisco light isn't merely bright and glowing like none other; it engages you in its battle with the fog, makes you an ally, sweeps you along, carries you with it (when you look out over the distance) as if you were not where you are standing but where you are looking. The pellucid, enthralling light of San Francisco is like one of those huge emerald waves in Hawaii through which surprised surfers break only to find themselves on the covers of magazines.

Light is the soul of San Francisco. It is responsible for the serenity and inner freedom that are otherwise inexplicable. It energizes. It enthralls. It redeems bad buildings and jerry-built neighborhoods and makes more beautiful the beautiful buildings and their surroundings. Most importantly, it, like the laws of proportion, is an agent that perpetually shapes the city—through human intentions, but beyond them. Unlike proportion, however, which underlies even the light itself, the light is something specific, active, and surprising. Once, I was walking in Fort Mason, under the shade of the trees. I came to a place on the path where the view gave out on the Golden Gate. The metal roofs of Fort Mason itself were hardly a shade different from the color of the bridge; beyond the bridge the cliffs were tinged in red; and beyond them something was in the air, an almost imperceptible glint of gold and red light. My line of sight, amplified by the resonance of the otherworldly red and gold, was like the trajectory of a rocket, which is perhaps why I suddenly felt as if I'd been shot out of a cannon. The sensation was that of flight, of tremendous velocity, of moving out of the dark, out of oneself, and into gravityless light. San Francisco is one of the few cities in the world where things like this happen not only to beatitudes and mystics but to newsboys, politicians, and donut-fryers. If it hasn't happened to you, perhaps you should move to Philadelphia.

In some ways, straining to achieve a beautiful city is useless, for cities become truly beautiful only when they breed and reconcile tensions—as is the case with a human being. Too much unreconciled and contending force, and they go nowhere. Too much reconciliation, too much ease, and they fail from want of substance and alacrity. In an increasingly homogenous America the sources of tension and reconciliation lie in most cases outside of any one city. In that sense, what happens to San Francisco depends upon the rest of the country and the Western world. Even the building materials used in cities are no longer local: the New York Stock Exchange was built from stone quarried thirty miles up the Hudson, but the steel in the World Trade Center comes from Seattle. The automobiles that have been ruinously unleashed upon San Francisco, like the Huns who destroyed Rome, come from Detroit.

But San Francisco is young, and youth is not only capable of adapting to instability and assault, it requires it for subsequent maturation. Boston and Philadelphia were once in much the same position, as were even Rome and Jerusalem. The principles by which they developed are precisely those by which San Francisco has developed, now engages, and will utilize in the future. You need not necessarily know them to honor them, as long as you are attentive to exhilaration, beauty, and equanimity. These qualities, in architecture as well as in anything else, have been preserved by repetition and imitation as much as by attempting to fathom what they are.

In a city the role of accident and destiny is insuperable. Beauty occurs where it has never been intended, in compressed views and sudden and surprising juxtapositions as protean light makes of a single city an infinitely varying work of illusion. But even accident and destiny are subject to the pull of certain forces and tend to favor themes and repetitions. Still, they cannot be forced or blocked, and this may account for the fact that destiny has so far favored San Francisco. Perhaps this is so because (despite all the challenges to it, and there have been many) the great equanimity that covers the city like a cloud, and is perhaps its most gorgeous and mysterious attribute, remains.

Despite the assaults and imperfections, it remains. Why is that? It is because San Francisco has a golden core—of light, color, proportion, of the feel of the air, the fog, and the blue of the bay. These are the steadfast perfections around which human endeavor organizes itself even at times without realizing it. They give a common language to science and to art. They provide the real continuity of history. And they are the true builders of cities.

Sally B. Woodbridge

Visions of Renewal and Growth: 1945 to the Present

With the ending of World War II, the quest for growth and prosperity was vigorously pursued throughout the United States. Growth in urban centers was tied to the renewal of inner-city areas, which had lost middle-class population to the suburbs and were unable to lure new investment. The vision of urban renewal matched the hopes for progress in the postwar world.

In reality, planning for San Francisco's future had continued unabated during the fallow building period of World War II. Soon after the war, architects, planners, city officials, and developers focused their attention on large urban areas. Some of these sites were recurrent loci for grand plans; others had never before been considered. Freeways became an important element of transportation, which figured prominently in national postwar planning. These roadways imposed a new level of speed and land occupancy on the smaller, older fabric of cities such as San Francisco, Boston, and Seattle.

The Ferry Building and the Foot of Market Street

One San Francisco area strongly affected by the increased use of the automobile was at the foot of Market Street. Since 1898 the Ferry Building had provided a major gateway to the city. As more and more automobiles and buses brought commuters across the Bay Bridge, ferryboat ridership declined. Coincidentally, in 1947 the World Trade Center Authority, a new state agency, launched a campaign to build an architecturally prominent headquarters for itself. The Authority's 1951 prospectus justified the choice of San Francisco because of its location at the geographical center of the Pacific coast and its status as the finan-

cial, insurance, communications, and transportation capital of the West. In the first phase of construction, a large seven-story building with 217,238 square feet of space was to be erected on the waterfront between the Ferry Building and Pier 1, at a cost of $600 million. The plan projected several more buildings surrounding a thirty-story tower, at a total estimated cost of $750 million.

The Center's architect, William Gladstone Merchant, envisioned a striking departure from the eclectic 1898 Ferry Building designed by A. Page Brown, which borrowed from the Giralda Tower in Seville. Merchant housed the Center in a complex of crystalline structures enclosing a succession of courts on both sides of a central tower (fig. 2). Fountains and terraces on the Embarcadero and port sides enforced an axial composition that, in every way but style, employed Beaux-Arts principles.

Funding for this grand vision fell so far short of its goal that Merchant had to set aside his proposed design and remodel the interior of one wing of the existing building to house the World Trade Center's immediate functions. But beyond the problem of inadequate funds, the larger project faced another obstacle. The plans for the new Embarcadero Freeway had moved forward in the late 1940s following cooperative studies carried out by city officials and Harbor Board engineers. In June 1953 the city and the State Highway Department executed an agreement that showed the route running parallel to the Ferry Building's façade (fig. 3). An editorial in the *San Francisco Chronicle* on August 24, 1953, stated that the freeway project deserved the backing of the entire Bay Area community. (Ten years later, October 7, 1963, an editorial in the same newspaper implored the Board of Supervisors to block construction of the ramps at Washington and Clay streets.) In 1954 Merchant revised his scheme to create a broad public terrace that would vault over the freeway and descend to the ground on the other side in

1 San Francisco, 1950s.
Courtesy Aero Photographers, Sausalito.
(Photo: Ed Brady)

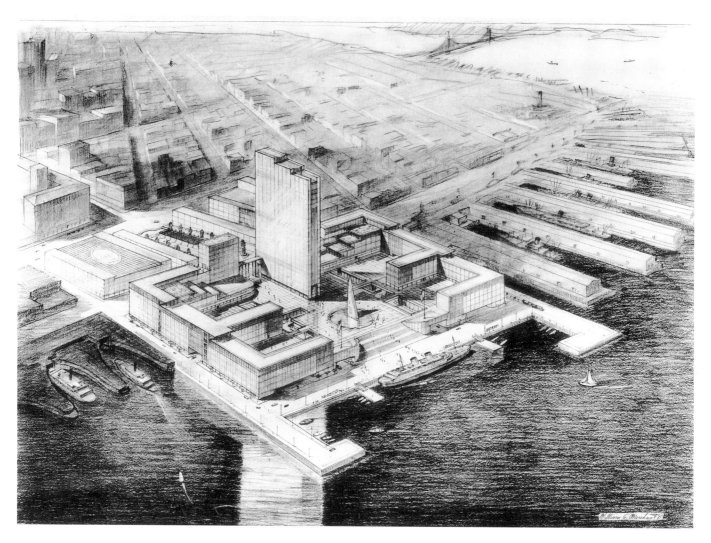

terraced steps and watercourses embraced by two building wings.

In the spring of 1955 a citizens' group proposed to the State Legislature that State Park funds assigned to San Francisco be used to create a park on the Ferry Building site.[1] When the proposal was turned down because it lacked a specific plan, the group approached the American Institute of Architects (AIA) and the California Association of Landscape Architects (CALA) to make studies. The two organizations named a joint committee chaired by Vernon DeMars from the AIA and Theodore Osmundson from the CALA; other members were architects William Merchant and Hans Gerson and landscape architect Douglas Baylis. In the fall they presented a proposal to the Citizens' Committee to curve the freeway 130 feet away from the planned right-of-way to provide ample space for a park.

The proposed twelve-acre park would have a central plaza and incorporate the municipal bus turnaround as the focal point for the end of Market Street. The Ferry Building was reinstated as a valuable historic landmark.[2] Since the state could not justify giving

2   *William G. Merchant. San Francisco World Trade Center proposal, 1951. Drawing.*
Courtesy Hans Gerson.
(Photo: Moulin Studios, San Francisco)

The Center was to house a full range of temporary and permanent exhibits, showrooms for domestic and foreign products, conference rooms, offices for banks and transportation interests, press headquarters, a library, and a world trade information bureau.

3   *Aerial view of the site for the Embarcadero Freeway, 1951.*
Courtesy Aero Photographers, Sausalito.
(Photo: Ed Brady)

money for a city improvement, honoring the Ferry Building became the reason for the proposal.

In December 1955 this proposal was rejected by another committee composed of important state officials.[3] Their report concluded that, in addition to the increased construction costs for the altered route, the delay of at least twenty-eight months in completing the freeway would be a serious mistake. The committee

members also doubted the aesthetic merit of moving the location of the freeway to a more prominent position in the lower Market Street area.

In the fall of 1956 citizens associated with the new Blyth-Zellerbach Committee—headed by Charles Blyth and J. D. Zellerbach and composed of prominent members of the business community—lost their battle to put the Embarcadero Freeway underground.[4] City Planning Director Paul Oppermann then commissioned a new plan for the Ferry Park from architect Mario Ciampi, using funds voted for the purpose by the Board of Supervisors.

Presented in July 1957, Ciampi's plan received rave reviews and won the endorsement of numerous city organizations. However, City Hall, the Harbor Commission, the World Trade Authority, the State Division of Parks and Beaches, and the San Francisco Redevelopment Agency were slower to respond. Newspaper editorials questioned the possible sources of funding.

State Harbor Commission Chairman Cyril Magnin soon raised objections to the plan, saying that demolition of the south wing of the Ferry Building would de-

prive the Harbor Board of $11,000 a month. At the August meeting of the State Division of Parks and Beaches, the four members voted unanimously against the plan. Mayor George Christopher reacted with deep disappointment. The *San Francisco Chronicle* editorialized on August 26, 1957, that "the bright and iridescent dream of a State Park has impaled itself and collapsed on the double-decker Embarcadero Freeway which the city planners approved incomprehensibly and the city administrators incontinently rushed to construction over protests of this newspaper and thousands of agonized San Franciscans."

In 1959 a municipal-bond issue for the Ferry Park failed. A San Francisco Port Authority plan of that year, called Embarcadero City, proposed the redevelopment of some eighty state-owned blocks between the Ferry Building and Aquatic Park as envisioned by architects John S. Bolles and Ernest Born. With a price tag of $300 million, this proposal also failed. However, prospects were bright for the Golden Gateway Redevelopment project, which included plans for a Ferry Park, and in 1960 the city appropriated money for it.

In 1961 the concerned agencies—Redevelopment, City Planning, and the Port Authority—joined together to award the contract for the park design to Mario Ciampi, John Bolles, and landscape architect Lawrence Halprin. Now called Justin Herman Plaza, the park was completed in 1971. However, the Embarcadero Freeway and the surface roads still formed a strong visual barrier between the Ferry Building and the public park. Subsequent visions for the building, to be discussed below, focus on its bay side.

Freeways

Freeways were an important part of both national and local planning programs in the postwar period. In San Francisco, the James Lick Freeway (fig. 4), completed in 1950, took traffic from the Bay Bridge and funneled it to downtown locations south of Market Street and farther south to the Bayshore Highway. The goal of the Embarcadero Freeway, under construction in the mid-1950s, was to connect to the Golden Gate Bridge. Another route to this bridge was projected from the Central Skyway through the Panhandle of Golden Gate Park, across 19th Avenue, and through the Presidio. In the opinion of many people, these high-speed transportation corridors would encircle the city like an unsightly moat.

Anti-freeway sentiment began with the planning of the Embarcadero Freeway and grew to a roar with the planning of the Panhandle route in the late 1950s. The issue was so politically sensitive that the Board of Supervisors requested that the State Department of Highways engage Lawrence Halprin to do a special urban-design study of the freeway. In 1962 he presented designs for making the freeway as unobtrusive as possible by means of sensitive landscaping, a sculptural handling of sunken corridors for the streets on either side of the Panhandle, and a tunnel under the park itself (fig. 5). However, public sympathy, fueled by the *San Francisco Chronicle*'s anti-freeway editorials, was overwhelmingly against any freeway through the park. Another report on the urban-design aspects of the Panhandle and Golden Gate freeways, prepared by Mario Ciampi and Associates with John Carl Warnecke and Associates and published in 1966, proposed additional criteria for the entire route linking the Central Freeway to the Embarcadero Freeway. But no matter how well designed, the freeways were anathema to the public. With the city's rejection of federal funds to build the proposed routes in 1966, all planning for freeway construction within the city ceased.

Urban Redevelopment and Transportation

Words such as "blight" and "cancer," borrowed from vocabularies of disease, became the standard jargon of urban renewal. Heart disease was a particularly useful metaphor for what ailed cities that were dying at the core, their health eroded by the exodus to the suburbs. And just as the surgery recommended to remove cancerous tissues might cause postoperative problems, the sweeping removal of substandard buildings resulted more often than not in a scarred landscape that remained a wasteland for years. The power of eminent domain given to the redevelopment agencies in the postwar era permitted razing buildings on a scale commensurate with the perceived need for slum clearance but could not guarantee that private developers would rush to rebuild and heal the wounds.

Concurrent with the publication of the city's master plan in 1948, the Board of Supervisors designated 280 blocks of the Western Addition—the city's major nineteenth-century streetcar suburb west of Van Ness Avenue—as a blighted area and established a Redevelopment Agency to administer a program for it (fig. 6).[5] In this early stage of urban redevelopment a local agency served primarily as a public real estate operation that, by means of the right of eminent domain, cleared confusing land titles, razed obsolete or deteriorated buildings, and assembled large parcels to sell at fair market prices to private developers who agreed to build according to a publicly approved plan. A certain percentage of properties within an area had to be declared blighted before a redevelopment area could be designated.

Early large-scale projects, such as the Western Addition, strained the capabilities of city administrations that generally lacked sufficient staff to manage them. Unaccustomed to urban-renewal planning on such a large scale, most local and even federal government agencies viewed the plans for such areas as mere artists' conceptions. Moreover, the human costs of relocating the residents, mainly poor minority groups, were underestimated and given little attention in face of the challenge of restructuring the city. Underfunded relocation programs for displaced residents provided neither adequate counseling nor alternative housing despite the fact that the 1949 National Housing Act had pledged "a decent home and a suitable living environment for every American family."

Opposition to razing the Fillmore area of the Western Addition and problems with the relocation program delayed the start of the project. Agency planners

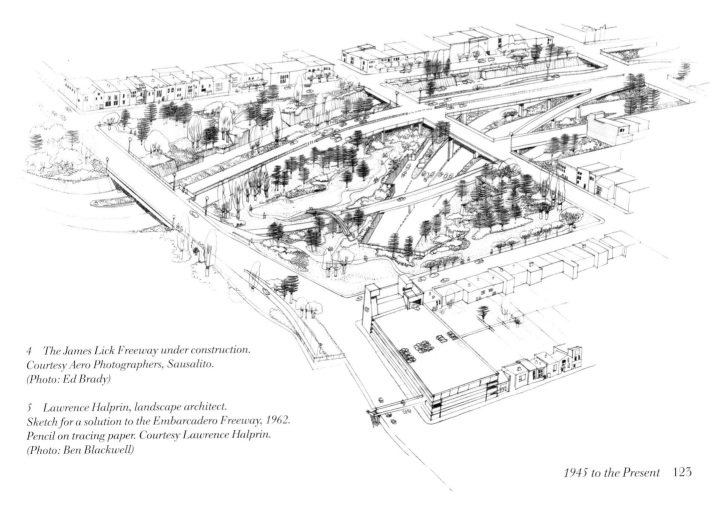

4   The James Lick Freeway under construction.
Courtesy Aero Photographers, Sausalito.
(Photo: Ed Brady)

5   Lawrence Halprin, landscape architect.
Sketch for a solution to the Embarcadero Freeway, 1962.
Pencil on tracing paper. Courtesy Lawrence Halprin.
(Photo: Ben Blackwell)

therefore turned their attention to Diamond Heights, a hilly, 325-acre site plotted in a grid system which resulted in an absence of streets in many areas where grades were too steep. In contrast to the densely settled Western Addition, Diamond Heights had few residents to relocate or property owners to contend with (fig. 7).[6]

In 1950 federal grants from the Housing and Home Finance Agency were approved for preliminary plans for a twenty-eight-block area of the Western Addition, called Area 1, and for Diamond Heights. The renewal process became so fragmented by delays (the Area 1 plan was not approved until 1956) that, by the late 1960s, much had been published to demonstrate that the exhausting and expensive federal effort had mainly produced vast wastelands and the depletion of low- and moderate-income housing.[7]

Urban redevelopment was also on the minds of members of the San Francisco business community. In 1956 the Blyth-Zellerbach Committee had allocated funds to the city's Planning Department to develop a proposal for alternative uses for the old produce market, a seventy-eight-acre area adjacent to the financial district. Previous plans to move the market to a location south of Market Street had stalled because of insufficient funds.

The Planning Department retained the San Francisco office of Skidmore, Owings & Merrill (SOM) to prepare the Area E plan (bounded by Clay and Battery streets, Broadway, and the Embarcadero), which was published in the spring of 1957 (fig. 11). The SOM master plan provided for the disposition of offices and parking. The block plan, based on the city grid, was designed to mesh with the adjacent areas. The controversy over the impact of traffic from the access ramps on Washington and Clay streets was addressed by having them adjoin a parking garage for 1,300 cars. Skywalks connected a landscaped plaza atop the garage to the office buildings on one side and the residential area on the other; stairs and escalators connected the plaza to the street.[8]

The office towers rendered schematically in the plan —ranging in height from six to twenty-two stories— were characteristic of the clean-cut, transparent forms that had become hallmarks of contemporary design. To the north of the office towers, set on fifteen acres, were five twenty-story apartment buildings containing 1,600 units. Although walk-to-work housing was available on the hills around downtown, none of it was new or located on flat land. The northernmost part of the site was devoted to eight acres of light industry that

preserved existing brick warehouses. A Ferry Park, now called Justin Herman Plaza, was included at the southern end. The SOM plan was approved and used as the basis for the Redevelopment Agency's first national architectural competition. The competition prospectus for the Golden Gateway was issued on September 1, 1959.

That year not only initiated the practice of holding architectural competitions to assist in planning the renewal of the city but also witnessed more construction than had been seen since 1907, the year after the major earthquake and fire. The Blyth-Zellerbach Committee and the San Francisco Housing and Planning Association joined to form the San Francisco Planning and Urban Renewal Association (SPUR).[9] In April, Mayor Christopher appointed Justin Herman director of the San Francisco Redevelopment Agency. Formerly the head of the regional office of the Housing and Home Finance Agency, Herman had been a major critic of the slow pace of redevelopment in the city. A brilliant administrator whose politics had been formed during Franklin D. Roosevelt's New Deal era, Herman brought enormous energy to his job, along with the belief that architectural design was important to the success of urban renewal.[10]

The results of the Golden Gateway competition gave the Redevelopment Agency its first triumph. The *Chronicle*'s editorial for March 10, 1960, announced, "The Golden Gateway Redevelopment Project has moved with stunning impact out of the realm of fancy. The proposal to transform a shabby, rundown area of downtown San Francisco into 44 acres of tower apartments, landscaped dwellings, shopping malls, parkways and ultra-modern urban amenities has abruptly become a strictly business proposition." The editorial referred to the results of the bidding on the Redevelopment Agency's Golden Gateway project, which had garnered nine eligible bidders, each of whom had spent about $100,000 on plans, models, and brochures to qualify themselves. It was the largest number of bids for any of the nation's redevelopment projects up to that time and offered proof that the city could attract serious developers for a practical project.

Mario Ciampi chaired a distinguished architectural advisory panel for the competition composed of architects Lawrence Anderson, Henry Churchill, Louis Kahn, Morris Ketchum, and Minoru Yamasaki and banker-developer Fred Kramer. Ciampi advised the contenders for the project that they were not only competing with one another but also with those who had produced the finest work in the history of architecture (fig. 8). The completed project was also intended to re-alize the urban-design goal of appearing as an integral part of the city. By August 2, 1960, the selection process had narrowed the choice to three; by October 5 Perini-San Francisco Associates, with architects Wurster, Bernardi & Emmons/DeMars & Reay, were announc-ed as the winners. The project area was cleared during the year, and Phase 1 of the residential development was built between 1961 and 1963. The office buildings and the mixed-use development called Embarcadero Center were completed by 1981, and the last phase of residential construction in the following year. Given its location next to the financial district on one side and the residential and commercial areas of the North Beach area on the other side, the Golden Gateway could hardly fail to become a vital part of the city. But from an urban-design point of view, the concept of creating a pedestrian environment by placing office

6   *Aerial view of the Western Addition and Fillmore areas, 1961. Courtesy Aero Photographers, Sausalito. (Photo: Ed Brady)*

7   *Aerial view of Diamond Heights, 1960. Courtesy Aero Photographers, Sausalito. (Photo: Ed Brady)*

8   Skidmore, Owings & Merrill. Entry for the Golden Gateway Competition, 1959.

Drawing on Le Corbusier's plan for Algiers of 1930, designer Charles Perry proposed curvilinear, slablike buildings for SOM's competition submission.

9   Jan Lubicz-Nycz and Mario Ciampi. Scheme for towers on Red Rock Hill, Diamond Heights Competition, 1961. Architectural model. Courtesy Mario Ciampi. (Photo: Dwain Faubion)

As if extruded from the hill itself, Lubicz-Nycz's crystalline towers provided the most visionary image of the four final competition schemes.

10   *Aerial view of San Francisco showing South of Market Street area and downtown, 1974.*
Courtesy Aero Photographers, Sausalito. (Photo: Ed Brady)

and residential buildings over parking garages was less than successful. The characterless walls of the garages have deadened the street; the open, often windy terraces, reached by drab stairways from the street, are not as inviting as the adjacent street-level park even though they are well landscaped and peaceful.

During the same period Diamond Heights also seemed headed for success. On February 24, 1961, the Redevelopment Agency released the prospectus for a second major architectural competition, targeting twenty-two acres of the Diamond Heights area known as Red Rock Hill. An architectural advisory panel composed of architects John Carl Warnecke, Ernest J. Kump, and Don E. Burkholder and developers Gerson Bakar and Sanford Weiss selected the ten best schemes—ninety were submitted—for the 990 apartments in multiple-residence buildings (fig. 9). Following a second phase of the competition, four schemes were selected and made available to interested developers, who were required to submit proposals based on one of the schemes. The winning design was by B. Clyde Cohen and James K. Levorsen,[11] but

the steep and windy ridge proved to be so unattractive to buyers that only one group of townhouses was built. Not until the 1970s did single-family houses, townhouses, and apartments fill the slopes. Today nothing about this pleasant and bland development suggests that a grand composition had been envisioned for the area.

Yerba Buena Center

The redevelopment area that has undergone the greatest transformation and has served to chronicle changing attitudes toward architecture and urban design over its long history is the 1,100-acre site originally called Area D, located south of Market Street (fig. 11). In 1954, the year after its designation by the Board of Supervisors, hotel entrepreneur Ben Swig promoted a Prosperity Plan for a convention center, sports stadium, high-rise office buildings, and a 7,000-car parking garage. The four blocks targeted by Swig for his project were bounded by 5th, Mission, 4th, and Folsom streets, out of the designated area and nearer

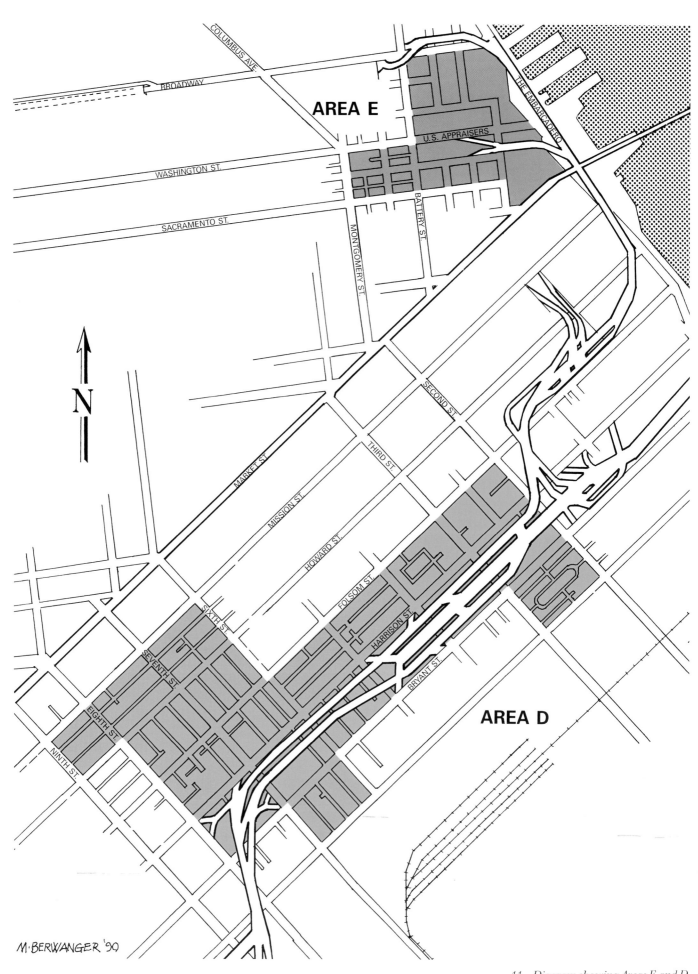

M·BERWANGER '90

11 Diagram showing Areas E and D.

to Market Street. After a study of the proposal, Planning Director Paul Oppermann judged that it did not meet federal standards for blight, and in 1956 the recommendation for designation of the area was rescinded. Swig withdrew his plan because of lack of support.

The city then proposed that twelve and one-third blocks of the original nineteen be targeted for project study under the 1954 amendments to the 1949 housing act, which permitted financial assistance for nonresidential projects.[12] The planners also recommended spot clearance of deteriorated industrial properties rather than total razing of the area. No mention was made of a major facility to enable San Francisco to compete for the growing tourist and convention trade.[13]

Plans for redeveloping the area south of Market in the mid-1950s were concurrent with those for redesigning the street itself. Although the longest of the city's major arteries, Market Street had never become a grand boulevard like the Champs-Elysées in Paris. Instead it remained a great divide nicknamed "the slot," punctuated with unrelated nodes of banking, retail, and theater activities.

In 1962 Planning Director James McCarthy commissioned Mario Ciampi to update the city's 1948 master plan. Ciampi's recommendation envisioned Market Street as the trunk of a tree with branches of development north and south.

James W. Keilty, author of the text for the plan, wrote eloquently of the need for its implementation in order to replace "the squalor of South of Market

12   *Redevelopment Agency. Schematic plan for Yerba Buena Center, 1964. Architectural model. Courtesy John Dykstra. (Photo: Dwain Faubion)*
The model shows varied structures sited, along with theaters and a museum, on the rooftop plaza of the parking garage.

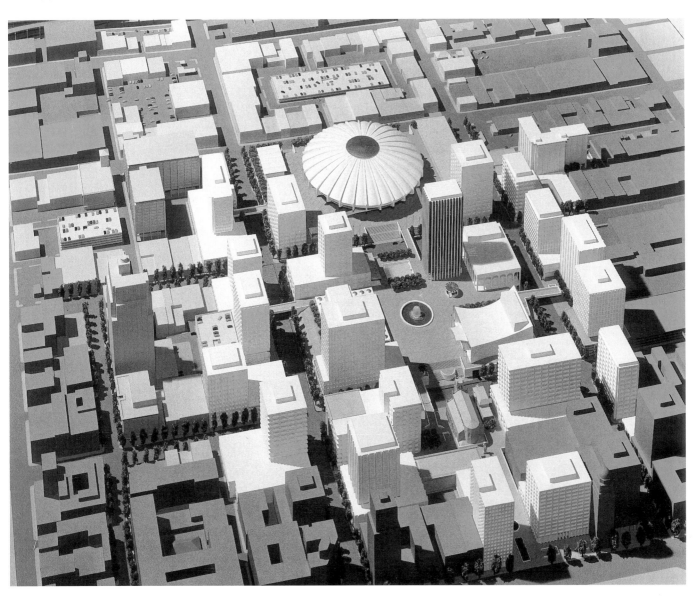

13 Gerald McCue (second from left), Kenzo Tange
(center), Justin Herman (second from right), and others
viewing the Yerba Buena Center model, 1969.
Courtesy John Dykstra. (Photo: Karl H. Riek)

14 Kenzo Tange, URTEC/Gerald McCue. Yerba Buena
Center central blocks, 1969. Architectural model. Collec-
tion of Calvin Imai, Architectural Models.
Courtesy John Dykstra. (Photo: Gerald Ratto)

The Tange/McCue scheme united the central blocks by
bridging them with two discontinuous parking garages
that overlapped in plan and, elevated above the streets,
were accessible through monumental circular towers
containing spiraling ramps. Office buildings, positioned
in line with the towers, occupied peripheral sites on 3rd
and 4th streets; the sports arena was sited at the corner of
3rd and Folsom streets.

15 Schlesinger/Arcon-Pacific. Plan for Yerba Buena
Center, 1973. Architectural model.
Courtesy John Dykstra. (Photo: Jeremiah O. Bragstad)

Alterations to the original scheme of 1969 included placing the parking facilities underground and introducing a
building in the middle of the site for the apparel mart.

Street" with a "safe and solid downtown." Keilty observed that the downtown area north of Market Street
was densely developed with vital financial and commercial activities, whereas the most important activities south of Market were manufacturing and
warehousing. Most of the city's important transportation corridors, including the James Lick Freeway,
were also south of Market. But since the freeway
ramps did not connect directly to Market Street, which
also was the meeting point of two disparate street
grids, access to it was limited. In recognition of Market
Street's isolation from through traffic, the plan proposed removing private vehicles and restricting the
street to public transit, such as the Bay Area Rapid
Transit (BART), and pedestrians. Landscaping was
proposed to make the thoroughfare more attractive.

The planners associated the upgrading of Market
Street with a similar transformation of the blocks south
of Market and adjacent to the central downtown area.

Activities related to those of the downtown core and
most in need of public transit would be located near
Market Street. Facilities such as a sports arena and
exhibition halls, related to conventions and more dependent on the private automobile, would be nearer
the freeway.

To facilitate private development south of Market
Street, in 1961 the city redesignated Area D after re-

ducing its size from 1,100 to 156 acres. In 1964 the Redevelopment Agency proposed a plan prepared by Livingston/Blayney and architect John Carl Warnecke for beginning development on ninety-six acres, thereafter called Yerba Buena Center (YBC). Yerba Buena was the name given to the city by its Spanish founders in 1776). Narrowing the focal area further, the plan identified three central blocks, approximately twenty-five acres, for mixed-use development, including office and retail facilities, two theaters, a museum, a convention center, and a sports arena.

Although the project area was cleared of buildings in the late 1960s (fig. 10), the rebuilding process became one of the longest board games in the city's history. But if the players have changed over the years, the pieces have remained remarkably constant since they were first exhibited in a model prepared by the Redevelopment Agency architects and planners in 1965 (fig. 12).

To launch the central blocks, Redevelopment Agency Director Justin Herman decided to forego an architectural competition in favor of a strong plan, prepared under the aegis of the agency and then offered to developers. Herman had visited Tokyo for the 1964 Olympic Games and was impressed by the dynamic gymnasiums designed by Kenzo Tange. He invited Tange to create his first project outside Japan—a master plan for the central blocks. Tange's local associates were architects John Bolles and Gerald McCue & Associates, with Lawrence Halprin as landscape architect. In 1969, with much fanfare, the agency unveiled the design for an imposing megastructure estimated to cost about $200 million (figs. 13, 14).

Unlike the Redevelopment Agency's model of the area, which showed the city blocks densely but conventionally planned in terms of both scale and accessibility, the Tange/Bolles/McCue scheme envisioned a futuristic urban setting. Its composition recalled a fortress with office buildings and garage towers for bastions. The structures rose three levels above the street and sank to about twenty feet below ground level. For Tange, the design reflected the international culture of architecture and projected an urban image that he also had in mind for Tokyo, where he was engaged in planning an enormous development of megastructures to bridge Tokyo Bay.

The imposition of such a monumental compound in the area south of Market expressed the agency's view that the existing environment lacked the potential to stimulate new development matching north-of-Market's Golden Gateway. The perception was that de-

velopers would cross over the Market Street "slot" only if they were not required to merge with its seedy environment. The Tange scheme was useful as a symbol, but its sculptural unity was gained at the expense of practicality. The floors of the office buildings were the size of those in Tokyo, or about half the size of what was considered appropriate for the large blocks south of Market Street. The spiral garage ramps were simply too big and too high for comfort and ease of access to the floors. The garages also overshadowed the central pedestrian mall, inhibiting its use as a public amenity.

Although the design received a great deal of attention in the press, it did not attract developers. Herman acknowledged that its cost was a deterrent but vowed that the search for developers would circle the globe. Support from the business community, officials, and the press was enthusiastic. Dismissed in all the excitement were threats from the Neighborhood Legal Assistance Foundation and the recently organized Tenants and Owners in Opposition to Redevelopment (TOOR) to file suits against the project in the federal courts because of its inadequate relocation plan for residents.

Developers responded slowly. Extension of the June 1969 deadline elicited only fourteen more expressions of interest. Only five developers actually entered the competition, and of these, only three were able to secure financing. In 1971 Lyman Jee, an architect/developer who headed the firm of Arcon-Pacific, in partnership with entrepreneur Albert Schlesinger, won what had become a very limited competition. In the meantime, TOOR's lawsuit halted the project. Other suits followed, which stalled construction on the central blocks until 1978. Another major setback for the project was the untimely death of Justin Herman in August 1971. With his passing, the city lost an effective supporter of urban redevelopment and a master builder who advocated architectural excellence. Even his detractors acknowledged that Herman was a financial wizard and a perfectionist who never shunned controversy.

In 1973 Schlesinger/Arcon-Pacific presented their plan (fig. 15). Gerald McCue's firm, now called McCue Boone Tomsick, became the executive architects for a team that included Kenzo Tange/Urtec, Lawrence Halprin, and Mario Ciampi as urban-design consultant. Although the new scheme was more fragmented than the one Tange had conceived for the Redevelopment Agency's initial offering, it retained its fortress-like appearance. The parking garages, which

16 Henry Adams, with
architects Wurster, Bernardi &
Emmons, and Lawrence Halprin,
landscape architect. Proposal for
the International Trade Mart,
1968. Architectural model.
Courtesy Wurster, Bernardi &
Emmons, Inc., Architects.
(Photo: Gerald Ratto)

This mammoth project helped to
mobilize public opinion in support of height limits for bayshore
development.

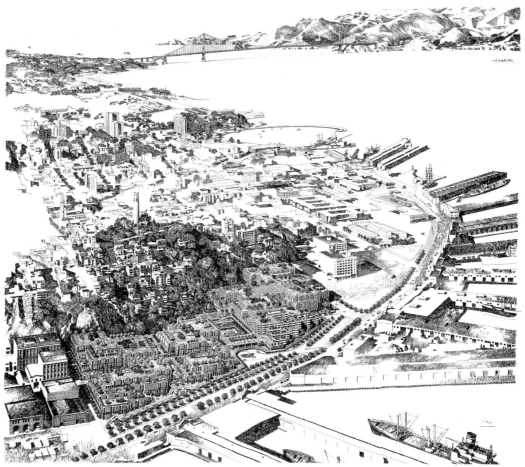

17 Henry Adams, with
architects Wurster, Bernardi &
Emmons, and Lawrence Halprin,
landscape architect. Proposal for
the International Trade Mart,
1968. Drawing.
Courtesy Wurster, Bernardi &
Emmons, Inc., Architects.

had been the most expensive component of the first scheme, were reduced in size and located underground. The exhibition hall—not yet called a convention center—was allotted more meeting space than in the original plan. Office buildings were traded for an apparel mart, and the various functions on the central blocks were well integrated. In 1974 plans for the sports arena were scrapped. Legal and budgetary woes presented additional hurdles for the project. Still more lawsuits were filed, and even the lowest construction bid in 1975 was $17 million higher than the $210 million bond issue could support.[14]

While plans for Yerba Buena Center slowly unfolded, increasingly negative reaction to Redevelopment Agency housing-relocation programs in the Western Addition and YBC took the form of more organized public opposition. San Francisco's elected officials have always shared their political power with strong citizen groups, many of which have their bases in the neighborhoods and do not view downtown as the most important part of the city. During the heyday of the Redevelopment Agency's power under Justin Herman, neighborhood organizations in the areas impacted by redevelopment gained support from the general public. The man who was to respond most sympathetically and effectively to neighborhood concerns was Planning Director Allan Jacobs, appointed in 1966 under Mayor Joseph Alioto. In an interview Jacobs recalled his impressions while visiting the city on the eve of his appointment. Standing on Nob Hill, he lamented the new high-rise buildings that blocked views of the Bay. The city seemed to be losing its distinctive form, and, for Jacobs, a top priority would be to define the positive aspects of that form and plan for its conservation by means of an urban-design element for the city's master plan. In its preliminary planning phase, which began in 1968, Jacobs and his staff carried their concern for the city as a whole to the neighborhoods. This educational effort bolstered citizen support for the environmental and preservation movements that grew to dominate planning efforts in the 1980s.

In *Making City Planning Work*—Jacobs' account of his years as city planning director, published in 1978, two years after he left office—he states, in answer to newspaper reporters' requests for a statement of his vision of the San Francisco of the future, "I was never able to come up with anything very different, physically, from what existed."

However, Jacobs' first years in office were not devoid of visions for projects that would change the city's form. Both private developers and the city's Port Authority proposed large-scale developments on and near the Bay waterfront. John C. Portman's design for the Embarcadero Center gained approval in 1966 as part of the ongoing development of the Golden Gateway; it was built in increments and completed in 1981. Though large in scale, the complex of four slender office towers, rising from podiums with three levels of shopping next to a hotel on Market Street, preserved views to the Bay in sixty-foot-wide corridors between the towers.

In 1968 a proposal for an International Market Center—a huge mixed-use project at the base of Telegraph Hill—presented a major challenge to Jacobs' policy of keeping a low profile for bayside development (figs. 16, 17). The Telegraph Hill Dwellers Association, joined by other organizations bent on preserving the waterfront, succeeded in stalling the project until height restrictions and financial problems caused its abandonment in 1971.[15] But in the intervening years two other major projects—the Ferry Port Plaza and the U.S. Steel Corporation's tower complex—became critical battles in the war over the issue of appropriate development for the waterfront.

In 1969 the Port Authority announced plans for the Ferry Port Plaza. Oceanic Properties, the developer, proposed building a 1,200-room hotel, offices, and shops on a pile-supported platform that would replace Piers 1 through 7. The proposed buildings, none higher than 125 feet, would occupy only fifteen percent of the forty-three-acre site; the rest would be open space for parks, promenades, and plazas. That same year the Port Authority encouraged the U.S. Steel Corporation to propose the development of a 550-foot office tower and associated buildings on nine acres of a site reclaimed from the demolition of Piers 14 to 24 next to the approach to the Bay Bridge. This proposal also included a generous amount of publicly accessible open space. As far as the city and the port were concerned, the jewel of the U.S. Steel proposal was a new terminal for passenger ships. But even before the project left the drawing boards of Skidmore, Owings & Merrill, who were also the architects for the Ferry Port Plaza, it overshadowed, literally and figuratively, all other proposals for development of the waterfront.

By the end of 1970 both projects had garnered an unprecedented amount of public disapproval and were confronted with legal barriers. The Bay Conservation and Development Commission could not approve the Ferry Port Plaza because state law did not permit filling the Bay for projects not oriented to water use. The

U.S. Steel project fell victim to the height limit of eighty-four to 175 feet for the waterfront between the Ferry Building and the Bay Bridge, which was approved on March 5, 1971.

Although the monumental vision of the waterfront embodied in these two proposals was rejected by a conservation-minded public, it was worthy of consideration from an architectural point of view. Edward C. Bassett, the SOM partner in charge of designing both projects, stated that he considered the U.S. Steel proposal more of a trial balloon than a serious venture. Reflecting on San Francisco's unmatched natural

shoreline, extending from Aquatic Park through the Golden Gate and southward along the Pacific Ocean, Bassett maintained that a strong composition of towers rising from the area south of Market Street, where the bridge rose to cross the Bay, would provide a fitting manmade counterpart to nature's achievement. His vision of the city as a sculptural work that could be fine-tuned through the judicious allocation of formal elements recalls Daniel Burnham's 1905 plan, which also took an Olympian view of the city's formal needs. By contrast, Jacobs viewed the city as an insider; from his viewpoint the city's form was worth preserving just as it was. By preempting views of the Bay, projects such as the U.S. Steel complex would deprive San Francisco's inhabitants of the attributes that made the city so livable.

The new height limits did not put a lasting damper on visions for the Ferry Building. The latest, designed by James Ingo Freed of the architectural firm of I. M. Pei and Partners, was proposed to the Port Authority in 1985 (fig. 18). The plan would restore the Ferry Building, removing the 1950s remodeling, and turn the landmark into a mixed-use building that would serve as the frontispiece for a lavish market and enter-

18 I. M. Pei. Ferry Park, 1984. Architectural model.
Courtesy Continental Development.
(Photo: Nathaniel Lieberman)

A grand vision for recapturing the historic importance of the Ferry Building site by means of a festive marketplace on one pier and a major office building on the other. In terms of the attractions it offered and the audience it hoped to appeal to, the program resembled that of Yerba Buena Gardens.

tainment complex at the waterside. On Pier 1 a huge office building would be used by state and Port employees. The fate of this plan has yet to be decided.

Yerba Buena Center from 1976 to 1990

In 1976 George Moscone was elected mayor of San Francisco. One of his first acts, in an effort to get Yerba Buena Center moving again, was to appoint a select committee whose members represented every shade of political opinion. The mayor gave the committee four months to produce recommendations for a plan that the voters would approve. Miraculously, in only five months the committee held fifty or so meetings and produced seventeen recommendations. Public concern was mainly for the environment; opinion was divided over the balance between housing and open space and whether the exhibit hall of the convention center should be above or below ground. Although the sub-committees on housing, real estate, and open space were referred to as the "warring tribes," their disagreements were resolved. Among the most important issues was historic preservation, addressed through the retention of several historic structures. To satisfy the public demand for open space, an urban theme park was to occupy the top of the new exhibit hall and a major part of the adjacent central block.

In 1977 Mayor Moscone made a series of key administrative appointments that led to the beginning of construction on Yerba Buena Center's central blocks.[16] A year later the environmental impact report was accepted, and the Board of Supervisors approved the project and bond issuance for the convention center. Although everything augured success, the celebration for the project was overshadowed by the assassination of George Moscone on November 27, 1978. The convention center, completed in late 1981, was named in honor of the mayor who had succeeded, after so many failures, in getting it built.

In 1980, following a request for qualifications issued by the Redevelopment Agency, a development team was granted exclusive negotiating rights for the design of the project by the Redevelopment Commission (fig. 19).[17] The concept for the design was agreed upon a year later (fig. 20). By this time, the area surrounding the central blocks had been redeveloped largely through private means and was no longer a risky venture. Instead of the urban fortress of the earlier proposals, the central blocks now seemed best suited to provide cultural amenities and open space for a growing residential and working population. For the top of

Moscone Center and part of the adjacent central block, Lawrence Halprin and Omi Lang conceived an urban theme park modeled on the famous Tivoli Gardens in Copenhagen (figs. 21, 22).

On May 1, 1984, Allan Temko, architectural critic for the *San Francisco Chronicle*, wrote enthusiastically of the master design team's published plans for Yerba Buena Gardens, "If the plan for Yerba Buena Gardens comes even partly true, with its 10-acre park, baroque fountains and glass-roofed pleasure pavilions, it will have been worth fighting 20 years to get a decent plan for the long-jinxed project." Temko noted that the total development would amount to about half of the original scheme and that large-scale development in the form of a hotel and office building, located at Market Street, would pay for low-rise cultural and entertainment facilities. (figs. 23-25)

In 1985 the Downtown Plan was adopted; its preservation elements and reduction of height limits and floor-area ratios for new buildings ensured that future large-scale development would shift from north to south of Market. Mission Bay—a new town in town first proposed in 1981 in a plan prepared by John Carl Warnecke—is a project equal in scope to those of the postwar era (fig. 26). Located on 195 acres one mile from the heart of downtown, the site had been a major railroad yard belonging to the Southern Pacific Railway Company. A comprehensive plan for Mission Bay presented in 1982 (fig. 27)[18] had as its focus a central island formed by a circuit of canals linked to public parks and open space. The massing of the buildings on the island conveyed the image of a dense urban development with a downtown marked by high-rise office towers.

The specter of past megadevelopments soon rose to haunt the proposed design. Revised guidelines were issued, and in 1985 the Department of City Planning, under the direction of Dean Macris, launched a planning process for what was called a new "urban neighborhood." The new plan, prepared by EDAW and associated architects and presented in 1987, reduced office space and emphasized housing, including up to

19 *Zeidler-Roberts Partnership/Architects and Olympia & York. Winning plans for Yerba Buena Gardens, 1983-84.*
Colored pencil and graphite on paper.
Courtesy Olympia & York. (Photo: Ben Blackwell)

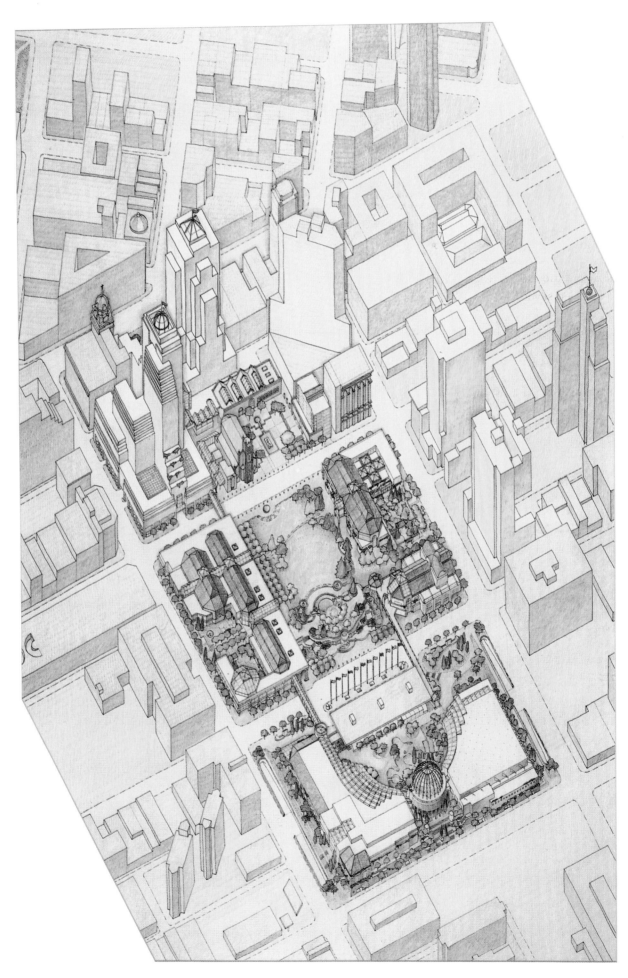

8,000 affordable units for a range of income groups, located adjacent to or near landscaped open space. With the election of Art Agnos as mayor of San Francisco in 1989, this proposal is being revised by Skidmore, Owings & Merrill to meet demands for more housing. (figs. 29-31)

The second half of the twentieth century has witnessed an ongoing debate in San Francisco about the issues of urban renewal and growth. In the decade following the end of World War II, city movers and shakers saw the regulatory machinery of urban redevelopment as the means to acquire, raze, and rebuild large areas of the inner city. Gradually, however, marketplace dynamics began to bring about the changes that redevelopment once promised. Community activism has altered the emphasis of development and, in the 1970s and 1980s, set limits to it that were unthinkable in the postwar era. Now, in the final decade of the century, demographic pressures for higher densities are increasing along with political pressure to encourage development in order to increase the city's tax base. After a period of restraint and reappraisal, San Francisco is in search of new ways to expand its horizon.

NOTES

1 Members of the Citizens' Committee were: Jerd Sullivan, president of the Crocker Bank; Thomas Mellon, president of the Chamber of Commerce; Edward Mills, president of the Downtown Merchants' Association; Paul Oppermann, city planning director; Cyril Magnin, chairman of the State Harbor Commission; Eugene Riordan, director of the Redevelopment Agency; and Benjamin Swig, a hotel entrepreneur. The apportioning of office, residential, and industrial space in the Area E plan reflected the need to meet the guidelines for federal grants-in-aid for development areas set by the Federal Urban Redevelopment Act.
2 At the time, the Ferry Building's north wing was being remodeled for the World Trade Center at a cost of $2 million to the state, while the south wing was proposed as a state historical museum.
3 Members of the committee were: T. A. Brooks, chief administrative officer for the city and county; Sherman P. Ducket, director of the Department of Public Works; Sidney Gorman, chief engineer for the Board of State Harbor Commissioners; and B. W. Booker, assistant state highway engineer. Although the second committee agreed that a park was desirable, the realignment of the freeway was fraught with practical problems such as what to do about the Harbor Belt Line Railroad that crossed the site, the proposed Greyhound bus station for lines serving Marin County, and the fact that all surface parking for the Ferry Building and adjacent piers would be eliminated by the park.
4 Nathaniel Owings, whose firm was designing a headquarters building on a Market Street site for the Crown-Zellerbach Corporation, had been one of the most vigorous proponents of putting the freeway underground.
5 The California Community Redevelopment Act, passed in 1945, was largely written by the San Francisco Chamber of Commerce and was later viewed as favoring real estate interests. In 1948 San Francisco became the first city to adopt the act. These legislative actions preceded the omnibus program of federal loans and grants established by Title One of the 1949 National Housing Act.
6 The designation of Diamond Heights as a redevelopment area provided the first court test of whether an underdeveloped area could be declared blighted. The case was settled favorably in 1954.
7 Anti-renewal sentiments continued to build, as people saw social ills go unaddressed and neighborhood character vanish. With public opinion increasingly opposed to clearing large urban areas, the emphasis of renewal shifted to rehabilitation. This shift is visible in the contrast between the Western Addition's Area 1—featuring the widened and improved Geary Boulevard, the large-scale development of the Japanese Cultural Center, and various new housing developments—and the 1970s development of Area 2, which mixes new housing with rehabilitated older housing.

8 The proportioning of residential and office space in the Area E plan reflected the guidelines set by the federal Urban Renewal Act for federal grants-in-aid for development areas.
9 This citizens' committee was required by law to serve as a liaison group between the city and the R. E. Redevelopment Agency.
10 Mayor Christopher stated in an interview with Jeanette Ryan of Olympia & York that he had appointed Herman because he was the agency's sharpest critic and he knew more about the federal field of operation than anyone else. Prior to Herman's appointment, the San Francisco Redevelopment Agency had no staff and had to borrow city staff, who, according to Christopher, were ineffectual.
11 The other winning designs were by: 1. A. N. Contopoulos, Russell Gifford, Albert R. Seyranian, Karl E. Treffinger, and Paul A. Wilson; 2. Reid, Rockwell, Banwell & Tarics, Rai Okamoto, and Royston, Hanamoto & Mayes; 3. Jan Lubicz-Nycz, and John Karfo with Mario J. Ciampi and Paul Reiter.
12 The National Housing Act was amended in 1954 to permit ten percent of the federal grants to be used for non-residential sections of a redevelopment project. The Urban Renewal Act required redevelopment plans to be tied to the master plan.
13 Brooks Hall, the underground exhibition facility at the Civic Center, was inadequate when it was completed in 1958.
14 The Transformation of San Francisco, by Chester Hartman (1984), gives a detailed account of the political history of Yerba Buena Center.
15 Two important benchmarks of the environmental movement were the founding of the Save San Francisco Bay Association in 1969 and Alvin Duskin's 1971 anti-high-rise initiative, which called for height restrictions of seventy-two feet for new downtown construction. When this initiative failed, Duskin wrote a second initiative proposing seventy-two to 160 feet as the height limit. This initiative also failed, possibly because it raised the potential height limit for residential buildings.
16 Roger Boas became the chief administrative officer with a mandate to initiate plans for the convention center; Wilbur Hamilton became director of the Redevelopment Agency; a new design team under Project Director John Igoe included architects Hellmuth, Obata & Kassabaum, engineers T. V. Lin International, Jack Young & Associates, and Hayakawa & Associates.
17 The development team included Olympia & York/Marriott Corporation/The Rouse Company; Zeidler Roberts Partnership/Beverly Willis and Associates, architects, and Lawrence Halprin & Associates/Omi Lang, landscape architects, in addition to other prominent firms.
18 The plan was designed under the aegis of the Southern Pacific Development Company for presentation to the city by James Ingo Freed of I. M. Pei and Partners/WRT Associates.

20   The 25-acre site for Yerba Buena Gardens as it
stood cleared, 1984. Aerial photograph.
Courtesy Olympia & York.

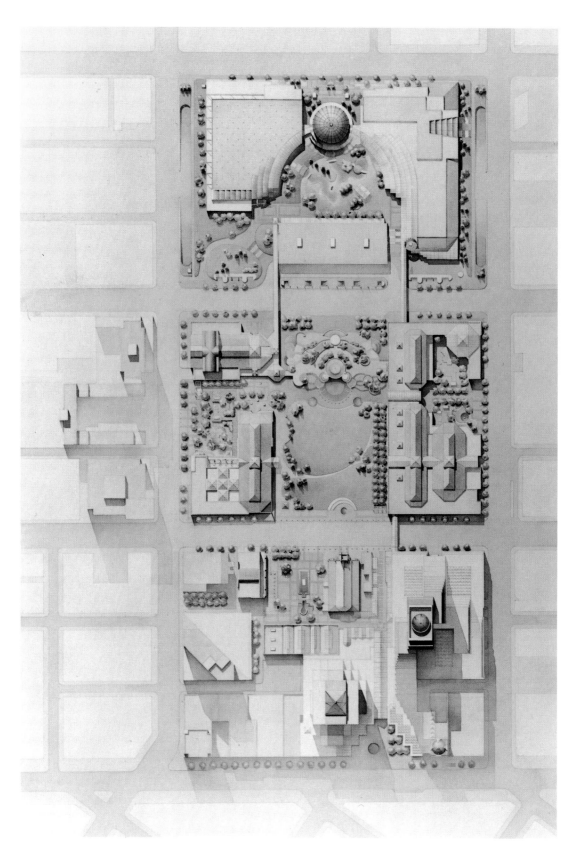

21   Lawrence Halprin and Omi Lang, landscape
architects. Garden plan for Yerba Buena Gardens ex-
ecuted in the office of Zeidler Roberts Partnerships/
Architects, 1981.
Watercolor on paper, 55½ × 35¼ in. (141 × 89.5 cm).
Courtesy Olympia & York. (Photo: Lenscape, Toronto)

The design for the Tivoli Gardens was inspired by the
Copenhagen park of the same name and featured a
grand fountain along with smaller, more specialized
areas such as the Children's Garden and the Chinese
Garden.

22 *Zeidler Roberts Partnership/Architects and Lawrence Halprin, landscape architect. Yerba Buena Gardens as proposed in the master plan, which was the basis of the land use agreement between the Redevelopment Agency and Olympia & York, 1984. Photomontage. Courtesy Olympia & York.*

The proposed uses for Yerba Buena Gardens included on Block 1: a 1500-room Marriott Hotel, 750,000 sq. ft. office tower, 80,000 sq. ft. retail space and market-rate housing. On Block 2: public gardens, visual-arts building, theater, 80,000 sq. ft. retail space, ice rink, 15,000 sq. ft. cinema center, IMAX theater, restaurants, and 45,000 sq. ft. entertainment facility. On East Block 2 (east of 3rd Street): 500,000 sq. ft. office tower, 300-500 units of market-rate housing.

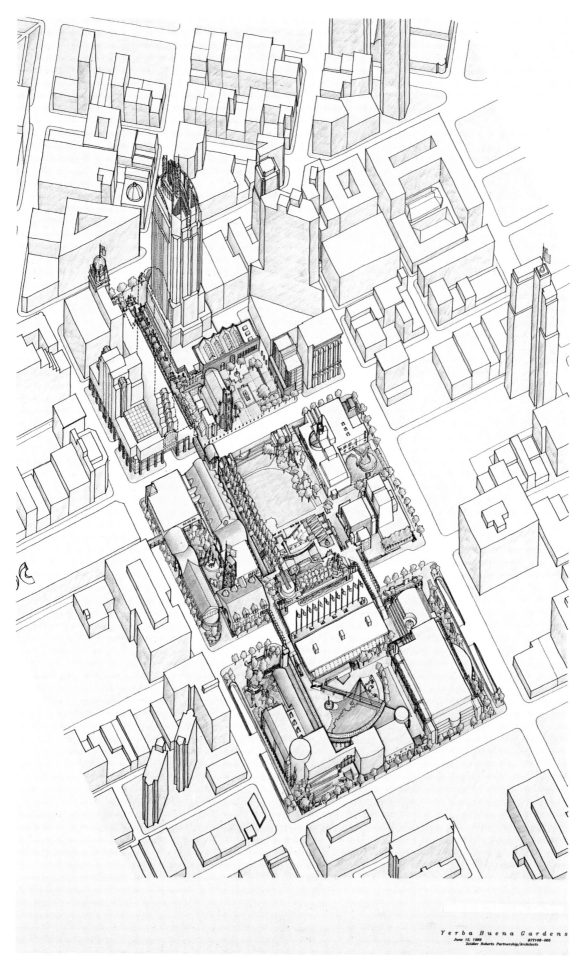

Yerba Buena Gardens
June 12, 1989
Zeidler Roberts Partnership/Architects
87T108-005

23 *Zeidler Roberts Partnership/Architects, with Lawrence Halprin and Omi Lang, landscape architects. Axonometric view of Yerba Buena Gardens, 1989.*
Ink and colored pencil on paper mounted on foam core,
50½ × 33¼ in. (128.3 × 84.5 cm).
Courtesy of Olympia & York.
(Photo: Ben Blackwell)

This overview of the project area reflects changes in the design of the central public gardens as a result of the expansion of the Moscone Convention Center located under the public gardens and cultural buildings. The gardens' design, by Mitchell/Giurgola Architects, features two principal north-south paths that rise to a higher level, terminating in two gardenlike partitions. The upper-level garden is built on the roof of the convention center.

24 *The Jerde Partnership.*
Plan for Yerba Buena Gardens, 1989.
Approx. 60 × 36 in. (152.4 × 91.4 cm).
Courtesy Olympia & York.
(Photo: Ben Blackwell)

In mid-1989 the Redevelopment Agency asked Olympia & York to retain The Jerde Partnership to advise on the overall planning of the retail and entertainment complex in the project. The diagrammatic plan of the central blocks emphasizes the interaction between the various facilities in the project, which serves to create a major urban "cultural park" that embraces all aspects of high culture (museums, theaters) and low culture (street entertainment, shopping).

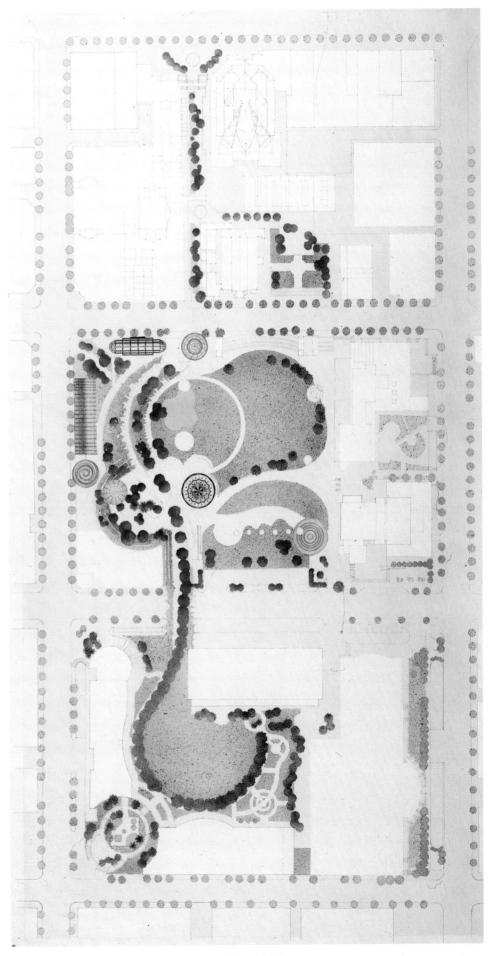

25 a   *The Jerde Partnership, 1989. East-west section/*
elevation for Yerba Buena Gardens, 1989.
Airbrush, ink, and colored pencil on paper,
approx. 36 × 120 in. (91.4 × 304.8 cm).
Courtesy Olympia & York. (Photo: Ben Blackwell)

Section through retail/entertainment complex, showing
the relationship to the central public gardens. A series of
landscaped terraces, reminiscent of Antoni Gaudí's
Parque Güell in Barcelona, is proposed to emphasize the
garden-like nature of the central block.

25 b   *The Jerde Partnership, 1989. North-south section/*
elevation for Yerba Buena Gardens, 1989.
Airbrush, ink, and colored pencil on paper,
approx. 36 × 120 in. (91.4 × 304.8 cm).
Courtesy of Olympia & York. (Photo: Ben Blackwell)

This view shows the public gardens extending from the
roof of the Moscone Convention Center to the central
block, approximately 1100 feet, from Howard to Mission
streets. An inclined plane is created over the convention
center to give visual prominence to the greensward be-
hind the convention-center lobby.

26   *View of Mission Bay area, 1989.*
Courtesy Santa Fe Pacific Realty.

This is the last large undeveloped area in San Francisco,
300 acres of land currently occupied by a major railroad
yard and several warehouses.

27   *Walter Vangreen, renderer.* Rendered Site Plan for
Proposed Mission Bay Development, *1983, Pei Cobb*
Freed & Partners, James I. Freed, Partner-in-Charge,
Charles T. Young II, Associate Partner.
Colored pencil on board, 41 × 60¾ in. (104.1 × 154.3 cm).
Collection of Pei Cobb Freed & Partners, Archives.

The planning of open spaces, integration of circulation
and transportation with the three street grids that meet
in the area, and emphasis on transit to link the new-
town residents to downtown workplaces – all were evi-
dence of a mature approach to achieving the long-held
objectives of a decent living environment replete with a
full range of urban amenities. However, the high density
of office and commercial space at the expense of housing
caused this plan to be abandoned.

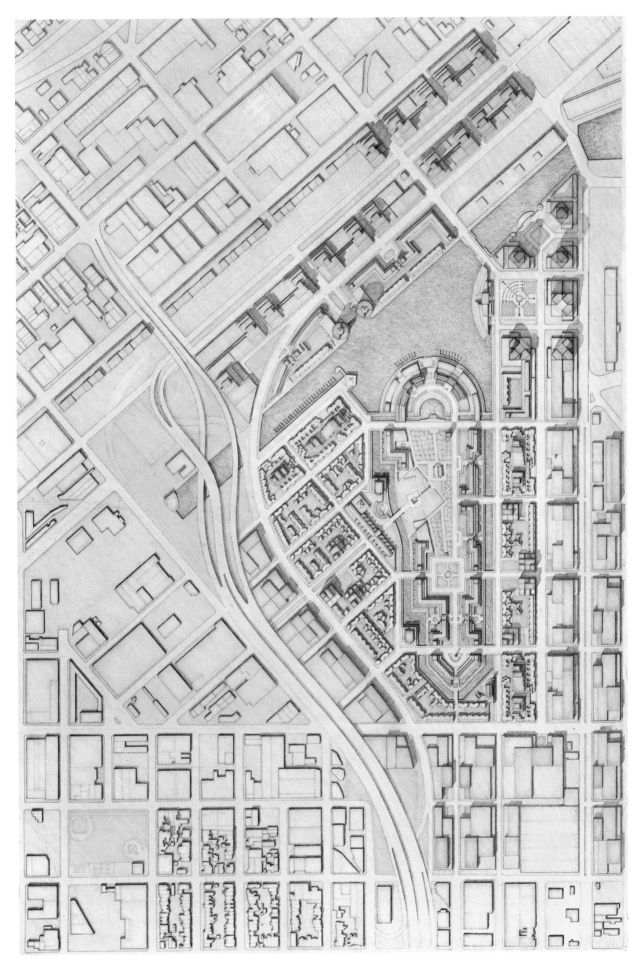

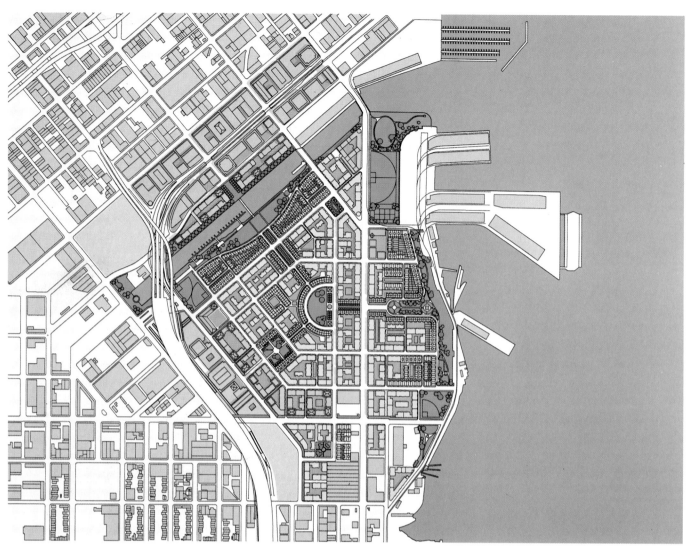

28   *Proposal for Mission Bay, plan.*
Courtesy Santa Fe Pacific Realty.

The proposed plan for Mission Bay emphasizes housing.
A large mixed-use development, it combines housing
with commercial facilities, a school, child care and
senior centers, a hotel, and 60 acres of recreational area.
It provides 3,000 new homes at affordable rates and
5,000 dwellings for a competitive residential market.
The area will be completely developed in twenty or
thirty years.

29   *Proposal for Mission Bay, bird's-eye view, 1990.*
Skidmore, Owings & Merrill. Photomontage.
Courtesy Skidmore, Owings & Merrill.

When completed, Mission Bay will be San Francisco's
newest, self-sufficient neighborhood. It will mix work
places and residences and emphasize their proximity to
public parks and recreational areas.

30 *Proposal for the Mission Bay waterfront.*
Courtesy Santa Fe Pacific Realty.

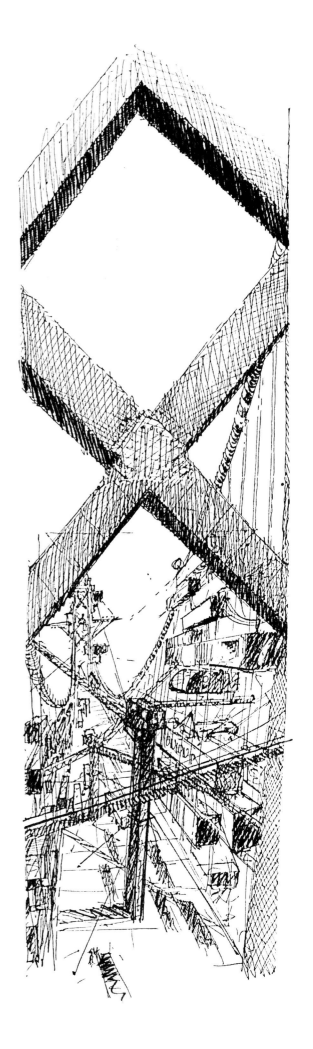

William Gibson

Skinner's Room

It's Halloween and she's found her way up into this old hotel over Geary, Tenderloin's cannibal fringe down one side and the gray shells of big stores off the other; pressing her cheek to cold glass now to spy the bridge's nearest tower—Skinner's room is there—lit with torches and carnival bulbs, far away, but still it reassures her, in here with these foreigners who've done too much of something and now one of them's making noises in the bathroom.

Someone touches her, cold finger on bare skin above the waistband of her jeans, sliding it in under her sweater and the hem of Skinner's jacket; not the touch that makes her jump so much as the abrupt awareness of how hot she is, a greenhouse sweat, zipped up behind the unbreathing horsehide of the ancient jacket, its seams and elbows sueded pale with wear, a jingle of hardware as she swings around— D-rings, zip-pulls, five-pointed stars—her thumbtip against the hole in the knife's blade, opening it, locked, ready. The blade's no longer than her little finger, shaped something like the head of a bird, its eye the hole that gives the thumb purchase. Blade and handle are brushed stainless, like the heavy clip, with its three precise machine screws, that secures it firmly to boot-top, belt, or wristband. Old, maybe older than

the jacket. Japanese, Skinner says. SPYDERCO stamped above an edge of serrated razor.

The man—boy, really—blinks at her. He hasn't seen the blade, but he's felt its meaning, her deep body-verb, and his hand withdraws. He steps back unsteadily, grinning wetly and dunking the sodden end of a small cigar in a stemmed glass of some pharmaceutically clear liquid.

"I am celebrating," he says, and draws on the cigar.

"Halloween?"

It's not a noun he remembers at the moment. He just looks at her like she isn't there, then blows a blue stream of smoke up at the suite's high ceiling. Lowers the cigar. Licks his lips.

"I am living now," he says, "in this hotel, one hundred fifty days." His jacket is leather, too, but not like Skinner's. Some thin-skinned animal whose hide drapes like heavy silk, the color of tobacco. She remembers the tattered yellow wall of magazines in Skinner's room, some so old the pictures are only shades of gray, the way the city looks sometimes from the bridge. Could she find that animal there?

"This is a fine hotel." He dips the wet green end of the cigar into the glass again.

She thumbs the blade-release and closes the knife against her thigh. He blinks at the click. He's having trouble focusing. "One hundred. Fifty days."

Behind him, she sees that the others have tumbled together on the huge bed. Leather, lace, smooth pale skin. The noises from the bathroom are getting worse, but nobody seems to hear. She shivers in the jungle heat of Skinner's jacket. Slips the knife back up under her belt. She's come up here for whatever she can find, really, but what she's found is a hard desperation, a lameness of spirit, that twists her up inside, so maybe that's why she's sweating so, steaming....

Saw them all come laughing, drunk, out of two cabs; she fell into step on impulse, her dusty black horsehide

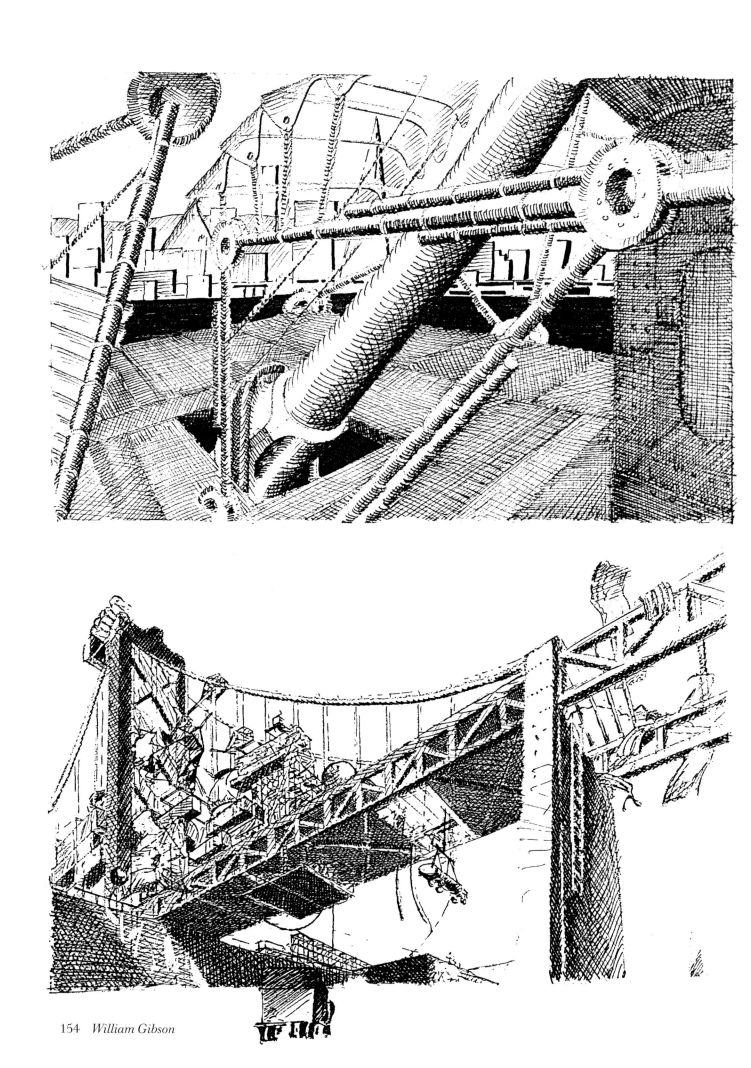

fading into the glossier blacks of silk hose, leather skirts, boots with jingling spurs like jewelry, furs. Sweeping past the doormen's braided coats, their stunners, gas masks—into the tall marble lobby with its carpet and mirrors and waxed furniture, its bronze-doored elevators and urns of sand.

"One hundred fifty days," he says, and sways, lips slack and moist. "In this hotel."

She's out of here.

The bridge maintains the integrity of its span within a riot of secondary construction, a coral growth facilitated in large part by carbon-fiber compounds. Some sections of the original structure, badly rusted, have been coated with a transparent material whose tensile strength far exceeds that of the original steel; some are splined with the black and impervious carbon fiber; others are laced with makeshift ligatures of taut and rusting wire.

Secondary construction has occurred piecemeal, to no set plan, employing every imaginable technique and material; the result is amorphous and startlingly organic in appearance.

At night, illuminated by Christmas bulbs, by recycled neon, by torchlight, the bridge is a magnet for the restless, the disaffected. By day, viewed from the towers of the city, it recalls the ruin of Brighton Pier in the closing decade of the previous century—seen through some cracked kaleidoscope of vernacular style.

Lately Skinner's hip can't manage the first twenty feet of ladder, so he hasn't been down to try the new elevator the African has welded to the rivet-studded

3 Ming Fung and Craig Hodgetts. Untitled, 1989.
Ink and xerography on paper, 9 × 11½ in. (22.9 × 29.2 cm).
Courtesy San Francisco Museum of Modern Art.
(Photo: Ben Blackwell)

Skinner's rooftop, slung above the massive bridge cable with nothing but air between it and the San Francisco skyline.

4 Ming Fung and Craig Hodgetts. Untitled, 1989.
Ink and xerography on paper, 9 × 11½ in. (22.9 × 29.2 cm).
Courtesy San Francisco Museum of Modern Art.
(Photo: Ben Blackwell)

As the bridge approaches land, the roadway suddenly stops, breaking its link with the city and protecting those who have become part of the collage.

steel of the tower, but he's peered at it through the hatch in the floor. It looks like the yellow plastic basket of a lineman's cherrypicker, cogging its way up and down a greasy-toothed steel track like a miniature Swiss train, motor bolted beneath the floor of the basket. Skinner's not sure where the tower's getting its juice these days, but the lightbulb slung beside his bed dims and pulses whenever he hears that motor whine.

He admires people who build things, who add to the structure. He admires whoever it was built this room, this caulked box of ten-ply fir, perched and humming in the wind. The room's floor is a double layer of pressure-treated two-by-fours laid on edge, broken by an achingly graceful form Skinner no longer really sees: the curve of the big cable drawn up over its saddle of steel. 17,464 pencil-thick wires.

The little pop-up television on the blanket across his chest continues its dumb-show. The girl brought it for him. Stolen, probably. He never turns the sound on. The constant play of images on the liquid crystal screen is obscurely comforting, like the half-sensed movements in an aquarium: life is there. The images themselves are of no interest. He can't remember when he ceased to be able to distinguish commercials from programming. The distinction itself may no longer exist.

His room measures fifteen by fifteen feet, the plywood walls softened by perhaps a dozen coats of white latex paint. Higher reflective index than aluminium foil, he thinks. 17,464 strands per cable. Facts. Often, now, he feels himself a void through which facts tumble, facts and faces, making no connection.

His clothes hang from mismatched antique coathooks screwed at precise intervals along one wall. The girl's taken his jacket. Lewis Leathers. Great Portland Street. Where is that? Jacket older than she is. Looks at the pictures in *National Geographic*, crouched there with her bare white feet on the carpet he took from the broken office block in . . . Oakland?

Memory flickers like the liquid crystal. She brings him food. Pumps the Coleman's chipped red tank. Remember to open the window a crack. Japanese cans, heat up when you pull a tab. Questions she asks him. Who built the bridge? Everyone. No, she says, the old part, the bridge. San Francisco, he tells her. Bone of iron, grace of cable, hangs us here. How long you live here? Years. Spoons him his meal from a mess kit stamped 1952.

This is his room. His bed. Foam, topped with a sheepskin, bottom sheet over that. Blankets. Catalytic heater. Remember to open the window a crack.

Skinner's Room 155

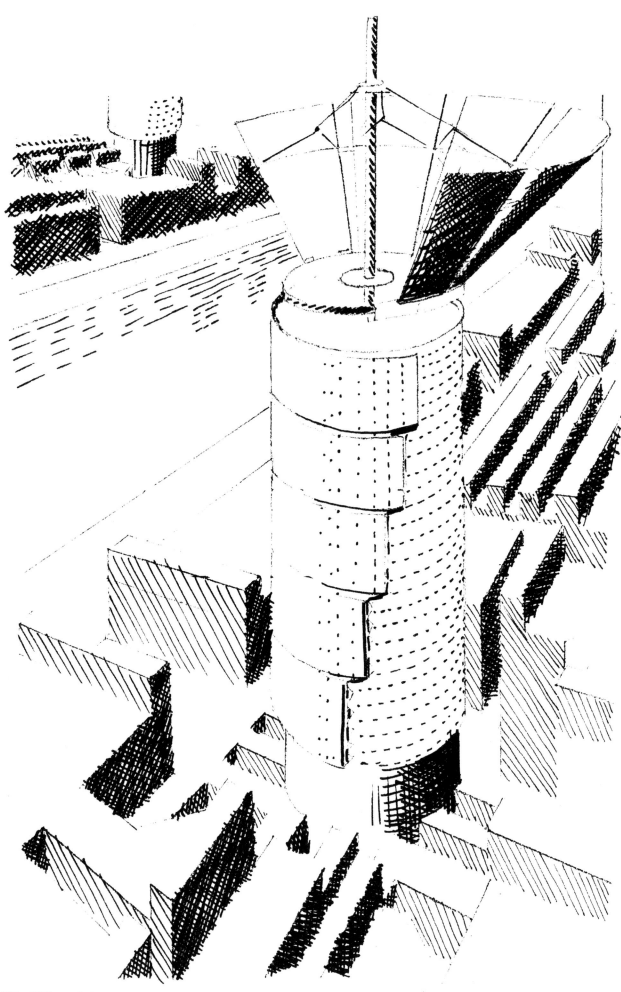

The window is circular, leaded, each segment stained a different color. You can see the city through the bull's-eye of clear yellow glass at its center.

Sometimes he remembers building the room himself.

The bridge's bones, its stranded tendons, are lost within an accretion of dreams: tattoo parlors, shooting galleries, pinball arcades, dimly lit stalls stacked with damp-stained years of men's magazines, chili joints, premises of unlicensed denturists, fireworks stalls, cut bait sellers, betting shops, sushi bars, purveyors of sexual appliances, pawnbrokers, wonton counters, love hotels, hotdog stands, a tortilla factory, Chinese green-grocers, liquor stores, herbalists, chiropractors, barbers, tackle shops, and bars.

These are dreams of commerce, their locations generally corresponding to the decks originally intended for vehicular traffic. Above them, rising toward the peaks of the cable towers, lift intricate barrios, zones of more private fantasy, sheltering an unnumbered population of uncertain means and obscure occupation.

Sagging platforms of slivered wood are slung beneath the bridge's lower deck; from these, on a clear day, old men lower fishing lines. Gulls wheel and squabble over shreds of discarded bait.

The encounter in the old hotel confirms something for her. She prefers the bridge to the city.

She first came upon the bridge in fog, saw the sellers of fruits and vegetables with their goods spread out on blankets, lit by carbide lamps and guttering smudge pots. Farm people from up the coast. She'd come from that direction herself, down past the stunted pines of Little River and Mendocino, Ukiah's twisted oak hills.

She stared back into the cavern mouth, trying to make sense of what she saw. Steam rising from the pots of soup vendors' carts. Neon scavenged from the ruins of Oakland. How it ran together, blurred, melting in the fog. Surfaces of plywood, marble, corrugated

5   *Ming Fung and Craig Hodgetts. Untitled, 1989.*
Ink and xerography on paper, 11½ × 9 in. (29.2 × 22.9 cm).
Courtesy San Francisco Museum of Modern Art.
(Photo: Ben Blackwell)
At the base of Sunflower Corporation tower is a mixture of offices, residences, and retail shops. At the top, a rotating, reflective umbrella concentrates solar heat on an absorptive steam-generation system that supplies electrical energy.

plastic, polished brass, sequins, Styrofoam, tropical hardwoods, mirror, etched Victorian glass, chrome gone dull in the sea air—all the mad richness of it, its randomness—a tunnel roofed by a precarious shack town mountainside climbing toward the first of the cable towers.

She'd stood a long time, looking, and then she'd walked straight in, past a boy selling coverless yellowed paperbacks and a café where a blind old parrot sat chained on a metal perch, picking at a chicken's freshly severed foot.

Skinner surfaces from a dream of a bicycle covered with barnacles and sees that the girl is back. She's hung his leather jacket on its proper hook and squats now on her pallet of raw-edged black foam.

Bicycle. Barnacles.

Memory: a man called Fass snagged his tackle, hauled the bicycle up, trailing streamers of kelp. People laughing. Fass carried the bicycle away. Later he built a place to eat, a three-stool shanty leached far out over the void with superglue and shackles. He sold cold cooked mussels and Mexican beer. The bicycle hung above the little bar. The walls were covered with layers of picture postcards. Nights he slept curled behind the bar. One morning the place was gone, Fass with it, just a broken shackle swinging in the wind and a few splinters of timber still adhering to the galvanized iron wall of a barber shop. People came, stood at the edge, looked down at the water between the toes of their shoes.

The girl asks him if he's hungry. He says no. Asks him if he's eaten. He says no. She opens the tin food chest and sorts through cans. He watches her pump the Coleman. He says open the window a crack. The circular window pivots in its oak frame. You gotta eat, she says.

She'd like to tell the old man about going to the hotel, but she doesn't have words for how it made her feel. She feeds him soup, a spoonful at a time. Helps him to the tankless old china toilet behind the faded roses of the chintz curtain. When he's done she draws water from the roof-tank line and pours it in. Gravity does the rest. Thousands of flexible transparent lines are looped and bundled, down through the structure, pouring raw sewage into the Bay.

"Europe . . . ." she tries to begin.

He looks up at her, mouth full of soup. She guesses his hair must've been blond once. He swallows the soup. "Europe what?" Sometimes he'll snap right into

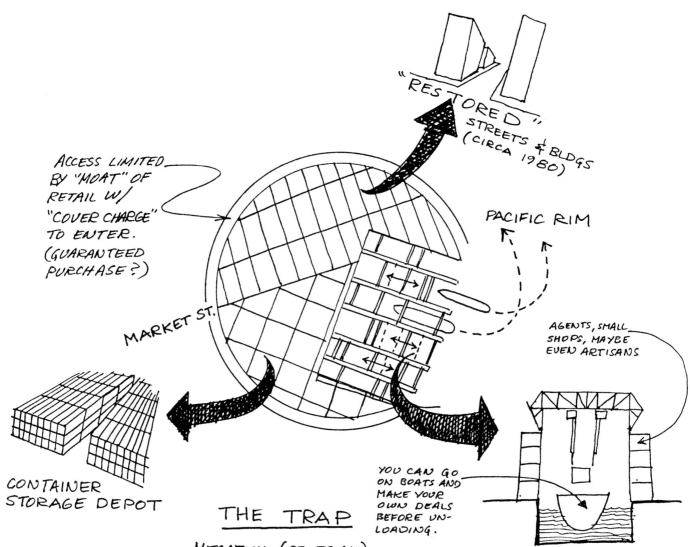

ACCESS LIMITED BY "MOAT" OF RETAIL W/ "COVER CHARGE" TO ENTER. (GUARANTEED PURCHASE?)

"RESTORED" STREETS & BLDGS (CIRCA 1980)

PACIFIC RIM

MARKET ST.

AGENTS, SMALL SHOPS, MAYBE EVEN ARTISANS

CONTAINER STORAGE DEPOT

YOU CAN GO ON BOATS AND MAKE YOUR OWN DEALS BEFORE UN- LOADING.

GANTRY UNLOADING AND FREE PORT SHOPPING AREA.

THE TRAP

MITSUBISHI (OR EQUAL) ASSEMBLES LAND IN THE TENDERLOIN & ADJACENT AREAS AND SUCCEEDS IN ESTABLISHING IT AS A MASSIVE "COST PLUS" DISTRICT WITH RES- TRICTED ACCESS FOR DIRECT IMPORT/EXPORT.

focus like this if she asks him a question, but now she's not sure what the question is.

"Paris," he says, and his eyes tell her he's lost again, "I went there. London, too. Great Portland Street." He nods, satisfied somehow. "Before the first devaluation...."

Wind sighs past the window.

She thinks about climbing out on the roof. The rungs up to the hatch there are carved out of sections of two-by-four, painted the same white as the walls. He uses one for a towel rack. Undo the bolt. You raise the hatch with your head; your eyes are level with gull shit. Nothing there, really. Flat tarpaper roof, a couple of two-by-four uprights; one flies a tattered Confederate flag, the other a faded orange windsock. Thinking about it, she loses interest.

When he's asleep again, she closes the Coleman, scrubs out the pot, washes the spoon, pours the soupy water down the toilet, wipes pot and spoon, puts them away. Pulls on her hightop sneakers, laces them up. She puts on his jacket and checks that the knife's still clipped behind her belt.

She lifts the hatch in the floor and climbs through, finding the first rungs of the ladder with her feet. She lowers the hatch closed, careful not to wake Skinner. She climbs down past the riveted face of the tower, to the waiting yellow basket of the elevator. Looking up, she sees the vast cable there, where it swoops out of the bottom of Skinner's room, vanishing through a taut and glowing wall of milky plastic film, a greenhouse; halogen bulbs throw spiky plant shadows on the plastic.

The elevator whines, creeping down the face of the tower, beside the ladder she doesn't use anymore, past a patchwork of plastic, plywood, sections of enameled steel stitched together from the skins of dead refrigerators. At the bottom of the fat-toothed track, she climbs out. She sees the man Skinner calls the African coming toward her along the catwalk, bearlike shoulders hunched in a ragged tweed overcoat. He carries a meter of some kind, a black box, dangling red and black wires tipped with alligator clips. The broken plastic frames of his glasses have been mended with silver duct tape. He smiles shyly as he edges past her, muttering something about brushes.

She rides another elevator, a bare steel cage, down to the first deck. She walks in the direction of Oakland, past racks of secondhand clothing and blankets spread with the negotiable detritus of the city. Someone is frying pork. She walks on, into the fluorescent chartreuse glare.

She meets a woman named Maria Paz.

She's always meeting people on the bridge, but only people who live here. The tourists, mostly, are scared. They don't want to talk. Nervous, you can tell by their eyes, how they walk.

She goes with Maria Paz to a coffee shop with windows on the Bay and a gray dawn. The coffee shop has the texture of an old ferry, dark dented varnish over plain heavy wood; it feels as though someone's sawn it from some tired public vessel and lashed it up on the outermost edge of the structure. Not unlikely; the wingless body of a 747 has been incorporated, nearer Oakland.

Maria Paz is older, with slate gray eyes, an elegant dark coat, tattoo of a blue swallow on the inside of her left ankle, just above the little gold chain she wears there. Maria Paz smokes Kools, one after another, lighting them with a brushed chrome Zippo she takes from her purse; each time she flicks it open, a sharp whiff of benzene cuts across the warm smells of coffee and scrambled eggs.

You can talk with the people you meet on the bridge. Because everyone's crazy there, Skinner says, and out of all that craziness you're bound to find a few who're crazy the way you are.

She sits with Maria Paz, drinks coffee, watches her smoke Kools. She tells Maria Paz about Skinner.

"How old is he?" Maria Paz asks.

"Old. I don't know."

"And he lives over the cable saddle on the first tower?"

"Yes."

"Then he's been here a long time. The tops of the towers are very special. Do you know that?"

"No."

"He's from the days when the first people came out from the cities to live on the bridge."

"Why did they do that?"

6 *Ming Fung and Craig Hodgetts.* The Trap, *1989.*
Ink and xerography on paper, 11½ × 9 in. (29.2 × 22.9 cm).
Courtesy San Francisco Museum of Modern Art.
(Photo: Ben Blackwell)

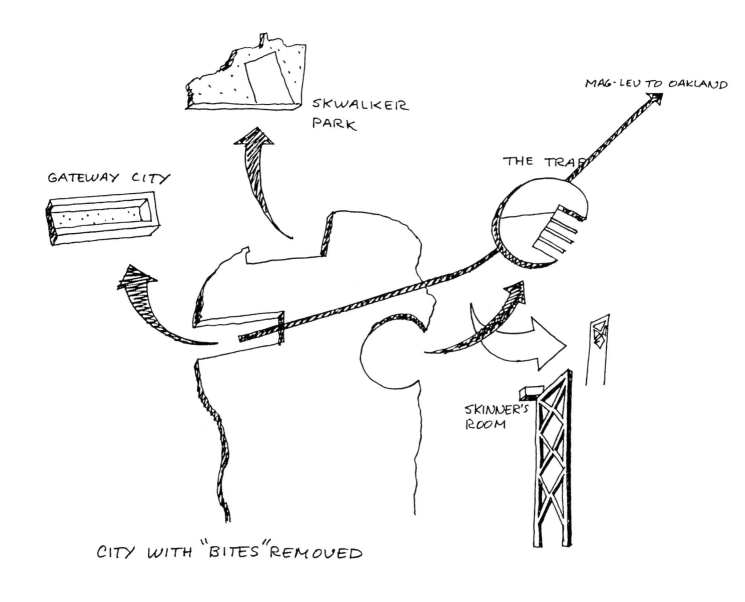

SKWALKER PARK

MAG-LEV TO OAKLAND

GATEWAY CITY

THE TRAP

SKINNER'S ROOM

CITY WITH "BITES" REMOVED

7   *Ming Fung and Craig Hodgetts.* City with "Bites" Removed, *1989.*
Ink and xerography on paper, 11½ × 9 in. (29.2 × 22.9 cm).
Courtesy San Francisco Museum of Modern Art.
(Photo: Ben Blackwell)

8   *Ming Fung and Craig Hodgetts.* Skywalker Park, *1989.*
Ink and xerography on paper, 11½ × 9 in. (29.2 × 22.9 cm).
Courtesy San Francisco Museum of Modern Art.
(Photo: Ben Blackwell)

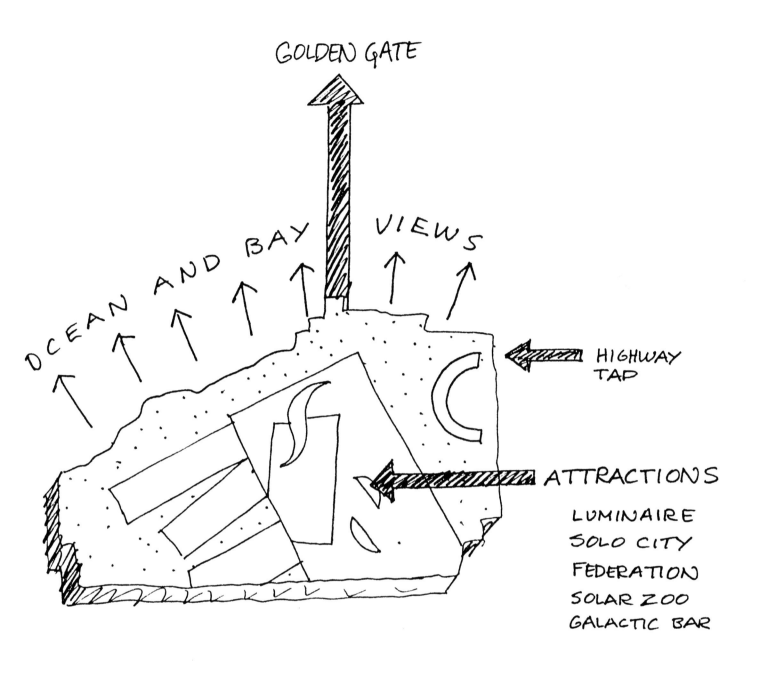

GOLDEN GATE

OCEAN AND BAY VIEWS

HIGHWAY TAP

ATTRACTIONS

LUMINAIRE
SOLO CITY
FEDERATION
SOLAR ZOO
GALACTIC BAR

SKYWALKER PARK

WITH NUKE PACT/CHEM PAK/DEFENSE
SLASH THE PRESIDIO WAS UP FOR GRABS,
AND LUSASPIEL GRABBED IT, OUTBIDDING
DISNEY AND SONY, TO TURN IT INTO
THEIR FLAGSHIP THEME PARK.

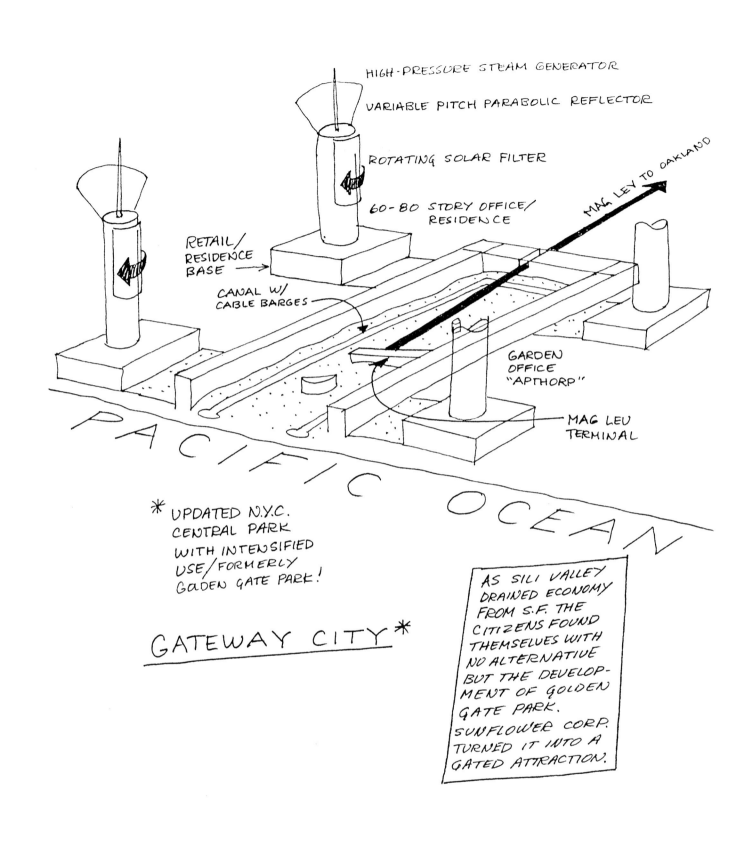

HIGH-PRESSURE STEAM GENERATOR

VARIABLE PITCH PARABOLIC REFLECTOR

ROTATING SOLAR FILTER

60-80 STORY OFFICE/RESIDENCE

MAG LEV TO OAKLAND

RETAIL/RESIDENCE BASE

CANAL W/CABLE BARGES

PACIFIC OCEAN

GARDEN OFFICE "APTHORP"

MAG LEV TERMINAL

* UPDATED N.Y.C.
CENTRAL PARK
WITH INTENSIFIED
USE/FORMERLY
GOLDEN GATE PARK!

GATEWAY CITY *

AS SILI VALLEY
DRAINED ECONOMY
FROM S.F. THE
CITIZENS FOUND
THEMSELVES WITH
NO ALTERNATIVE
BUT THE DEVELOP-
MENT OF GOLDEN
GATE PARK.
SUNFLOWER CORP.
TURNED IT INTO A
GATED ATTRACTION.

Maria Paz looks at her over the Zippo. Click. Tang of benzene. "They had nowhere else to go. They were homeless in the cities. The bridge had been closed, you see, closed to traffic, for three years."

"Traffic?"

Maria Paz laughs. "But it was a *bridge*, darling. People drove back and forth in cars, from one end to the other." She laughs again. "There were too many cars, finally, so they dug the tunnels under the Bay. Tunnels for the cars, tunnels for the maglevs. The bridge was old, in need of repair. They closed it, but then the devaluations began, the depression. There was no money for the repairs they'd planned. The bridge stood empty. And then one night, as if someone had given a signal, the homeless came. But the legend is that there *was* no signal. People simply *came.* They climbed the chainlink and the barricades at either end; they climbed in such numbers that the chainlink twisted and fell. They tumbled the concrete barricades into the Bay. They climbed the towers. Dozens died, falling to their deaths. But when dawn came, they were here, on the bridge, clinging, claiming it, and the cities, dear," she blew twin streams of smoke from her nostrils, "knew that the world was watching. They were no longer invisible, you see, the homeless people; they'd come together on this span of steel, had claimed it as their own. The cities had to be cautious then. Already the Japanese were preparing an airlift of food and medical supplies. A national embarrassment. No time for the water cannon, no. They were allowed to stay. Temporarily. The first structures were of cardboard." Maria Paz smiles.

"Skinner? You think he came then?"

"Perhaps. If he's as old as you seem to think he is. How long have you been on the bridge, dear?"

"Three months, maybe."

"I was born here," says Maria Paz.

The cities have their own pressing difficulties. This is not an easy century, the nation quite clearly in decline and the very concept of nation-states called increasingly into question. The squatters have been allowed to remain upon the bridge and have transformed it. There were, among their original numbers, entrepreneurs, natural politicians, artists, men and women of previously untapped energies and talents. While the world watched, and the cities secretly winced, the bridge people began to build, architecture as *art brut.* The representatives of global charities descended in helicopters, to be presented with lists of tools and materials. Shipments of advanced adhesives arrived from Japan. A Belgian manufacturer donated a boatload of carbon-fiber beams. Teams of expert scavengers rolled through the cities in battered flatbeds, returning to the bridge piled high with discarded building materials.

The bridge and its inhabitants became the cities' premier tourist attraction.

Hard currency, from Europe and Japan.

She walks back in the early light that filters through windows, through sheets of wind-shivered plastic. The bridge never sleeps, but this is a quiet time. A man is arranging fish on a bed of shaved ice in a wooden cart. The pavement beneath her feet is covered with gum wrappers and the flattened filters of cigarettes. A drunk is singing somewhere, overhead. Maria Paz left with a man, someone she'd been waiting for.

She thinks about the story and tries to imagine Skinner there, the night they took the bridge, young then, his leather jacket new and glossy.

She thinks about the Europeans in the hotel on Geary. Hard currency.

She reaches the first elevator, the cage, and leans back against its bars as it rises up its patched tunnel, where the private lives of her neighbors are walled away in so many tiny, handmade spaces. Stepping from the cage, she sees the African squatting in his tweed overcoat in the light cast by a caged bulb on a long yellow extension cord, the motor of his elevator spread out around him on fresh sheets of newsprint. He looks up at her apologetically.

"Adjusting the brushes," he says.

"I'll climb." She goes up the ladder. Always keep one hand and one foot on the ladder, Skinner told her, don't think about where you are and don't look down. It's a long climb, up toward the smooth sweep of cable. Skinner must've done it thousands of times, uncounted, unthinking. She reaches the top of this ladder, makes a careful transfer to the second, the short one, that leads to Skinner's room.

9   Ming Fung and Craig Hodgetts. Gateway City, 1989.
Ink and xerography on paper, 11½ × 9 in. (29.2 × 22.9 cm).
Courtesy San Francisco Museum of Modern Art.
(Photo: Ben Blackwell)

He's there, of course, asleep, when she scrambles up through the hatch. She tries to move as quietly as she can, but the jingle of the jacket's chrome hardware disturbs him, or reaches him in his dream, because he calls out something, his voice thick with sleep. It might be a woman's name, she thinks. It certainly isn't hers.

In Skinner's dream now they all run forward, and the police, the police are hesitating, falling back. Overhead the steady drum of the network helicopters with their lights and cameras. A light rain's falling now, as Skinner locks his cold fingers in the chainlink and starts to climb, and behind him a roar goes up, drowning the bullhorns of the police and the National Guard, and Skinner is climbing, kicking the narrow toes of his boots into chainlink, climbing as though he's gone suddenly weightless, floating up, really, rising on the crowd's roar, the ragged cheer torn from all their lungs. He's there, at the top, for one interminable instant. He jumps. He's the first. He's on the bridge, running, running toward Oakland, as the chainlink crashes behind him, his cheeks wet with the rain and tears.

And somewhere off in the night, on the Oakland side, another fence has fallen. And they meet, these two lost armies, and flow together as one, and huddle there, at the bridge's center, their arms around one another, singing ragged wordless hymns.

At dawn, the first climbers begin to scale the towers. Skinner is with them.

She's brewing coffee on the Coleman when she sees him open his eyes.

"I thought you'd gone," he says.

"I took a walk. I'm not going anywhere. There's coffee."

He smiles, eyes sliding out of focus. "I was dreaming . . . ."

"Dreaming what?"

"I don't remember. We were singing. In the rain . . . ."

She brings him coffee in the heavy china cup he likes, holds it, helps him drink. "Skinner, were you here when they came from the cities? When they took the bridge?"

He looks up at her with a strange expression. His eyes widen. He coughs on the coffee, wipes his mouth with the back of his hand. "Yes," he says, "yes. In the rain. We were singing. I remember that . . . ."

"Did you build this place, Skinner? This room? Do you remember?"

"No," he says, "no. Sometimes I don't remember . . . . We climbed. Up. We climbed up past the helicopters. We waved at them. Some people fell. At the top. We got to the top . . . ."

"What happened then?"

He smiles. "The sun came out. We saw the city."

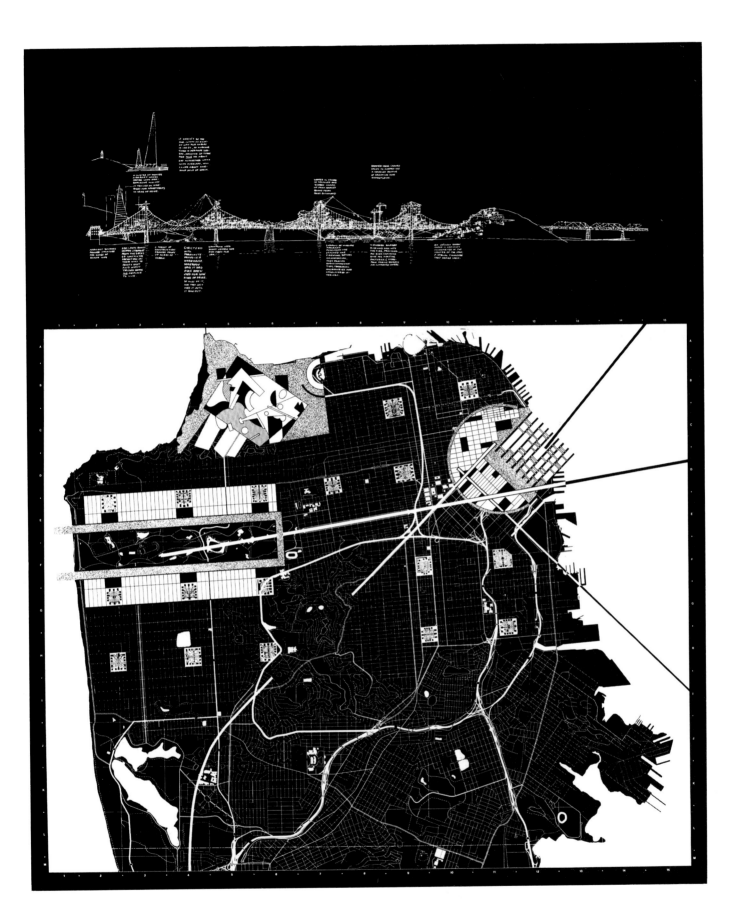

10   *Ming Fung and Craig Hodgetts.* Map of San Francisco, *1989.*
Ink, xerography, and collage on paper, 24 × 20 in. (61 × 50.8 cm).
Courtesy San Francisco Museum of Modern Art.
(Photo: Ben Blackwell)

Appendix

Suggested Reading

San Francisco: The City Beautiful
Gray A. Brechin

The American Renaissance: 1876-1917. Exhibition catalogue, The Brooklyn Museum. New York: Pantheon Books, 1979.

Benedict, Burton et al. *The Anthropology of World's Fairs: San Francisco's Panama Pacific International Exposition of 1915.* Berkeley, Calif., and London: Lowie Museum of Anthropology and Scolar Press, 1983.

Burnham, Daniel Hudson, and Edward H. Bennet. *Report on a Plan for San Francisco.* San Francisco: The City of San Francisco, 1905.

Corbett, Michael. *Splendid Survivors: San Francisco's Downtown Architectural Heritage.* San Francisco: California Living Books, 1979.

Limerick, Patricia Nelson. *The Legacy of Conquest: The Unbroken Past of the American West.* New York and London: W. W. Norton & Co., 1887.

Longstreth, Richard, and Robert A. Stern, eds. *On the Edge of the World: Four Architects in San Francisco at the Turn of the Century.* Cambridge, Mass., and London: MIT Press, 1983.

Moudon, Anne Vernez. *Built for Change: Neighborhood Architecture in San Francisco.* Cambridge, Mass.: MIT Press, 1986.

Muscatine, Doris. *Old San Francisco: The Biography of a City.* New York: G. P. Putnam's Sons, 1975.

Partridge, Loren W. *John Galen Howard and the Berkeley Campus: Beaux-Arts Architecture in the "Athens of the West."* Berkeley, Calif.: Berkeley Architectural Heritage Association, 1978.

Scott, Mel. *The San Francisco Bay Area: A Metropolis in Perspective.* Berkeley, Los Angeles, and London: University of California Press, 1959, 2nd ed. 1985.

Starr, Kevin. *Americans and the California Dream: 1850-1915.* New York: Oxford University Press, 1973.

A Vivacious Landscape: Urban Visions between the Wars
Daniel P. Gregory

There are no comprehensive histories of visionary design in San Francisco during the 1920s and 1930s. The most important records for the period are local newspapers, architectural journals, official reports and files. A selective bibliography follows:

The Architect and Engineer (professional journal). San Francisco, 1920s and 1930s. Bound volumes at San Francisco Public Library.

Corbett, Michael. *Splendid Survivors: San Francisco's Downtown Architectural Heritage.* San Francisco: California Living Books, 1979.

Corn, Joseph, ed. *Imagining Tomorrow: History, Technology and the American Future.* Cambridge, Mass.: MIT Press, 1986.

Dillon, Richard, Thomas Moulin, and Don De Nevi. *High Steel: Building the Bridges Across San Francisco Bay.* Berkeley, Calif.: Celestial Arts, 1979.

Gilliam, Harold. *San Francisco Bay.* Garden City, N. Y.: Doubleday, 1957.

The Golden Gate Bridge: Report of the Chief Engineer to the Board of Directors. San Francisco: Golden Gate Bridge and Highway District, September 1937.

Hansen, Gladys. *San Francisco Almanac.* San Francisco: Presidio Press, revised ed. 1980.

Neuhaus, Eugen. *The Art of Treasure Island.* Berkeley: University of California Press, 1939.

Reinhardt, Richard. *Treasure Island: San Francisco's Exposition Years.* San Francisco: Scrimshaw Press, 1973.

Report of the Hoover-Young San Francisco Bay Bridge Commission to the President of the United States and the Governor of the State of California. August 1930.

Scott, Mel. *The San Francisco Bay Area: A Metropolis in Perspective,* Berkeley: University of California Press, 1959, 2nd ed. 1985.

Sky, Alison and Michelle Stone. *Unbuilt America: Forgotten Architecture in the United States from Thomas Jefferson to the Space Age.* New York: Abbeville Press, 1983.

Stackpole, Peter. *The Bridge Builders: Photographs and Documents of the Raising of the San Francisco Bay Bridge 1934-1936.* Corte Madera, Calif.: Pomegranate Press, 1984.

Van der Zee, John. *The Gate: The True Story of the Design and Construction of the Golden Gate Bridge.* New York: Simon & Schuster, 1986.

Willis, Carol. "Drawing Toward Metropolis." In Hugh Ferriss, *Metropolis of Tomorrow.* Princeton, N. J.: Princeton Architectural Press, 1986.

Works Progress Administration. *San Francisco: The Bay and Its Cities.* New York: Hastings House, 1940.

Woodbridge, Sally and John M. Woodbridge. *Architecture, San Francisco, The Guide.* San Francisco: 101 Productions, 1982.

Visions of Renewal and Growth: 1945 to the Present
Sally B. Woodbridge

Downtown Plan: An Ordinance of the City and County of San Francisco. San Francisco: Office of the Clerk, Board of Supervisors, 1985.

Hartman, Chester. *The Transformation of San Francisco.* Totowa, N.J.: Rowman and Allenheld, 1984.

Hirten, John E. "Our San Francisco Tomorrow." *Town and Country* 5, no. 19 [1962]: 16-19.

Jacobs, Alan. *Making City Planning Work.* Chicago: The American Society of Planning Officials, 1978.

Lathrop, William H., Jr. "San Francisco Freeway Revolt." *Transportation Engineering Journal.* Proceedings of the American Society of Engineers, February, 1971.

The Mission Bay Plan: Proposal for Citizen Review. San Francisco: Department of City Planning, 1987.

San Francisco Department of City Planning. *The Urban Design Plan for the Comprehensive Plan of San Francisco.* San Francisco: Department of City Planning, 1971.

Scott, Mel. *The San Francisco Bay Area: A Metropolis in Perspective.* Berkeley: University of California Press, 1959, 2nd ed. 1985.

"Urban Renewal, Remaking the American City." *Time* 84 no. 19, (Nov. 6, 1964): pp. 60-75.

List of Illustrations

6 Bird's-eye view of central Paris on the Right Bank.
Courtesy Institut Géographique National and Norma Evenson.

7 Emile Benard. First-prize perspective, *Roma*, from finalist drawings for Phoebe Hearst International Competition, 1899.
Ink and watercolor on paper, 27 × 61½ in. (68.6 × 156.2 cm).
College of Environmental Design Documents Collection, University of California, Berkeley.

8 Willis Polk. *Proposed Peristyle and Arch at Foot of Market Street*, 1897.
Pen and ink on paper, 41 × 66½ in. (104.1 × 168.9 cm).
College of Environmental Design Documents Collection, University of California, Berkeley.

9 Panhandle Extension, *San Francisco Examiner*, September 24, 1899, pp. 26-27.
Courtesy of the *San Francisco Examiner*.
(Photo: Ben Blackwell)

10 Daniel H. Burnham. *Map of the City and County of San Francisco*, from *Report of D.H. Burnham on the Improvement and Adornment of San Francisco*, September 1905.
Collection of Albert R. Schreck.
(Photo: Ben Blackwell)

11 Burnham Plan. Telegraph Hill, looking east.
Collection of The Bancroft Library, University of California, Berkeley.

12 View of Powell Street from Market Street, c. 1930.
Courtesy Gabriel Moulin Studios, San Francisco.

13 Bird's-eye Perspective of Entire City as World's Fair, *Sunset Magazine*, September 1911, pp. 338-339. Reprinted from *Sunset Magazine*, © Lane Publishing Co., 1990.
(Photo: Ben Blackwell)

14 Jules Guerin. *Bird's-eye View* of the *Panama-Pacific International Exposition*, 1913.
Ink and watercolor on paper, 49 × 97 in. (124.5 × 246.4 cm).
Collection of the Exploratorium, San Francisco. (Photo: Ben Blackwell)

15 Jules Guerin. Court leading to the Column of Progress, 1912.
Pencil and watercolor on paper, 50 × 37 in. (144.8 × 94.0 cm).
Collection of the San Francisco Public Library. (Photo: Ben Blackwell)

16 Jules Guerin. *Court of Honor*, c. 1912.
Pencil and watercolor on paper, 26 x 65 in. (66 × 165.1 cm).
Collection of the San Francisco Public Library. (Photo: Ben Blackwell)

17 Bernard Maybeck. Palace of Fine Arts, elevation, 1914.
Charcoal on paper, 26 x 57½ in. (66 × 146.1 cm).
Collection of Hans Gerson.
(Photo: Ben Blackwell).

18 B. J. S. Cahill. Perspective of Memorial Court for Civic Center with Cannons, c. 1909.
Pencil on paper, 17 × 20½ in. (43.2 × 52.1 cm).
College of Environmental Design Documents Collection, University of California, Berkeley.

19 Arthur Mathews. *The City* (sketch for mural in California State Capitol), c. 1913.
Watercolor and pencil on paper, 27⅞ × 21⅞ in. (70.8 × 55.6 cm).
Collection of the Santa Barbara Museum of Art, gift of Harold Wagner.

Richard Rodriguez
Sodom: Reflections on a Stereotype
pp. 62-77

1 Sohela Farokhi and Lars Lerup. *Section, Typical Plan, and Moveable Furniture*, 1989.
Ink on vellum, 14 × 17 in. (35.6 × 43.2 cm).
Courtesy San Francisco Museum of Modern Art. (Photo: Ben Blackwell)

2 Sohela Farokhi and Lars Lerup. *Site and View in Context*, 1989.
Ink on vellum, 14 × 17 in. (35.6 × 43.2 cm).
Courtesy San Francisco Museum of Modern Art. (Photo: Ben Blackwell)

3 Sohela Farokhi and Lars Lerup. *Elevation in Recess*, 1989.
Ink on vellum, 14 × 17 in. (35.6 × 43.2 cm).
Courtesy San Francisco Museum of Modern Art. (Photo: Ben Blackwell)

4 Sohela Farokhi and Lars Lerup. *House of Flats: Working Drawing #1*, 1989.
Mixed media on Bristol paper, 22⅝ × 30³⁄₁₆ in. (57.5 × 76.7 cm).
Courtesy San Francisco Museum of Modern Art. (Photo: Ben Blackwell)

5 Sohela Farokhi and Lars Lerup. *House of Flats: Working Drawing #2 (Lot Size and Type)*, 1989.
Mixed media on Bristol paper, 22⅝ × 30³⁄₁₆ in. (57.5 × 76.7 cm).
Courtesy San Francisco Museum of Modern Art. (Photo: Ben Blackwell)

6 Sohela Farokhi and Lars Lerup. *House of Flats: Working Drawing #3 (Space Shaping)*, 1989.
Mixed media on Bristol paper, 22⅝ × 30³⁄₁₆ in. (57.5 × 76.7 cm).
Courtesy San Francisco Museum of Modern Art. (Photo: Ben Blackwell)

7 Sohela Farokhi and Lars Lerup. *Moveable Furniture: Closet/Chest, Club, Recorb*, 1989.
Graphite and acrylic on Bristol paper, 22⅝ × 30³⁄₁₆ in. (57.5 × 76.7 cm).
Courtesy San Francisco Museum of Modern Art. (Photo: Ben Blackwell)

8 Sohela Farokhi and Lars Lerup. *Moveable Furniture: Which Way Chair*, 1989.
Graphite and acrylic on Bristol paper, 22⅝ × 12¼ in. (57.5 × 31.1 cm).
Courtesy San Francisco Museum of Modern Art. (Photo: Ben Blackwell)

9 Sohela Farokhi and Lars Lerup. *Rooms of Obsession: Fragment of Room Painting*, 1989.
Gilded wood, graphite, and acrylic on Bristol paper, 30³⁄₁₆ × 22⅝ in. (76.7 × 57.5 cm).
Courtesy San Francisco Museum of Modern Art. (Photo: Ben Blackwell)

10 Sohela Farokhi and Lars Lerup. *3 × 3 Postcards: 2 Kalmar Slott, Rutsalen; Ercolano, Casa del Tremezzo di Legno; 3 Mantova, Castello, Sala degli Sposi; 2 Mantova, Palazzo Te, Sala dei Cavalli; Ercolano, Casa del Mobilio Carbonizzato*, 1989.
Postcards, 12¼ × 17½ in. (31.1 × 44.4 cm).
Courtesy San Francisco Museum of Modern Art. (Photo: Ben Blackwell)

Daniel P. Gregory
A Vivacious Landscape:
Urban Visions between the Wars
pp. 78-103

1 San Francisco, 1930.
Courtesy Gabriel Moulin Studios, San Francisco.

2 450 Sutter Building, 1989.
Courtesy Gabriel Moulin Studios, San Francisco.

3 San Francisco, 1927.
Courtesy Gabriel Moulin Studios, San Francisco.

4　Hugh Ferriss, delineator. *Winning Entry for the Pacific Stock Exchange Competition,* J. R. Miller and T. L. Pflueger, Architects, 1929.
Pencil and charcoal on paper, 25¼ × 20⅜ in. (64.2 × 51.7 cm).
Courtesy Butterfield & Butterfield, San Francisco.

5　Hugh Ferriss, delineator. *Pacific Telephone & Telegraph Co. Building,* J. R. Miller and T. L. Pflueger, Architects, 1924.
Charcoal and pencil on paper, 32½ × 20 in. (82.5 × 50.8 cm).
Courtesy Butterfield & Butterfield, San Francisco.

6　Hugh Ferriss, delineator. *Pacific Edgewater Club,* J. R. Miller and T. L. Pflueger, Architects, 1927.
Charcoal on paper, 31¾ × 46¾ in. (80.6 × 119 cm).
Courtesy Butterfield & Butterfield, San Francisco.

7　Timothy Pflueger, J. R. Miller and T. L. Pflueger, Architects. Perspective study sketches for a skyscraper, 1920s.
Pencil and charcoal on paper; colored pencil and pastel on paper, 29½ × 12 in. (74.9 × 30.5 cm) each.
Courtesy Butterfield & Butterfield, San Francisco. (Photo: Ben Blackwell)

8　Downtown San Francisco, c. 1930.
Courtesy Gabriel Moulin Studios, San Francisco.

9　Louis Christian Mullgardt. Bridge-skyscraper proposal, 1924, from *The Architect and Engineer,* March 1927.
Courtesy the San Francisco Public Library. (Photo: Ben Blackwell)

10　Lewis P. Hobart, architect. *The Embarcadero, San Francisco, Proposed Aviation Platform and Elevated Highway,* 1926.
Courtesy San Francisco Archives. (Photo: Ben Blackwell)

11　J. R. Miller and T. L. Pflueger, Architects. *Bird's-eye View of the Proposed China Basin Airport,* c. 1928.
Charcoal and pencil on paper, 14½ × 20¼ in. (36.8 × 51.3 cm).
Courtesy Butterfield & Butterfield, San Francisco.

12　Peter Stackpole. *Waiting for Rivets and Steel,* 1935, from the portfolio *When They Built the Bridge: Photographs of the San Francisco-Oakland Bay Bridge, 1934-1936,* 1985, 12/35.
Gelatin silver print, 7 × 9⅜ in. (17.8 × 23.8 cm).
Collection of the San Francisco Museum of Modern Art, gift of Ursula Gropper. (Photo: Ben Blackwell)

13　Chesley Bonestell, renderer. *Diagrammatic Study of San Francisco Pier Showing Caisson and Fender Construction,* Golden Gate Bridge, c. 1932.
Oil on canvas, 39½ × 58½ (100.3 × 148.6 cm).
Collection of the Golden Gate Bridge, Highway and Transportation District, San Francisco. (Photo: Ben Blackwell)

14　Chesley Bonestell, renderer. *A Proposed Easterly San Francisco Approach to Golden Gate Bridge,* c. 1932.
Oil on canvas, 23⅛ × 31⅛ in. (58.7 × 79.1 cm).
Collection of the Golden Gate Bridge, Highway and Transportation District, San Francisco. (Photo: Ben Blackwell)

15　The San Francisco end of the Bay Bridge, 1989.
(Photo: Paolo Polledri)

16　Eudori, renderer. Cutaway view of central pier, San Francisco-Oakland Bay Bridge, *The Architect and Engineer,* October 1934.
Courtesy Cal Trans Library, Sacramento.

17　Carl Nuese, delineator. *The San Francisco-Oakland Bay Bridge Approach and Anchorage from Rincon Hill to the Embarcadero, San Francisco,* 1934.
Pencil and charcoal on paper, 18 × 83 in. (45.7 × 210.8 cm).
Courtesy Butterfield & Butterfield, San Francisco.

18　Bernard Maybeck, architect. *West View Bay Bridge,* c. 1939.
Watercolor, ink, and colored pencil on illustration board, 30 × 20 in. (76.3 × 50.8 cm).
Collection of Timothy Tosta. (Photo: Ben Blackwell)

19　Bernard Maybeck, architect. *San Francisco Ideal City,* c. 1939.
Watercolor, ink, gold paint, and pencil on illustration board, 20 × 30 in. (50.8 × 76.3 cm).
Collection of Timothy Tosta. (Photo: Ben Blackwell)

20　E. A. Burbank, renderer. *Site of the Golden Gate-International Exposition, "A Pageant of the Pacific,"* c. 1938.
Collection of the San Francisco Archives. (Photo: Ben Blackwell)

21　Chesley Bonestell. *Tower of the Sun,* Golden Gate International Exposition, Treasure Island, 1938.
Oil on canvas, 48¼ × 28¼ in. (122.5 × 71.7 cm).
Collection of The Oakland Museum.

22　Walter Dorwin Teague. U. S. Steel's exhibit, "San Francisco in 1999," Golden Gate International Exposition, 1939.
Courtesy San Francisco Public Library.

23　Walter Dorwin Teague. U. S. Steel's exhibit, "San Francisco in 1999," Golden Gate International Exposition, 1939.
Courtesy San Francisco Public Library.

24　Aerial view of San Francisco, c. 1940.
Courtesy Gabriel Moulin Studios, San Francisco.

Mark Helprin
The True Builders of Cities
pp. 104-117

1　Barbara Stauffacher Solomon. *The Green Rectangle = Paradise,* 1989.
Graphite and colored pencil on vellum, 24 × 18⅞ in. (61 × 47.9 cm).
Courtesy San Francisco Museum of Modern Art. (Photo: Ben Blackwell)

2　Barbara Stauffacher Solomon. *The Green Rectangle = Play-ground,* 1989.
Graphite and colored pencil on vellum, 24 × 18⅞ in. (61 × 47.9 cm).
Courtesy San Francisco Museum of Modern Art. (Photo: Ben Blackwell)

3　Barbara Stauffacher Solomon. *Installation at the SFMOMA – Rotunda, 33 Tables/84 Players, The Green Rectangle = Paradise,* 1989.
Graphite and colored pencil on vellum, 24 × 18⅞ in. (61 × 47.9 cm).
Courtesy San Francisco Museum of Modern Art. (Photo: Ben Blackwell)

4　Barbara Stauffacher Solomon. *Table Tennis Installation at the Marina Green,* 1989.
Graphite and colored pencil on vellum, 24 × 18⅞ in. (61 × 47.9 cm).
Courtesy San Francisco Museum of Modern Art. (Photo: Ben Blackwell)

5 Barbara Stauffacher Solomon. *Tennis Courts in the Backyards*, 1989. Graphite and colored pencil on vellum, 24 × 18⅞ in. (61 × 47.9 cm). Courtesy San Francisco Museum of Modern Art. (Photo: Ben Blackwell)

6 Barbara Stauffacher Solomon. *After October 17th*, 1989. Graphite and colored pencil on vellum, 24 × 18⅞ in. (61 × 47.9 cm). Courtesy of the artist. (Photo: Ben Blackwell)

Sally B. Woodbridge
Visions of Renewal and Growth:
1945 to the Present
pp. 118-151

1 San Francisco, 1950s. Courtesy Aero Photographers, Sausalito. (Photo: Ed Brady)

2 William G. Merchant. San Francisco World Trade Center proposal, 1951. Drawing. Courtesy Hans Gerson. (Photo: Moulin Studios, San Francisco)

3 Aerial view of the site for the Embarcadero Freeway, 1951. Courtesy Aero Photographers, Sausalito. (Photo: Ed Brady)

4 The James Lick Freeway under construction. Courtesy Aero Photographers, Sausalito. (Photo: Ed Brady)

5 Lawrence Halprin, landscape architect. Sketch for a solution to the Embarcadero Freeway, 1962. Pencil on tracing paper. Courtesy Lawrence Halprin. (Photo: Ben Blackwell)

6 Aerial view of the Western Addition and Fillmore areas, 1961. Courtesy Aero Photographers, Sausalito. (Photo: Ed Brady)

7 Aerial view of Diamond Heights, 1960. Courtesy Aero Photographers, Sausalito. (Photo: Ed Brady)

8 Skidmore, Owings & Merrill. Entry for the Golden Gateway Competition, 1959.

9 Jan Lubicz-Nycz and Mario Ciampi. Scheme for towers on Red Rock Hill, Diamond Heights Competition, 1961. Architectural model. Courtesy Mario Ciampi. (Photo: Dwain Faubion)

10 Aerial view of San Francisco showing South of Market Street area and downtown, 1974. Courtesy Aero Photographers, Sausalito. (Photo: Ed Brady)

11 Diagram showing Areas E and D.

12 Redevelopment Agency. Schematic plan for Yerba Buena Center, 1964. Architectural model. Courtesy John Dykstra. (Photo: Dwain Faubion)

13 Gerald McCue (second from left), Kenzo Tange (center), Justin Herman (second from right), and others viewing the Yerba Buena Center model, 1969. Courtesy John Dykstra. (Photo: Karl H. Riek)

14 Kenzo Tange, URTEC/Gerald McCue. Yerba Buena Center central blocks, 1969. Architectural model. Collection of Calvin Imai, Architectural Models. Courtesy John Dykstra. (Photo: Gerald Ratto)

15 Schlesinger/Arcon-Pacific. Plan for Yerba Buena Center, 1973. Architectural model. Courtesy John Dykstra. (Photo: Jeremiah O. Bragstad)

16 Henry Adams, with architects Wurster, Bernardi & Emmons, and Lawrence Halprin, landscape architect. Proposal for the International Trade Mart, 1968. Architectural model. Courtesy Wurster, Bernardi & Emmons, Inc., Architects. (Photo: Gerald Ratto)

17 Henry Adams, with architects Wurster, Bernardi & Emmons, and Lawrence Halprin, landscape architect. Proposal for the International Trade Mart, 1968. Drawing. Courtesy Wurster, Bernardi & Emmons, Inc., Architects.

18 I. M. Pei. Ferry Park, 1984. Architectural model. Courtesy Continental Development. (Photo: Nathaniel Lieberman)

19 Zeidler-Roberts Partnership/Architects and Olympia & York. Winning plans for Yerba Buena Gardens, 1983-84. Colored pencil and graphite on paper. Courtesy Olympia & York. (Photo: Ben Blackwell)

20 The 25-acre site for Yerba Buena Gardens as it stood cleared, 1984. Aerial photograph. Courtesy Olympia & York.

21 Lawrence Halprin and Omi Lang, landscape architects. Garden plan for Yerba Buena Gardens executed in the office of Zeidler Roberts Partnerships/Architects, 1981. Watercolor on paper, 55½ × 35¼ in. (141 × 89.5 cm). Courtesy Olympia & York. (Photo: Lenscape, Toronto)

22 Zeidler Roberts Partnership/Architects and Lawrence Halprin, landscape architect. Yerba Buena Gardens as proposed in the master plan, which was the basis of the land use agreement between the Redevelopment Agency and Olympia & York, 1984. Photomontage. Courtesy Olympia & York.

23 Zeidler Roberts Partnership/Architects, with Lawrence Halprin and Omi Lang, landscape architects. Axonometric view of Yerba Buena Gardens, 1989. Ink and colored pencil on paper mounted on foam core, 50½ × 33¼ in. (128.3 × 84.5 cm). Courtesy of Olympia & York. (Photo: Ben Blackwell)

24 The Jerde Partnership. Plan for Yerba Buena Gardens, 1989. Approx. 60 × 36 in. (152.4 × 91.4 cm). Courtesy Olympia & York. (Photo: Ben Blackwell)

25a The Jerde Partnership, 1989. East-west section/elevation for Yerba Buena Gardens, 1989. Airbrush, ink, and colored pencil on paper, approx. 36 × 120 in. (91.4 × 304.8 cm). Courtesy Olympia & York. (Photo: Ben Blackwell)

25b The Jerde Partnership, 1989. North-south section/elevation for Yerba Buena Gardens, 1989. Airbrush, ink, and colored pencil on paper, approx. 36 × 120 in. (91.4 × 304.8 cm). Courtesy of Olympia & York. (Photo: Ben Blackwell)

26 View of Mission Bay area, 1989. Courtesy Santa Fe Pacific Realty.

27 Walter Vangreen, renderer. *Rendered Site Plan for Proposed Mission Bay Development*, 1983, Pei Cobb Freed & Partners, James I. Freed, Partner-in-Charge, Charles T. Young II, Associate Partner. Colored pencil on board, 41 × 60¾ in. (104.1 × 154.3 cm). Collection of Pei Cobb Freed & Partners, Archives.

28 Proposal for Mission Bay, plan. Courtesy Santa Fe Pacific Realty.

29 Proposal for Mission Bay, bird's-eye view, 1990. Skidmore, Owings & Merrill. Photomontage.
Courtesy Skidmore, Owings & Merrill.

30 Proposal for the Mission Bay waterfront. Courtesy Santa Fe Pacific Realty.

William Gibson
Skinner's Room
pp. 152-165

1 Ming Fung and Craig Hodgetts.
Untitled, 1989.
Ink and xerography on paper, 11½ × 9 in. (29.2 × 22.9 cm).
Courtesy San Francisco Museum of Modern Art. (Photo: Ben Blackwell)

2 Ming Fung and Craig Hodgetts.
Untitled, 1989.
Ink and xerography on paper, 11½ × 9 in. (29.2 × 22.9 cm).
Courtesy San Francisco Museum of Modern Art. (Photo: Ben Blackwell)

3 Ming Fung and Craig Hodgetts.
Untitled, 1989.
Ink and xerography on paper, 9 × 11½ in. (22.9 × 29.2 cm).
Courtesy San Francisco Museum of Modern Art. (Photo: Ben Blackwell)

4 Ming Fung and Craig Hodgetts.
Untitled, 1989.
Ink and xerography on paper, 9 × 11½ in. (22.9 × 29.2 cm).
Courtesy San Francisco Museum of Modern Art. (Photo: Ben Blackwell)

5 Ming Fung and Craig Hodgetts.
Untitled, 1989.
Ink and xerography on paper, 11½ × 9 in. (29.2 × 22.9 cm).
Courtesy San Francisco Museum of Modern Art. (Photo: Ben Blackwell)

6 Ming Fung and Craig Hodgetts.
The Trap, 1989.
Ink and xerography on paper, 11½ × 9 in. (29.2 × 22.9 cm).
Courtesy San Francisco Museum of Modern Art. (Photo: Ben Blackwell)

7 Ming Fung and Craig Hodgetts.
City with "Bites" Removed, 1989. Ink and xerography on paper, 11½ × 9 in. (29.2 × 22.9 cm).
Courtesy San Francisco Museum of Modern Art. (Photo: Ben Blackwell)

8 Ming Fung and Craig Hodgetts.
Skywalker Park, 1989.
Ink and xerography on paper, 11½ × 9 in. (29.2 × 22.9 cm).
Courtesy San Francisco Museum of Modern Art. (Photo: Ben Blackwell)

9 Ming Fung and Craig Hodgetts.
Gateway City, 1989.
Ink and xerography on paper, 11½ × 9 in. (29.2 × 22.9 cm).
Courtesy San Francisco Museum of Modern Art. (Photo: Ben Blackwell)

10 Ming Fung and Craig Hodgetts.
Map of San Francisco, 1989.
Ink, xerography, and collage on paper, 24 × 20 in. (61 × 50.8 cm).
Courtesy San Francisco Museum of Modern Art. (Photo: Ben Blackwell)

Index of Names

Figures in *italics* refer to captions